Stepping
Off
The
Edge

Published by Compass Flower Press

an imprint of AKA-Publishing
Columbia, Missouri USA
www.AKA-Publishing.com

ISBN: 978-1-942168-83-6

Stepping
Off
The
Edge

Faith and Fiasco in a Philippine Mission

Deborah Tuhy Simmons

Compass Flower Press
Columbia, MO

DISCLAIMER

This is a work of non-fiction. It is a compilation of my original letters from the Philippines, and selections from my daily journal entries. I edited these materials for length, interest, and relevant content, and sometimes combined or rearranged them for clarity and chronology.

My letters (often written well after an event) and journal entries were dependent on my memory, which has never been infallible. My view of events and characters was also filtered through my opinions, expectations and cultural background. There's always another side to every story . . . I just wrote what I saw.

To protect the privacy of the people in these stories, I have changed all their names, and, in some instances, their physical properties, occupations, and places of residence.

The newsletters were mostly written by my husband, Art, with a few words from me in each one. Again, all names and identifying properties have been changed. The images in the newsletters were either from church clip art packages that we purchased at the time, or simple drawings made by Art or myself.

For

Art

who lived it all

and for

Tim and Mindy

who heard it all

Table of Contents

Maps ix

Introduction xi

1. Arrival—Discoveries and Decisions: Manila 1

2. Preparation—Strength Training: Davao City 13

3. First Steps—Setting the Stage: Davao, Malungon, Lumabat 31

4. Edging In—Testing the Waters: Malungon 47

5. Hanging On—Battling the Obstacles: Malungon 63

6. Still Hanging—Battling the Obstacles: Malungon, Part 2 73

7. Interim I—Touching Home: U.S.A. 83

8. Here and There—Final Steps: Malungon, Lumabat 89

9. The Back of Beyond—Finally: Lumabat 102

10. Digging In—Getting Established: Lumabat 115

11. Interim II—Furlough: U.S.A. 127

12. Second Verse, Same as the First—Back to Work: Lumabat 131

13. Keep On Keeping On—Carrying On: Lumabat 143

14. Staying the Course—Persevering: Lumabat, with Side Trips 159

15. Interim III—The Far Reaches: India and Nepal 173

16. Bye!—Reaching the End: Lumabat, and Out 181

Newsletters 197

Gallery 229

Acknowledgments 239

About the Author 241

PHILIPPINES

South China Sea

Luzon

MANILA O

Philippine Sea

Visayas

CEBU O

Sulu Sea

Mindanao

O DAVAO

MALAYSIA

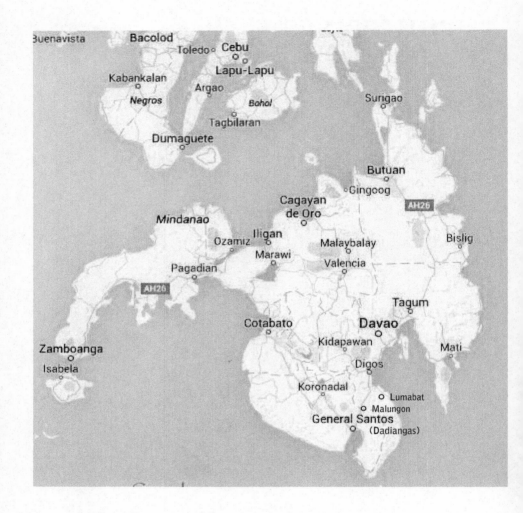

Introduction

The Proposal
Early 1980s

Way down in the southern Philippines, in off the road and back up the dirt trails into the mountains, there is a tribe of people called the Tagakaulo Kalagans. There are a lot of them but no one knows how many—maybe 60,000, maybe 100,000. They stay alive, more or less, by subsistence farming. They plant corn on hillsides so steep they have to roll the corn down to harvest it, and then sell it for rice to eat. They live in bamboo huts with straw roofs, and most of their kids die young. For water to wash in, to clean or butcher their animals in—and to drink—they have the river. For health care, they have witch doctors. They can't read or write or figure numbers, and when they come out to the road for trade, they routinely get cheated. They believe in spirits who are largely indifferent or evil, and fate has convinced them that that's life.

They have their own language, so a survey team came through from an international, church-based translation and literacy group. A husband and wife team volunteered, set up a house close to the road and began writing the language for the first time. They developed a literacy primer and started some Bible translation.

Then the church figured it was time to do another survey, and decided it was a perfect place to start a mission. Plans would include adult literacy, basic health care, better farming techniques, a mutual-trust relationship with the people, all presented through the Christian faith and supported by a Filipino-American partnership. It would be a multi-year project, until self-sufficiency was gained on all levels. The new program needed to be site-based and dependable for the long run.

Then the linguistics couple encountered a life-threatening health problem, and left. The work shut down. Plans were cancelled, and things settled back into the old ways, the routines of a hard, short life. Somebody needed to go back in there.

Somebody needed to go.

The Setting
1986-1992

And so, we went.

Six years ticked by. When we finally packed up and went home, we left behind water wells, literacy programs, medicines, health care, local pastors in training, gardens, knowledge, true friends—and most of my sanity.

I seemed to have plenty of it when we arrived, but when the plane lifted off for the last time, most of that sanity was far below—buried deep in cockroaches and coup attempts, mud and landslides, dysentery, earthquakes, giant spiders, and famines.

Our lives there took place in a curious time. These were the transitional 1980s and early 90s. The world was shoving the door open on technology, and all the science fiction fantasies were finally coming true. You couldn't properly be stunned by one discovery, or even figure out how to use it, before the next one came along. Little of this touched our mountain area, but it was coming closer. After we left, aid workers, missionaries, relief organizations and do-gooders of all kinds would continue to filter into those remote areas. But they would all be equipped with technology. They'd have communication: a lifeline to mentors, friends, and support. They'd have information, and the instant answer to all the most urgent questions. They'd never be alone. Our years were the last ones of the old world—years of self-reliance, judgment calls, danger, isolation and adventure.

I sometimes wonder what life would've been like if the nearest telephone weren't a three-hour hike plus two-hour drive away. If a letter and its reply didn't take over a month. If urgently needed information came reliably on the spot, instead of out of a well-thumbed, ten-year-old book with pages missing. Well, it would've been a lot easier. But the stories wouldn't have been as good.

Trouble is, they were stories I couldn't tell anybody. They weren't about mission and ministry. They didn't reflect goals and encourage supporters. Art wrote bright newsletters which highlighted our accomplishments – and left all the hard-fought background unsaid. But everybody has one good friend they can tell the truth to. We were fortunate enough to have two: Tim and Mindy. We had spent ten years together in Wisconsin. We enjoyed each other, trusted each other, and could pretty well tell each other anything. So that's what I did—I told them the truth. And the TimMindy letters began.

1

Arrival
Discoveries and Decisions: Manila
Fall/Winter 1986

Dear Tim & Mindy,

We are here! It only took about thirty hours, thousands of miles, another date (it's tomorrow, your time), a variety of crammed planes, and at least three movies, all of which I'd seen. At some point late in the trip we went through other airports—maybe Seoul or Tokyo. I was comatose. No, it must've been Tokyo because the pilot pointed out Mt. Fuji in the setting sun. It looked just like it does on all the postcards (what a coincidence).

Right before we landed in Manila, the rich Filipina sitting in front of me started stripping off all her gold jewelry and stuffing it under the dirty diapers in her baby's diaper bag. Not having any diaper bags ourselves—or any gold besides those pawnshop wedding rings we picked up in Chicago—we breezed right through Customs. A driver from the mission was there to pick us up, and we piled out into the smog.

Now we're staying at the mission's Hospice Center, fondly known by the other families as the Hostage Center. It's a square, two-story flat-roof concrete block house with a big wall around it topped by killer barbed wire. Don't know yet if that's to keep burglars out or culture-shocked Americans in. We have the upstairs apartment. Most folks would call it shabby but I like it. Some American mission pastor from up north has just moved into the downstairs apartment with his countless kids and about 5 yapping dogs. I think he brought them down here to sell them (the dogs, not the kids, but both would be a good idea). The uproar all night is amazing, but since we're a long ways from sleeping at night (cruel jet lag) it doesn't much matter.

About Manila, I guess we'd say, "that's different." At eight million people, it's slightly larger than home sweet Stevens Point, and so polluted I can't figure how folks survive here for long. Imagine the black cloud of fumes that come out of the back of a Point Transit bus when they step on the gas. Multiply that by a million, then hang it over the city and live in it. Even inside, everything has a black oily film on it. If I wash plates after breakfast and leave them in the drainer, I can come back in an hour and write my name on them in the soot. Since I'll be eating a lot of soot, I wonder what the nutritional value of it is. Remember how I always loved black hot dogs? OK, I'm looking at the bright side here.

Speaking of food, we went over to the Farmers' Market yesterday—a fryingly hot metal shed about three blocks long—to learn how to buy our mangoes, rice and lapu-lapu fish. I didn't get any of the giant live squid, chicken feet (appropriately called Adidas), pig snouts or manta rays, but who knows when I might be tempted.

Everyone says it's been pretty cool here for December—only in the high 80s and not much rain. I guess that's a tad warmer than the snowdrifts, icy roads and constantly frost-bitten face that sent me screaming out of Wisconsin and over here to the tropics. Haven't seen any of the giant spiders yet but the 4" cockroaches are something else. I'm going to put a leash on the one in the bathroom, call him Fred and take him for a walk.

And on top of it all, in true church fashion, they don't even know what they're going to do with us yet! The head mission boss is sending Art and Wayne, the missionary personnel coordinator, down to Mindanao in a couple weeks to see if it's really feasible to start that tribal mountain mission there. They won't take me because of all the communist insurgent activity down there, so Fred (see above) and I will just have to stay here and keep each other company. There are a couple other nebulous, made-up options, but who knows when they'll find out. So please keep an eye out for all the people who bought the junk at my rummage sales and prepare to get it all back for me. I'll keep you posted. Don't forget to write! Bye for now, Debb & Art

❧ Journal Entry

All the water in the apartment keeps stopping in the middle of the afternoon. When you turn on the faucet, the pipes just moan. I finally learned how to handle it though. First thing this morning, after doing the dishes from yesterday, I filled the huge red bucket. There was a supposedly dead giant cockroach in the kitchen; when I reached for it with a paper towel to throw it out, it came to life and tried to crawl up my arm. Art ran after it and stomped it while I screamed and hopped around. Lesson: upside down does not equal dead. No water again tonight but I have some in the bucket. Ha ha.

❧ Journal Entry

Read in the paper about the farm workers' riot over by the palace. Fourteen were killed near the Mendiola bridge. Rode a jeepney to the mission office, and while Art makes plans with Wayne, they're having me edit and rewrite some of the Bible correspondence courses. We got one of the last jeepneys back—another strike was starting. Met some loudspeaker opposition near our mission house street, but got through. After supper we would've watched TV, but the protesters are still holding the TV stations.

Dear Tim and Mindy,

    Things are all quiet here at the old apartmentstead. Art and his boss flew down to Mindanao yesterday to see who's shooting who(m) and where they're doing it. They're looking to see if that proposed mountain area is relatively out of the cross-fire. It's kind of a toss-up down there between the communist rebels (called the NPA, or New People's Army), who tend to kidnap people as a fund-raising project, and the Muslim separatists, who prefer throwing hand grenades into packed movie theaters.

While we wait we've been keeping ourselves entertained. Now that we have terminal Black Lung, we don't even worry about pollution anymore and go all around the city by jeepney. Now there's a carnival ride for you. A jeepney is a jeep (you don't say) where the back has been extended, and bench seats face each other on both sides. They don't have regular stops but troll the street edges looking for riders and battle each other to the curb (hopefully not crushing the waiting passenger) whenever someone raises a hand. You leap up the steps in the back, usually while it's still moving, squash onto the seat with the other thirty riders and bang on the roof when you want to get off.

We also played good tourista and went to see some of the more famous sights. The Tondo garbage dump called Smoky Mountain was probably the most gruesome. It's acres and acres of putrid steaming trash with a whole city of shacks built on top of it. The people who live there (whole families) stay alive by scrounging through the mounds with hands and sticks, looking for anything resellable. But you would love the Chinese cemetery—it's like a whole empty town for the dead with actual 2-story houses for the coffins. Some are air-conditioned, and some have maids to cook daily meals which they set out for the dead ancestors. I should have it so good.

Speaking of food, we're starting to eat some decidedly strange stuff ourselves. There's this kind of vegetable called ube, which is a violent purple color—they use it to make purple cakes and ice cream that taste sort of cinnamony. I like it but you have to shut your eyes to eat it. Last night I made beef and sayote (squash) over bihon (rice noodles) with pancit palabok (like spicy paprika). Tasty but time-consuming. I wonder when it'll come out in TV dinner form.

Just made a trip to the bathroom where I found, and was forced to slaughter, an immense cockroach, one of Fred's big brothers. This is bad news as it means that the lizard behind the toilet tank isn't doing his job. Now both Fred and the Lord are mad at me because I had to mash the cockroach with my Bible.

Sorry about that Lord, but it was the biggest book in the place.

We're managing to stay well. Last Thursday we were thinking about going down to the palace because it's free visitors' day, but decided to go to the library instead. As that was the day all those protestors got shot near the palace, I feel we made a good choice. I'll try and mail this tomorrow but the unions are calling a general strike on everything, so who knows when you'll get it. We sure miss your smiling faces. Love, Debb and Art

❦ Journal Entry

There was all kinds of screeching and uproar outside tonight. Art says it was only the guy across the street—he came out to pee on his wall and hit the cat that was digging through the trash pile. Things just got quiet again when the balut seller came by—11 p.m. on the dot. He hollers "Baloooooooot!" and bangs on his pail. Balut are fertilized duck eggs with a semi-formed duck embryo inside—makes them crunchy. It's supposed to be an aphrodisiac, but sounds more like a barfiac to me. Judging by the packed population of this place though, there must be something to it.

❦ Journal Entry

It's Revolution Day—commemorating People Power and the overthrow of the Marcos regime last year. We woke to completely silent streets; all buses and jeepneys were rerouted off Edsa, the huge main street. We walked out to the Araneta overpass to see the People Parade—hundreds of thousands of people marching down the street, some marching bands, everyone wearing yellow. We followed as far as the camps until it was too dense to move, and then headed back against the crowd. Felt like a spawning salmon. Back at the apartment, the kids across the street were playing revolution: half of them barricaded themselves in the garage, while the other half marched around shouting slogans.

Spring 1987

Dear Tim and Mindy,

I'm finally sending some pictures so you can see what a thrilling place this is. Could you send them on to Lois? Then when you get them back, please just put them in a shoebox and stick them in a closet somewhere. When we come back in ten years or two months or whenever, I'll have all the materials I need for my memoirs entitled, "Really Stupid Things You Can Do With Your Life."

Well, they still haven't decided where they're going to send us yet. They're still thinking of that remote mission down on Mindanao but now it depends on getting a seminary grad to join us and form a team. That depends on a Mission Board vote, which depends on timing and bureaucraziness, which depends on us putting up with this officialese fighting until they make up their minds next century or we go home in a huff. Whichever comes first.

To keep us from full-blown mutiny, they've started us in language school. It's a weird language. Trying to start a word with ng is like coughing while throwing up, and takes dedicated practice. They only have one pronoun (siya) for both he and she, so when they speak English they often call men "she" and women "he" - think of the confusion on your His n' Hers printed guest towels. And we were doing idioms the other day. Slang for "we're all out of food" is "it's time to hang the dog now." What a way with words.

All our earthly possessions finally arrived from the movers more or less in one piece. They delivered the crate to the office but there's no secure storage there so day by day we've been hauling stuff to the apartment in the little blue Suzuki Beaver, which is sort of like a pastel squashed-in jeep that they let us drive. On one trip, we had a fold-up cot in the top luggage rack and it blew off right in the middle of Manila traffic. I jumped out and ran back to collect it (a street vendor had dragged it over to the side) and was standing there with traffic zooming around me while Art doubled back in a series of creative illegal

U-turns. In his last turn he succeeded in cutting everybody else off and came face to face with a street cop, of course. So he got to pay his very first bribe. Now we feel like we really live here.

I had my first piña colada the other night. They whack the top off a fresh buko (young green coconut), fill up the inside with whatever liquor they have, and give you a straw. Then you get a big spoon to scrape out the insides of the buko. It's tasty but you look immensely stupid sitting there sipping at a giant green bowling ball. It's OK, I'm used to looking stupid, especially here. I've also been having a little bit of stomach trouble lately, but it's probably just the Lenten Special sardine and cheese pizza I had for lunch yesterday.

Missionary life continues to be rough. Last Sunday Graham, the pastor of the expat church, and his wife Peg invited us over to their club to swim. After floating around for a bit, I was taking the sun in my deck chair, watching the goats wander around (hoping they wouldn't eat my towel) and dozing off. I must've come about three feet off my chair when this big rooster stalked over and crowed a big one right in my ear. Not your average country club. Keep those letters coming! Love, Debb & Art

❧ Journal Entry

We caught the 9 a.m. Victory Liner bus for Olongapo and got the last two seats in the back, but at least there was air con. Met up with Roger and Bill, who are chaplains at the Subic and Clark U.S. military bases, to get their advice on mission starts. We toured the Midway aircraft carrier, and had lunch at Bill's house on base: lunch meat and real potato chips! Flashback USA! We visited some orphanages, then all had supper at the Officers' Club: drinks, veal cutlets, wine, fresh salads, fresh vegetables, and a live band with singers in black dresses slit up to their ears. Pretty posh. Roger took us down to Magsaysay St., infamous strip with all the bars, hookers and hustlers. He works with abandoned street kids—the ones sold off (no age too young) by their mothers to the soldiers for whatever kinky sex they can imagine. It's a huge and lucrative business. When the little kids are dumped, Roger takes in as many as he can, and tries to rebuild their lives. We went back to the service center, and in the night sky saw the Southern Cross for the first time.

ꙮ Journal Entry

Up early, flagged over a bus, and headed for church. Halfway there, the bus pulled over, smoke pouring from the floorboards by the clutch. Most of the people stayed put, waiting to see what the driver would do. He sauntered out, lifted the hood and flames roared up. It looked pretty hopeless so we all bailed out. Got a cab the rest of the way to church.

Dear Mindy and Tim,

It looks like there are miracles after all! No, I don't mean the power stays on and we get water in the afternoons, but some unsuspecting seminary grad has agreed to come over and round out the team, thereby freeing us up to leave charming Manila and move south. So it will be the Tagakaulo Kalagan tribal area in southern Mindanao for us after all! Art and Wayne went back down to set things up, and this time I got to go along. They must figure if I'm going to live there I better get used to getting shot at.

We'll be starting out based in Davao City, which is tiny compared to Manila, at only about 8 hundred thousand people. We'll do more language school, but this time in Cebuano, which is the main southern language, and different from the Tagalog they speak up in Manila. Go figure. We also met Tinong, pastor of the church in town, and saw the house where we'll be living. It's a rambling old concrete two-story place with a giant kitchen, three bedrooms, a garage, big screened windows (but without glass— it's never cold enough to close windows), and running water that so far seems to stay on in the afternoon. An ancient, wheezing air conditioner hangs out the window of one bedroom, and looks like it might work a couple times a year, if coaxed. There's also a big walled yard with trees—mango, papaya, calamansi, coconut and avocado—and a monkey living next door.

We had to start looking for furniture so the next morning Art and I walked pretty far to Santa Ana street where Tinong said the furniture stores were. I was browsing along when wham, some guy slams into the back of me and starts trying to rip my purse off my shoulder. At this point we won't go into how stupid it is for a gringo to carry a purse out in the open, and—double stupid—I had our plane tickets and all our money in there. So there I was, jumping up and down, screaming like a banshee, dancing around playing tug of war with this guy over my purse, which was caught on my wrist, until Art, who was walking ahead, finally noticed what was going on and came rushing back. At that point, the guy ran off (without my purse) and all the interested, but non-participatory bystanders went back to their daily routines. As your average American, I was a whole lot taller than the would-be bandito and probably outweighed him by about 30 pounds, but was lucky I didn't get knifed. Later in the day, Tinong tells us we should've gone to the Santa Ana *district*, not Santa Ana *street*.

While down south we also got to cram into Tinong's jeep and head a couple hours way out of town into the rural mountain area where we'll finally be based. Miles and miles of coconut palms, some banana plantations, but no it does not look like a Tarzan movie and there will be no vine-swinging. We got to the roadside town of Malungon in time to find out that Viktor (one of the village high officials), several of his wives and a bunch of the other village big-wigs were already there but they couldn't chat yet because it was a fiesta and they had their horses entered in the big horse-fight. Much later, after the fights, endless coffee and rounds of rice n stuff (don't ask, just eat it) we finally started hiking into the mountains—Lumabat, their main village, is about 7 miles in. No road, just a really steep track which they see no reason to switchback (wastes time). About halfway in they got me a horse, which saved them having to tote my dead body the rest of the way. We stayed overnight at Viktor's house, which was sort of like a two-story shed, with floor mats to sleep on. At one point in the evening I went outside to the bathroom (big mistake), which was mainly just a hole in the ground with little bamboo walls around it. When I shined my flashlight inside, I couldn't figure out why the walls seemed to be moving and gleaming, until I realized it was just the hundreds of cockroaches rushing to get away from the light. Oh well, he's actually got a bathroom, as opposed to everyone else, who just uses the river.

So, long conversations went on (everyone and his dog has to have his say, or it's rude) and the long and short of it is they have invited us to live and work with them. Now all we have to do is learn a couple of languages, build a house (in which I will personally supervise the bathroom), plan a bunch of programs, and go for it. Hiked back out, drove to Davao, flew to Manila, where there is now no water most of the mornings, as well as afternoons. There was a big fire in our area while we were gone (which they couldn't put out because of no water) and my favorite grocery store and the McDonald's burned down. Well, I guess the McDonald's is no loss (they serve hamburgers with rice instead of fries) but the grocery store actually had corn flakes! Write soon about nice normal things. Love, Debb and Art

✤ Journal Entry

Art left early to go preach at the graduation service of the mission grade school. When I arrived, he told me there'd been a shooting at our mission office last night. Amboy, the secretary's brother, came in high on drugs, wanting to steal money. He shot and killed the new security guard, and badly wounded a local pastor's son. Held one of the workers hostage for awhile, then shot the lock off Wayne's house and went in. Wayne had hidden Nora and the kids first in the bathroom, then in a closet. He went outside to draw Amboy out—kept him talking in the yard. By that time the police were coming, so Amboy ran—shot at them but missed. The police gunned him down by the gas station and he's dead. Had to keep it quiet in church because Tami (Peg's helper, and a Sunday School teacher there) was Amboy's fiancée, is pregnant and didn't know about the shooting. Graham brought her over to our mission house where her relatives, the Reyes's, are the caretakers.

✤ Journal Entry

Up late, made pancakes. Had to have cheese on them as all the butter melted (hot season is in full swing and the power is off). Art headed over to the Toyota dealer on the far side of town to see about buying us a truck to take down to the mountains. Came back late in the afternoon saying the place was abandoned—the government had shut it down.

Hi Tim and Mindy,

We're still alive and still getting ready to head south to Mindanao. Yesterday we had to go downtown to Immigration to be fingerprinted for our visa forms. Ought to take 15 minutes, right? Wrongo. After playing demolition derby with every bus, jeepney, taxi and bozo in town, we get to this huge office building filled with people reading the paper, putting on their makeup, playing checkers and eating snacks. These are the workers. The rest of us are jammed up around their desks (we don't do 'lines' here) trying to capture their attention with our bothersome and pitiful requests to help us comply with government regulations. Five hours. We were there five hours to get our fingerprints taken (twelve seconds) and then have every Filipino that God ever created initial our documents and send us to every other office in the place. We get to the last room and the guy says he can't complete our papers until we get them signed at Quarantine. Quarantine is not at the Immigration building. It is at the Port Authority. Across town. We went home. Art had beer(s). I had piña colada(s). We will never go back. They can throw us out of the country if they want to. Maybe we will see you soon.

Enough of such jolly news—on to other things. Last Friday was our final day of language school up here—hurray! So that torture is over until mid-June when we start our next course in Davao. We finally got to verbs, can carry on a simple conversation, and Art can say important things like "I will not get out of bed." I couldn't pass up the opportunity to send you a copy of "The Four Spiritual Laws" tract so you're all ready in case you run into any Cebuanos. I could read about half of it if I wanted to, but I prefer my copy of the Old Testament in comic book form, with Adam and Moses and Noah all speaking Cebuano. More action.

As always, and with the current excuse that it's so hot, our exercise program is going backwards. Now that spring has sprung over there, I guess you're back to jogging again. I saw a good one featured in our paper the other day: "The Bataan Death March Memorial Run." That's actually the name of it.

I bet the T-shirts are great, but at least they don't call it a fun run. Art says as far as he's concerned, every running event is a death march.

Well, it's Holy Week and the whole town is emptying out as everyone goes to the provinces. Absolutely everything is closed from Wednesday to Sunday—even a lot of the TV and radio stations go off the air. I suppose we could go downtown to some of the older Catholic churches and see the guys beating themselves, hauling around huge crosses and then crucifying themselves, but I imagine I can find more fun things to do. Unless some of them happen to be the guys from Immigration. Then it could be a worthwhile sight. Keep us up on how everything is going! Bye for now, Debb and Art

❧ Journal Entry—Good Friday

Decided to go with Frank and Leah over to the Tondo area anyway. Crowds gathered early at the tiny church in Navotas. The flagellantes started to arrive, singly or in groups, wearing black hoods. They would beat themselves with ropes with barbs on the end while walking, or sometimes lie down on the street and have their partners beat them. We had to really stand back so we didn't get sprayed with blood—the nearer crowds were getting covered with it. Others came by dragging crosses. One group had the whole crowd, Roman soldiers, women etc. all in costume. Headed home. About 5:30, a long procession came down our own street: nuns, kids all in white, a wagon with a Jesus statue in it surrounded by flowers. Soon after, tremendous lightning and thunder (for real). Hmmmm—wasn't that in the original?

❧ Journal Entry

Did a last clean-up on the apartment. The ants are back in all the cupboards again, including in the rice. Washed the cupboards. Then washed the rice (dead ants float), and set it out to dry. Got our last Heptavax B shots. Wayne and his family are leaving for the States on a furlough. We head down to Davao in two days. And we are on our own.

2

Preparation
Strength Training: Davao City
Spring 1987 (continued)

Hi Tim and Mindy,

Thanks for the magazines. I stare at them for hours, especially the recipes. I tried to eat the picture of Chocolate Chocolate Intensity with Mint Sauce, but it lacked the flavor of the original. Needless to say, none of the ingredients are available here to make any of the recipes. Now if they featured Rice Rice Overkill with Ant Sauce it would be a different matter.

We figured it was finally time to move out of Manila, seeing as how flood and typhoon season will be starting soon. First we waited until the elections were over (less chance of getting shot). Couple days later there I was, sitting in the Manila Domestic terminal waiting for our flight, reading the funnies, half my Dunkin Donut in my mouth, when this priest comes in, sets up a table by the shrine in the corner and starts having Mass. *Everybody* stands up and joins in. The counter people and ticket takers whip out their missals and are reading along. I put down my donut and tried to look reverent. I also looked around for Rod Serling and his Twilight Zone. I didn't see him but I could hear the music.

So now we're in Davao, home of the durian (world's retchingly smelliest fruit) and the Alsa Masa (the anti-communist vigilante group). We have to go through about 10 Alsa Masa roadblocks on our way to language school, our helicopters are military gunships instead of traffic copters, and fully half the people walk around carrying rifles. Yes, I know there's a State Department warning to Americans not to come down here. So much for that.

Our church-owned house, which we'll share with other families that drop around like in Manila, is a mansion (well, size-wise anyway). Come on over this weekend and we'll have a housewarming. San Miguel will be there in his little brown bottles (we're used to beer over ice now) and we can even play croquet in the huge yard if we don't bother the neighbor's monkey, pigs and chickens. The giant cockroach situation is pretty much under control for now, only 5 or 6 a week, but I'm battling it out with the 5,372 mice. The two caretaker women who used to live here—along with their kids, boyfriends, extended families, livestock, chance acquaintances, strangers off the street, etc.—weren't too tidy and the mice loved it. So I've been setting out my tasty mac n' cheese/rat poison special, and we scraped all the dried-out dead mouse bodies out of the bottom of the stove where they loved to hide. We'll see who wins.

My latest adjustment is that I now have a 'helper' - what some might call a maid but I would say is more along the lines of a personal slave. Her name is Marcey. She has her own big room and bathroom downstairs and reminds me of Radar O'Reilly— you turn around and she's silently right there behind you, giving you a heart attack. Today she waxed all the upstairs floors, did our week's laundry (by hand), fixed our meals and is now out there cutting the front lawn with a grass clippers. For all this I pay her the better-than-going rate of $15 a month and she gets Sundays off. Actually I didn't want a helper and would have the raging guilties if Tinong hadn't explained the whole helper situation to us, and told us we had to have one (or more). Marcey's case is typical in that she's one of a large rural family, and when the girls get older and the parents can't feed them all, they get kicked out to fend for themselves. Unless they can get a job (not likely) they end up as prostitutes, have a lot of illegitimate kids and die young. Anyway, Marcey is a nice kid, but this is the first time she's ever been a helper, so we're going to learn together.

Well, I've been rambling on and on so I better end. Our location, so you can get to the housewarming party, is on Mars Hill in Davao City, on the way up to the Holy Infant Jesus of Prague Shrine. Telephone number 83-28-7, but it's a party line of about seven people and only works on random days anyway. Bye for now, Debb and Art

❦ Journal Entry

Went grocery shopping, then stopped by the ice cream place and had a halo-halo: purple (ube) ice cream, chipped ice, custard, corn, munggo beans and jello. Who thinks up this stuff?

❦ Journal Entry

The monkey screeching in the night woke me up again. It started to rain, and right after that came a big hatching of moths—the lizards on the ceiling were stuffing themselves sick. I don't know how the moths were getting in, but they were pouring into the house. Art was bashing at them with a flyswatter and Marcey was attacking with a broom.

❦ Journal Entry

I went downtown to the post office to mail the mail. I keep getting my leg clutched by the beggar lady under window 6—she had such a grip on me today I almost took a header into the street.

Summer 1987

Dear Mindy and Tim,

Excitement plus! June 21—we just had the longest day of the year! The sun finally set at 6:05, as opposed to 6:00, when it sets on the shortest day of the year. Aren't those extra 5 minutes great—we can do yard chores, go for long evening walks, have picnics. Living just off the equator is a thrill.

Just got your letter earlier this week. There we were in the Gaisano's junk food restaurant, stuffing down our hamburgers (the ValuePak: hamburger, rice and Coke) and reading away. You know how things hit you sometimes. I got to the part you wrote, Mindy, when you said my gazing globe lawn decoration was still shiny and the little blue flowers were blooming next to the garage, and I got all teary-eyed right there. Hopefully the 43 people who are always staring at me just thought I bit into one of those sharp little pieces of bone to be found in every piece of ground meat sold in this country.

Speaking of food (as always) I finally got my oven fixed. Even after we chiseled all the dead, dried-out mouse bodies out of it, it still wouldn't run so we got some guy to haul it out for repairs. It's back, but the trouble is, there aren't any numbers on the temperature dial, and it wouldn't matter even if there were because no matter how you twist the dial, the gas stays at the same level—it's either on or off. Interesting cooking effects are to be had from this arrangement.

We managed to get most of our household chores done before language school started, including breaking into our (locked) file cabinet, finding the remaining leaks in the roof (most of which were over our bed), and getting a guy from church to come and pick all our ripe coconuts. He left me three for myself so we got this long wicked-looking machete called a bolo, like you see the natives carry in all those jungle movies, to cut them open with. I'm going to try and prune my mango trees with it, like I see everyone else doing, and will probably hack my arm off. . . . Now I'm back after a morning of pruning trees. Holy Toledo, that bolo is nothing less than a 15-inch razor blade—whole tree limbs with one whack. No wonder headless and armless corpses are always turning up in the rivers around town.

So now we are in school. Last Monday we headed off, along with every little kid in the country being hauled to the jeep stop by their mothers, feeling pretty much the same way. But not to worry, so far we're loving it. We've even settled into a routine: arrive, boot the dogs out of my little tape-lab room (especially Winston, who has his nose pasted to my lunch bag from the time I get out of the car), sounds class (ng, ng, roll those r's), drill, tape. Then snack time! Warm pineapple upside-down cake last Friday. Couple more sessions, then Mass, games time (including folk dances), or just strolling around the beach. Art found our first-ever whole sand dollar the other day. Then lunch. Unpack the bag to see what Marcey's given us that day (always an adventure). Back to my own little room, get out my fold-a-cot for the siesta nap hour. Then afternoon sessions: more tape work, more drills, more baby-level conversation. And so goes another day. I figure if I play it real stupid, I can stretch this language school business out for a couple years. It's worth a try.

The other students at school are fascinating to talk with, too. There aren't many of us, but we're diverse. Sister Io (Samoa) helped us all celebrate Sister Pat's (New Zealand and Tonga) birthday last week by bringing taro root cooked in coconut milk. Great stuff. Father Pierre (France) had to run up to Manila a few days ago to help present a French government award to the woman who worked so hard to get him released when he was kidnapped by the Muslims last year. He's still living in the same area, working with the same Muslims now. Father Brendan (Ireland, of course), Honi (from Germany, and a Lutheran like us) and the Hempels (a nice Mennonite couple from the States) pretty much round out the crew.

Not much else going on. There was a baptism in church this morning and the kid had 21 sponsors! When we asked why so many, one of the youth group kids shortly and simply explained all: "more gifts!" These folks are smart; we could learn many things from them.

Better end now. I feel a snack coming on—it's Marcey's day off and I can raid the place at will. Bye for now,   Debb & Art

🦋 Journal Entry

Doug and Jan—the seminary grad and his wife who will be joining us soon to form a mission team, called from the States. They have two toddlers (!) and will soon be at the same place in Fresno where we did our orientation and training. Things are moving along.

Journal Entry

Up at 5 and headed off to the mountains. I got to go along this time to ask literacy program questions. Just outside Digos, the really bad road starts—extremely rough, lots of holes and trenches. It's pretty painful riding in the back of the Beaver (no springs). Came down on my spine a couple of times. It's over a three-hour trip for what is barely 60 miles—can't ever get above 20 mph on those roads. Tinong explained the national 70/30 principle of road building: the contractor gets the job with the lowest bid, puts 70% in his own pocket, uses 30% to build the road, everybody knows, nobody cares. Roads usually last less than a year before falling apart. We finally arrived in Malungon, and turned straight down the road for Asterio's house. He knew the old translator couple and will be helping get the proposed literacy project started. I discovered I'm able to understand a lot more Cebuano this time.

Journal Entry

It's the fiesta of St John the Baptist today—large crowds of folks thronged the beach to swim, so they won't get sick in the coming year. In town, kids throw buckets of filthy street water on passers-by and on whole jeeps full of people, especially if riders are dressed for the office. Lots of fights. Heard in Manila more wet passengers are just shooting the water-throwers.

Hi Mindy and Tim,

It's a good time to write a letter. We're having what they like to call 'monsoon rains.' That means after the first ten minutes you start roaming the house looking for materials to build your ark. After twenty minutes, you go around again, lining up all the lizards, mice, rats and cockroaches two by two, ready to board. I don't know yet what happens after thirty minutes but the assembled creatures are getting restless and I hope this typewriter is waterproof.

Art was pretty sick for awhile. He came home from school one day and said he felt a little warmish, so would I take his temperature. 102. At first I thought it might be malaria or dengue fever, but none of the other symptoms ever showed up, so it was just the flu. But his temp wouldn't come down for three days, so I was a tad worried. The third day I had him directly in front of the fan, and then the power company came by to start tinkering with our phone pole and shut the power off—all day!—including afternoon siesta, when they sack out all over their truck with handkerchiefs over their faces. So I was wetting washcloths with cold water and putting those on Art until all the water stopped. I don't know how he managed to survive, but he always was a stubborn cuss.

Language school is still going along OK. Megan the Dog had her puppies (8) so now there are eleven dogs, most of them crawling around and chewing on our feet. We had to write and give our first drama-drama for the rest of the students, so we turned Little Red Riding Hood (bringing Dunkin Donuts to her grandma) into a Kung Fu action picture. Let me get off the subject here to say I have discovered Kung Fu movies—they are great! Jackie Chan will be forever in my heart. Thank heavens there are always 5000 Kung Fu pictures to select from on TV. They have no plot so the 15-minute banks of commercials don't interrupt the flow, and the funny dubbing is a bonus. Anyway, we're finally learning some Cebuano but I feel like I'm always on those plateaus they talk about where you can't understand a thing, everything you say is wrong, and you're going backwards. Oh well, the snacks are still good.

I also seem to be experiencing some trouble with the reptile world lately. Lizards keep falling on me. Generally, I don't mind them roaming around the house, but I think they're losing their grip (pun intended). I took a pot out of the cupboard the other day and a lizard fell in my lap. I took the timer down off the shelf and a lizard fell out of the back. And now we're having snakes at school. Last week we had a three-snake day. Someone hollers "snake!" and the yard-keepers come running up and bash at them with broom handles, but they (the snakes) generally escape up the coconut trees. That's real encouraging, since we usually sit under the trees for our lessons. They're not real fat snakes but are about three feet long, and they can really move. The teachers say they're some kind of cobra.

Art has to go up to a pastors' conference all next week. I'm just not fond of the idea. It's being held near Iligan City on the north coast of Mindanao, because that's where the district president lives, so that means Art and Tinong have to drive ten hours to get there. But the bad part is they have to go right smack dab through the middle of Muslim territory, past Marawi, the Muslim capital. Just last week, Muslim separatists kidnapped sixteen people—a whole jeepney-load of professors and students from Mindanao State University, and want 6 1/2 million pesos ransom. Well, maybe with those sixteen on their hands, they won't bother about kidnapping Art and Tinong. A couple weeks ago there was a big communist massacre out in the area of our village. Twenty-four civilians, including a bunch of the Tagakaulos, were killed, so things are just not too bright all over.

On a happier note, since Art will be gone all next week and I can't get ahead of him at school, I figured I'd have myself a bit of a break. Peg and Jayne (my friends in Manila) and I thought we'd fly up to Hong Kong for a few days. I know that sounds exotic, but going to Hong Kong from the Philippines is only like flying to Kansas City from Wisconsin. Probably more fun. Now I really better go—I see the neighbor has his goats on my front lawn again. Bye for now, Debb and Art

🦋 Journal Entry

Art and Tinong went to Lumabat to check on the lumber for the house we're planning to build there. Viktor wasn't around but they got to talk awhile with two of his wives: the first wife had a disability, so gave permission for him to marry a second wife. I think the first wife had all the money, so in this case her permission was needed, or at least wise. Then Viktor got the house-helper pregnant, and rather than abandon her, the second wife gave permission for the helper to be the third wife, but she still functions as the helper. In the afternoon Art saw some kabogs—huge bats the size of eagles, which the people also eat. They hiked out and fixed their latest (5th) flat tire before driving home.

🦋 Journal Entry

Tinong brought Viktor to s
next cash advance for our ho
seminarians half to death. 1
was, and with the big bulge in
grenade) they thought he was
in. I guess they lean to the le
After classes, we were almost ho
stopped in the middle of the roa
driver was just holding up traffic
start pouring out. Cars in front o
blew up—what a jam.

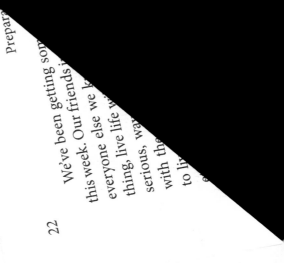

🦋 Journal Entry

We decided to see what the advertised 'concert' was about at the big
Apo Duwaling festival downtown. We arrived 45 minutes late (we're
learning) but still had to wait. The chairs all around us started to fill up
with baclas (transvestites) in various stages of female array, all preening
and swishing. I was jealous—I sure wish I could look that good in gown
and heels. The concert turned out to be some excruciating amateur
contest so we left after the second song.

🦋 Journal Entry

Ann, from school, reported she had a good trip to Midsayap—the bridge
was out at one point so they had to take an overloaded (80 people) dug-
out type boat with no outriggers across. She said they all had to sign
their names before starting out in case a casualty list was needed later.

Hi—It's Me,

I keep promising to drop a few lines, so I shall now do so.
All our teachers went to a funeral this afternoon—they didn't say
whose, but I expect it was some poor student whose brain blew
up from too many verb affixes. So we have some nice time off.

e interesting letters from the States
Texas are having a baby, like just about
now. They were the original 'do your own
ld and free' kind of people—and were actually
back when, about wanting us to go homestead
m in Canada. I said—are you crazy! I am not going
e in the boonies and kill chickens and cook over candles,
tc. So now he's some big government official with a baby and
a big house in the suburbs and here I am, living out in the . . .
chickens . . . candles . . . Life is so strange.

So as not to feel totally left out, we are having our own addition
to the family: decided to take one of Megan the Dog's puppies.
Oh boy, yapping, whining, puddles on the floor, legs chewed off
the furniture. I was looking over the litter, and while all the rest
were fighting over lunch on mom, one came staggering over to
me and tried to eat the toes off my foot, so I chose that one. He's
going to be a big one when grown—a good watchdog—so I'm
calling him Bantay (bon-tie), which means "guard!"

Now we're back to another round of New People's Army
(the commies) attacks and coup attempts. It's getting irritating,
as it's holding up our plans. Couple days ago, Art and Tinong
were going to drive down to Malungon to hike into Lumabat,
and pick a site for our house. They ate their rice n stuff early,
left about 5:15, and were back home again in less than an hour.
They decided not to go any farther when they heard that two
radio stations in Davao had been bombed by the NPA, and five
people killed. The NPA got away heading south for the hills—
exactly where Art and Tinong were going. A lot of military and
Alsa Masa (the vigilantes) were on the move, and it looked to
be shaping up for a sizeable fight. So, home again and back to
boring old school. A couple of the students from the Bajada
section said the bombing and gunfire there kept them awake
most of the night. How are we supposed to learn verb affixes
with all this noise going on?

The mail has at least been getting through, and it gives us a
chance to keep up with the folks in Manila. Our friend Jayne,
who is Australian and works as an exec in the World Bank, has
a good eye for detail. She was telling me about this Filipino

wedding she went to: the giant reception was held at the swanky Manila Hotel, with sappy music from the band and a dry ice machine blowing pink clouds on the floor when the bride came out to dance. There was a huge tiered wedding cake and above it from the ceiling, a big bell with streamers. The bride and groom are each supposed to pull one, the bell opens, and 2 doves supposedly fly out. Jayne has seen this before and says that what with the heat and all, often the streamers are pulled and two dead birds plop down on the cake. Anyway, these were alive and went zooming around the crowd. Jayne saw the bride's mother snag one, wring its neck under the table and stuff it in her purse to take home for later. Anybody that recognizes a free snack has all my admiration.

That's about it for now—don't forget to keep writing! Love, Debb and Art

🦋 Journal Entry

By afternoon, I had one of the worst sinus headaches ever. There's always something burning around here—either garbage, cooking fires or coconut shell charcoal—and the fumes go right up my head. Marcey's mother was over again. She says, this time, that her husband hasn't been paid where he works, and they need 700 (more) pesos. Also, she went on a rant, saying to never trust tribal people—the food they give you is always poisoned. Doesn't look good for Marcey to want to go along when we finally move out there.

🦋 Journal Entry

My urinary tract infection was so uncomfortable I finally went to Ann's doctor, who sent me all the way across town to the San Pedro hospital to give a urine sample (you have to provide your own jar). They told me I have a UTI (what a surprise) but I still can't get the needed meds until they release the results to the doctor . . . maybe tomorrow. Maybe not. The hospital was interesting—no window screens, no air conditioning, flies everywhere and smelled like a truck stop. Went home to calm down only to be cornered again by Marcey's money-demanding mother. Torrential rains pounded down for about four hours. The roof is leaking like a sieve.

🦋 Journal Entry

Tinong's boys arrived to fix the roof leaks. The dog went wild with excitement, slid through the mud by the garage and then tried to climb my leg. Picked him up to put out back and found all the neighbor's chickens eating everything out of his food dish. Art finally got back—said a road into the mountains has been promised by November (ha). Viktor's daughter is getting married as soon as she has the baby—big bride price: 2 carabaos, 5 horses, and more.

Fall 1987

Hi Mindy and Tim,

So what's new around here? They have us cranked into high gear at language school—only one and a half months left to cram 100,000 vocabulary words into us. And now we're only supposed to speak Cebuano. Yes, that calls for a great deal of smiling and nodding when I haven't the faintest clue what's been said (which is at least half the time). God alone knows what I've agreed to with all these people. Maybe I'm the new commander of the Civilian Home Defense Force and I volunteered for night patrol.

Art and Tinong keep making trips out to the boonies to see how things are going with the lumber, the supposed road into the hills, etc. They always see something unique every time—you'll like this latest. They were tooling along this little side road to the Baptist Agricultural Research Station when they come upon this broken-down bus in the middle of the road (second most common sight in this country, after palm trees). Broken down things never pull off the road, they just stop where they are. So Art and Tinong stop too, as they can't get around it.

The bus's battery is dead, so the people decide they're going to *push* it up this hill, and then roll it down to jump-start it (this is a full-size bus). About half the people get off to help push, and the rest of them *stay on*—and start reading magazines and stuff. Of the ones who get off, some of them drift around to the front, and the rest mill around to the back, and they both start pushing . . . against each other! Finally someone notices what's going on, takes charge and gets everyone to the front to push. They're all heaving away when someone else notices there's no driver inside to steer. In hops the driver. Now they're all pushing and actually get the thing moving, but the driver doesn't steer properly to turn the bus up the hill, and they push it into a tree. At this point Art and Tinong couldn't stand to see anymore (they'd been helping to push) so they left.

They said the Ag. Research Station was a great place, though. They teach hill farming for soil conservation, show how to raise tasty upo, kang kong and kalabasa for the table, and build their goat and duck houses on stilts over the stream so all that good animal poop falls in the water to fertilize the rice fields. I better start learning something from those folks. The Tagakaulos just gave us a whole hectare of land, and the only knowledge of farming this city-kid has comes from watching old Farmer Brown cartoons as a kid.

Next week Art has another week-long meeting up in north Mindanao at Cagayan de Oro City, so he'll head off in the blue Beav on Monday with as many extra people from church as they can stuff in there (it's a 4-passenger vehicle so they ought to be able to get in 8 or 9). The NPA has been blowing up bridges in the north lately, including a big one in Cagayan, so I don't know how they're going to get there. I guess they'll just have to (yup, you guessed it) cross that bridge when they come to it.

So while he's living the high life up north, eating his rice and sleeping on his floor mat, I'll have visitors. Doug (the seminary graduate), his wife Jan and their two toddlers have finally arrived in Manila. Doug will be attending the seminar with Art while Jan and the kids visit with me. Doug and Jan are terrific people—super friendly, open and sharing, real down-to-earth sorts—I think we're going to make a great team. Danny and Kerry, their kids, are your regular toddlers (I think Kerry is about 4, and Danny 2). I call them the Terror Twins. We ate with them at this one restaurant in Baguio when they first arrived. Little Danny is a championship eater. He had a circle of food chunks, toys, dinnerware and silverware around his chair about six inches deep. The waiters took turns going into the kitchen to cry. So now the kids will be roaming our house for a week. I'm stripping the place of moveable objects but it's still my bet they'll have the ears torn off the dog in the first ten minutes.

Well, I better be ending now—it's almost 9 o'clock, so way past my bedtime. Still miss you! Bye for now, Love, Debb and Art

✎ Journal Entry

Found cockroaches had been in the dresser drawers again, tearing up everything paper and starting to eat my driver's license right through the plastic. I had put cockroach powder in the drawers, but that did absolutely nothing, except maybe poison my underwear. So I took the drawers out to the garage and drenched them in Drelanox, which is this mega-serious insecticide. That stuff ought to work—it's banned in the States.

✎ Journal Entry

We headed off to Paradise Island in Davao Bay with friends from language school. The water was deep and clear so we did lots of snorkeling. Saw terrific live corals of all sorts, plus amazing tropical fish, including a big butterfly fish and some very weird-looking fish which had a red and green tartan head and striped body. Really. Got an incredible sunburn, especially on my back. And learned you should never try to say, "Wow! Look at that!" with your head under water.

✎ Journal Entry

I asked Marcey to burn leaves and stuff away from the house now, down under the mango tree at the edge of the yard. That will mean more mosquitoes in the house but, hopefully, fewer headaches. Smoke is now pouring into the yard of the guy with the 4 a.m. roosters—sweet revenge!

Hi Tim and Mindy,

Just got your letter with its cluster of great picture stamps, which I gave to Magda, our grammar teacher. The gift's main objective, of getting her off my back, failed miserably as she still finds something wrong with every sound that comes out of my mouth, but she did give me this gigantic sea urchin for my shell collection. I know, life ain't fair, it ought to be *your* sea urchin because they were *your* stamps. So in the interest of justice, I'll hand it over next time you drop by.

Well, Doug and Jan and the kids have come and gone on their big visit to Davao. Lucky Art got to attend a seminar up north with Doug, while guess who got to host Jan and the kids. No problem though—I almost have my hearing back in both ears again, the scars are healing, the plants and telephone can be replaced, the furniture reupholstered, and if I load enough gifts and movie magazines on Marcey, maybe she won't walk out after all.

My God, what a week. Those kids have a scream on them that'll rip your eardrums out. This is no joke. I was going to meet them in the grocery store and wondered how I'd find them, but didn't have to worry. In the entryway I just listened for the screaming and sure enough, it led me right to them. Mealtimes were especially relaxing. I didn't dare take them out to our favorite restaurants or I'd have a revenge grenade tossed in my front yard some night, so we ate at home. Enough of these fond memories. They're moving down here in a couple months to start language school, and will be renting a house on the *other* side of town (the Lord is indeed merciful). Doug and Jan are great people and the kids are actually pretty cute—when they're sleeping. Speaking of sleep, everyone is finally gone, the silence is just uncanny . . . there's the pillow . . . couple minutes . . . nap . . .

Back again. Had another interesting day earlier. Folks don't celebrate Halloween here but they have All Souls Day on November 1, which is even better. Everyone loads up food, kids, dogs and neighbors and they all go out to the cemetery. They find the graves of their special near-and-dear, spruce things up, put out flowers, light candles, and then spend the whole night out there. We went up the hill to have a look. What was usually just a big expanse of grass had become a giant city—lights and candles everywhere, tents and marquees set up as well as loudspeakers for the music (disco) later. Everyone had their food bags and sleeping mats along. They cook the favorite food of their dead relative and eat that while swapping memories. Then the guys get out the beer, the women set up the mah jongg table, the kids all run wild, and the dogs try not to be somebody's favorite food. When morning comes, they all go home.

Well, that's about it from us. Enjoy your Thanksgiving (which they don't have here either—think about it) and be sure to have a mound of stuffing, a big piece of crispy turkey skin, and a huge wedge of pecan pie (I'm killing myself here!) for me. Bye for now, Love Debb and Art

P.S. Today it was grey and rained all day long. Brother Declan (sure and isn't he from Ireland) said from great experience that a day like today is good for only two things: "for the bed or for the high stool." Whereupon he and Art had to be forcibly restrained from rushing over to the Insular Hotel next door to visit San Miguel and the garlic peanuts.

🦋 Journal Entry

I visited the town library, but it's pretty bad—it has a section of about 50 ancient fiction books in English, including such must-read gems as "The Leatherstocking Saga." So I decided to join a 'book club', which is really a store that rents used paperbacks. There's a $10 fee to join and each book costs about 50 cents to rent for one week, but it's the only game in town. Then went to church for choir practice—Mila finally showed up to direct. Half the choir was singing the piece in 4/4 time and the rest was singing it in 3/4 time, but no one would explain this to Mila, as it is rude to correct a teacher or leader. Interesting effect sound-wise.

❦ Journal Entry

Another one of those days. The garage door wasn't open wide enough, so when Art backed out, he tore the whole side mirror off the truck. On getting back to the truck after school, we discovered a flat tire. Art changed the flat but then found that the new one was flat too. We limped on to a vulcanizing place, where we sat endlessly on the bench and read ancient (hey, just like America) Cebuano magazines while the tires were fixed. Art discovered he has a chipped tooth and his side truck window is broken and won't roll up. Also lost the spare tire padlock. Sigh.

Dear Tim and Mindy,

Well, we did finally graduate from language school—it's hard to believe. Now if we could only speak the language, we'd be all set. The Big Day of graduation included tons of food, a caroling contest in Cebuano so we could start making fools of ourselves, more food, a gift exchange with our 'secret friends' (I'm a sucker for that kind of stuff), lots of snacks, the actual graduation ceremony, and then some food.

Since we were the stars of the day, we were required to make some sort of presentation to show our command of the language, so we came up with a drama-drama for the group. They had made us study this series of Filipino folk tales called Juan Tapulan (Lazy John) where this guy is so useless that his parents try to kill him off, but that always fails and he meets an enchanted animal that helps him marry the beautiful princess and live happily ever after. We just revised the idea a tad bit, and made our play about Stude Tapulan, the Lazy Student. He's always first out to morning snacks, but he grumbles about class so much that the teachers try to kill him off with the cobras in the yard and dropping coconuts on his head. Finally he meets the enchanted, mercury-eating fish out of the bay who helps him graduate by bribing the teachers, so he can marry the beautiful princess that he met during happy hour. I think the teachers then graduated us just to get us out of there. Luckily, Maryknoll (the owner of the school) espouses non-violence, so they couldn't throw vegetables during the performance.

Now that school is over we can concentrate on Christmas— which is sort of out there on the horizon somewhere. The town and store decorations have all been up since September (if the month ends in –ber, it is officially in the Christmas season). I bought my plastic Christmas tree and little twinkle lights at the department store and put everything up. Our friends in Manila have this swank congregation for business expats, one of whom had a couple of *real* Christmas trees flown in for himself from the Black Forest in Germany—which is a little more complicated than pointing one out at the Jaycees lot at the Y, but there are no pine trees in this country. Anyway, he gave one of the trees to our friends, and they sent down a branch for us. I took it to school—the teachers all examined it like the curiosity it was, and the expat students were all smelling it and getting teary-eyed.

The folks around here do great decorations, though. My favorite is the papaya tree down at the gas station that has big colored lights glommed around the cluster of papayas. The make-your-own trees at the other gas stations were also nice, with all the shiny oil cans hanging up for ornaments. And the Santa's sleigh made out of oil drums was truly prize-worthy.

Your big box arrived, and of course we would not cheat and unwrap any of the packages this early! But you would laugh if you could've seen how we smoothed out every single sheet of newspaper you used for packing material, and read every word on all of them. Bye for now, Love, Debb and Art

❧ Journal Entry—Christmas Day

Got up real early, read for a bit, and played my Handel's Messiah tape. About 8:15 a.m. I put through a call to Dad—it was 7:15 p.m. Christmas Eve over there. I got to chat for about 10 minutes before the line went hopelessly dead. They got fourteen inches of snow! Grandma is apparently not doing very well, so everyone is a little worried. Dad is alone for Christmas, but he has his tree up. I felt pretty sad for awhile.

❧ Journal Entry

I forgot to look, but sometime in the last weeks or so: One Year Down.

3

First Steps
Setting the Stage: Davao, Malungon, Lumabat
Winter 1987-1988

Dear Tim and Mindy,

Christmas was great and your presents were excellent! How did you ever guess that a Far Side calendar would fit our lifestyle so well? Gift shopping turned out to be a bit of a challenge this season. I got Art a nice can of Del Monte sweet corn from the exotic imported foods section of the grocery store (he had been looking longingly at it for some time). He said he's saving it for a special occasion. I also got him a book on chess, which is the only sport they cover regularly in the sports page. Yes, I know you can hear his comments about that, at the height of the football season.

Well, the elections here are finally over with, thank God. They were conducted in special, time-honored national fashion: last one left alive on election day wins the position. They managed to bump off over a hundred people. There was actually a box on the front page of the paper every day with the number of election-related deaths—sort of like a score card. And since it's going to take them at least another month to count all the ballots, I imagine several more will be shot or blown up or whatever. I'm just enjoying the peace and quiet, without those loudspeaker trucks blaring by the house every ten minutes. I think if I hear "La Bamba" one more time, I will run amok with the machete.

And now that the elections are over, Thea's neighbor can have her operation. On New Year's Eve, everyone shoots off fireworks for hours, and at midnight all the guys fire their automatic rifles and other fancy weapons into the air to make a lot of jolly noise. I don't know where those potato-heads imagine the bullets are going to come down, but a lot of the time it's on other people. Thea, one of our language school teachers, has a young daughter who was standing out in their yard with her best friend, when the friend was hit in the head by a bullet. The bullet is still lodged in her brain, and first they had to wait for the swelling to go down. But then they said they wouldn't operate until later anyway, as they had to keep the doctors and all the spare blood ready for the operations that were going to be necessary the last week before the elections.

Now we're getting ready for Wayne, Art's boss, to arrive tomorrow, but I don't think he's going to be in too good a mood. The office in Manila got a fancy new white Ford Laser, and Wayne wouldn't let anyone else drive it or even breathe on it in case something happened. He hired a brand-new driver to care for it, told the guy to take it out and get it washed, and the guy just drove off and never came back. Chances of getting it back are one in a billion.

Bantay the Brainless, fearless watch-puppy, is getting bigger all the time—in body, but unfortunately not in intellect. He was down at the end of the yard trying to bite butterflies for about half an hour yesterday. He does fulfill his one necessary function though— to bark his head off and hurl himself against the gate whenever anyone comes up to the yard (unless he happens to be sleeping).

Well, I've been babbling on so I better end. Keep writing! Bye for now, Debb and Art

❦ Journal Entry

Got up before 5, threw the water jugs and three butt-cushion pillows (hopeless) in the Beav, and took off for Malungon. Last week Art and Tinong talked with Viktor, who told them the foundation for our Lumabat house is poured and drying. Then they met up with Franco, the local guy overseeing the construction, who said the foundation isn't started yet as the sand (which Viktor last came to get money for) hasn't been delivered. When we arrived, Franco wasn't there—he was in Dadiangas, and there's still no wood. Franco's wife said Viktor took the advance for himself, refuses to pay the workers for any hauling, and even 'borrowed' P300 from Franco, and Franco is afraid. We went on to Nestor's house—he's also been collecting money all along. He swears Viktor has five carabao ready and the wood will be hauled by Saturday. We scanned the sky but did not see any pigs flying or other fairytale characters to enhance this story, but knew they were there. Drove back, stopped in Digos for a lunch of squid and fish balls. Yesterday there was an ambush in Santa Cruz, which we went through today – 7 military killed. No wonder there are so many military around today.

🦋 Journal Entry

Bantay the Brainless finally caught a chicken this morning. Marcey handed back what was left of it to the neighbors. Hope they're not too mad.

🦋 Journal Entry

Got the phone bill today. Our call to the States over Christmas, which was barely 10 minutes, was $75! I sure wish we could afford to call more often, but it looks like Christmases will be it.

Hi Mindy and Tim,

Guess what? I had cornflakes for breakfast this morning. I just had to share that excitement with someone. One grocery down here stocks a couple American things but I could never bring myself to pay $6 for a tiny box of cereal. Now for the first time they've got Filipino-made cornflakes, just like in Manila. There's no stopping progress.

Wayne, Art's boss from Manila, finally made it down here a couple weeks ago. He, Art and Doug got together in Doug's fancy new Nissan double-cab pickup truck and drove down to visit Lumabat. They had heard the new road to the village was finished, so they were all going to drive right up to Viktor's front door in luxury. Well . . . the highway part was at least OK, despite all the holes and trenches. But when they passed Malungon, crossed the creek and attempted the first uphill pull of the new road—absolutely no way. They had told Doug in Manila, "go ahead, just buy a 2-wheel drive, don't worry about special tires, the roads down there aren't that bad." The guys tried about an hour to get Doug's truck up that hill, different angles, everybody pushing—not a ghost of a chance. So now he has a brand new, incredibly expensive, useless truck. They just turned around and came back. He's kind of discouraged.

So Wayne, on the way back to town, saw a yard full of geese and decided he was going to buy a pair to take back to Manila. Only he happened to be staying in a hotel, so guess whose yard he wanted to keep them in for five days. I didn't mind—they were kind of nice waddling around the place. But the family guardian, Bantay the Brainless, was not so happy. He'd chase the things in laps around the house barking, and they'd be screeching and honking—until they got tired of it and turned around to start chasing him (same noises). The neighbors were real happy, I bet.

No, we're not getting any of those new TV programs you mentioned, or much of anything else watchable for that matter. Last time, Art counted commercial blocks of 14 minutes each, and then they cut the show. I broke down and decided to watch a movie (in real English) on TV the other night because I hadn't seen one in so long. It was "Supergirl" (listen, what are my choices) and pretty stupid, but I was finally getting into it, despite the commercials. Supergirl was getting ready for the big battle to rescue her boyfriend from the evil witch Selina, when the clock turns 12:30 and the station just goes off the air. Click . . . dark. I'm sitting there with my mouth open, staring at the snow on the screen, wondering whether I should rush outside and start screaming, or just go to bed. Went to bed.

And thanks for the new recipes, Mindy, but it's still no go on most of the ingredients. Although I think I could modify that rum cake and get it to work. With rum costing an actual 25 cents a fifth (they have to do something with all that sugar they grow when the rest of the world wants NutraSweet) I can afford to try the recipe several times until I get it just right—or fall into the sink, whichever comes first. Keep those letters coming. Love, Debb and Art

✿ Journal Entry

Went to Davao city hall to get our yearly alien residence certificates. We got directed to about three different places, upstairs and down, and finally found the window out in the back yard. A huge crush of people (of course no line) were all jamming and elbowing each other in front of the one window. Friends were letting others in and it looked hopeless, so we gave up.

[Next day] Got to city hall just as it was opening. We were about fifth in the crush, but we managed to get helped before the real mob scene started shortly after. People were putting their papers on the counter, then others would reach around and put theirs on top, the first ones would rearrange the stack—looked like a fight ready to break out. Didn't stick around to see.

✿ Journal Entry

Doug and Jan finally moved down to Davao and we went over to their place for spaghetti. Jan opened a cupboard over the stove and a big cockroach fell into the boiling water as we all watched. Extra protein I guess. But real homemade brownies!

✿ Journal Entry

Tinong says the sickness out at Samal Island, where we all go swimming, is an outbreak of leprosy. There are still many cases of it here.

Dear Tim and Mindy,

Big doings up in the mountains, and I've been waiting to write you all about it. I know—you're saying it's about time something interesting and letter-worthy happened around here. Art and Tinong were invited to Lumabat to officiate the wedding (finally) of Viktor's daughter. This being an occasion of great importance—and much food—I thought I better go along too. It turned out to be, as I have come to call them here in the Philippines, a 'do anything you want' trip. That's where you say over and over, "Dear Lord, if you just get me out of this, I'll do anything you want for the rest of my life!" We piled into the trusty Suzuki Beaver so we could get over the hill, and sure enough, in super-low 4-wheel drive, it inched us up the hill. Trouble is, the entire rest of the 'road' was the same way—they'd only scraped out a little dirt from the old horse trail, leaving all the grades just as steep and narrow, with curves banked to the outside of drop-offs. It was terrifying, and will only last until the first rain, but it saved us several hours of walking. Still had to hike about half an hour down the last hill.

We arrived just in time for rice n stuff, sat around, and strolled down to see our house. The wood which they swore had all been delivered weeks ago still hadn't been hauled out of the forest, and the advance money doubtless ripped off to spend on the late election, where some relative of Viktor's was running for office. At least they finally had the concrete poured for the support posts—the whole house will be up on stilts, like most of them build theirs. Then Art and Tinong wanted to get together with the couple, as the wedding was to be early the next morning (Wednesday). That's when we learned that there had been a communication mix-up with the groom's parents and the wedding wasn't going to be until Thursday, and we were going to continue sitting around for an extra day.

It was actually really nice. We strolled around a lot, chatting with people and getting to know them, except everywhere we went they kept feeding us (native coffee and rice n stuff) until I thought I would blow up. We had some good talks. The people are great, but the poverty is desperate in this area, and they have some awfully high expectations of what we're going to be able to do for them. But we're anxious to get started.

In the meantime, people from other barrios had started to swarm in and then things really got going. The women made paper flowers for decorations (I helped out) and others worked on cleaning the rice. From big flat baskets, they'd throw the rice up in the air to let the wind blow off the impurities, just like in those old bathrobe and head-towel filmstrips they used to show us in Sunday School. I counted the rice sacks and they started with about 400 lbs., but guests kept bringing more. The guys butchered seven pigs (incredible squealing), or else strutted around looking important with all their rifles, ammo belts and machetes. About dusk they hauled out the wooden drum and the women in all their belled and beaded costumes did some native dances. I said to myself, "Debb, this is not a National Geographic special, these people are your neighbors," while all the kids waited impatiently for them to finish. Then the high point of the evening: they brought in a couple car batteries (you remember this place has no electricity), hooked up the huge speakers, and started the DISCO music! It was right next to Viktor's house, at a level to crack your eardrums, and went on *all* night long, without letup.

Having slept about two hours the night before, due to freezing to death like I always do in the mountains when the temp drops into the 70s, and lying on the floor on a paper-thin woven mat, I was tired out of my mind. So I took my flashlight, went up to our little cubicle, lay down on the mat, and noticed on the wall the biggest damn spider I have ever seen in my entire life. Bulgy body and a leg span the size of a sandwich plate. I am not making this up. Back downstairs. Told Art and Tinong the spider better be removed in about three seconds. Tinong went upstairs, swatted at it with a shoe, and of course the thing hopped (they don't crawl here, they jump) somewhere. Looked everywhere, couldn't find it. So there I am in the dark, with a gigantic spider that I have no idea where it is. Lay down again, turned on the flashlight, there it was right over my head on the underside of a low board. Back downstairs. I was going to borrow an automatic rifle from one of the guys (hop away from that, sucker) when Tinong convinced me he could get it this time. Whacked at it again, and of course it hopped away, but at least this time it hopped out the window. So I spent the rest of the night listening to the nice disco music and waiting for it to hop back in again.

Finally, it was time for the wedding. It was supposed to start at 7 a.m., and only got underway three hours late, not too bad. All went well—the poor young couple (I don't think either one of them is older than 15) were scared out of their wits, normal wedding stuff. Tinong gave the wedding message, and Art conducted the ceremony and the vows. Then came the big feed—a whole roast pork on the table and so much other stuff you couldn't move without knocking something over. Actually, this was not a good deal—they ate up all the food in that village for the next couple of months, just like at a fiesta. A lot was wasted and now they're going to starve, with the weaker folks, and children, picking up disease and dying. The government is trying to crack down on this kind of imbalance but there's really nothing they can do. It was finally time to leave, which meant hiking back up the steepest part of the trail for an hour and back down the same fun road. We survived.

We're still trying to get plans worked out to take some kind of little vacation for a few days—haven't done that in a couple of years. I guess I don't count dozing through boring lectures and learning to eat raw bugs at missionary training school in Fresno as a true vacation. The office scheduled a pastors' conference in Manila for the end of the month, so we'll try and hook our trip onto that. I don't want to get my hopes up too high but if it works out, I'll send you some thrilling postcards. Bye for now, Love, Debb and Art

❦ Journal Entry

Had a glass of Coke beside my bed and when I woke up this morning there was a lizard floating in it. I emptied him out carefully, he staggered around for a bit (caffeine buzz) then took off. I did errands in town all day. Came home, had a Coke and ice cream (no lizard).

🦋 Journal Entry

There's incredible flooding throughout the city from recent downpours. Water was thigh deep and they were seining the streets for fish in front of Central Bank—getting some whopping big catfish too. I'm starting to drive like Art and the locals—cutting people off, passing on the right, leaning on the horn, driving an inch off the back bumper of the car ahead. This is not going to go over well back in the States. Art went over to Tinong's in the afternoon to help him sweep water out of the church.

🦋 Journal Entry

The kitchen sink is completely blocked again. I wrestled with the phone to get plumbers to come but they (probably wisely) never showed. Finally, Art decided to fix it himself and got this super strong Japanese drain cleaner from Gaisano's. He poured it in, stood back, and watched it eat clear through the pipes. Now when you turn the water on, it pours out straight onto the floor. Sigh.

Spring 1988

Hi Mindy and Tim,

Your last letter took a long time reaching us—they've got another new system going down at the post office now: every incoming piece of foreign mail is listed in a book, you get a slip of paper for it, then have to go into the back room and collect. This adds about a week to mail time, but is supposed to help stop pilferage. My usual comment: ha.

So then, our little vacation trip to New Zealand was great. I froze my parts off, but the natives tended to think it was still autumn (remember their seasons are upside down). They're all strolling around in shorts and T-shirts, while I'm huddled in long pants, sweater, jacket, wool scarf and gloves—with chattering teeth. Despite the arctic ambience, we went on to have an ace good time. Hope you got our postcards.

Before we went on this vacation, we had to fly up to Manila for a staff conference, and, while there, got a chance at some Culture in the Big City. I went with friends to the Bamboo Organ and Opera Festival, like I did last year, but Art declined to go on the grounds he didn't want to be bellowed at by some fat lady. He later regretted it, though, when we reported that we couldn't figure out how the alto, a woman of some heft, managed to stay inside her dress for the whole performance.

While in Manila, we also picked up our new truck. It is an animal. It's one of those 4-wheel-drive monsters, stuck way up in the air, with all-terrain tires. I feel like it ought to have a gun rack in the back, plus a CB radio, and I should be wearing a seed corn cap and spitting tobacco juice out the window. Needless to say, Art loves it, especially the dumb-looking (editorial comment) red racing stripe down the side. He freely admits he's having an attack of the second childhoods. Well, we didn't have a lot of choice. At the time, it was THE only 4-wheel drive (not model, I mean the *only* truck) available in Manila. I'm a little distressed at the incredible amount of money we had to shell out for it, but at least it ought to get us over that 'road' to our village. Cross your fingers.

Doug and Jan, our partner couple, are turning out to be pretty sturdy stuff. While we were away, they decided to take the little blue Suzuki Beav (remember their truck can't pull the hills) and drive into Lumabat, to keep up contacts. Halfway there, they came upon a big group of people, waving them down on the highway. A farmer had been shot (dead) and his son wounded in the leg. So they loaded the son into the front seat, with a neighbor squashed in front of him, trying to stop the bleeding, neighbors stuffed in the back, neighbors up on the roof, and set off for Malungon, the nearest clinic. Being Saturday, it was closed, so they took him to the police station, but not a lot of interest was shown there, either. I think the neighbors finally put the poor guy on the bus to Dadiangas, for the nearest hospital. So after they cleaned most of the blood out of the Beav, they decided to go on to Lumabat, and figured they would take the new 'road' because it was supposed to be flatter. Nobody told them it crosses the river seven times, most of the time at an angle. Tinong, who went along, got out each time to check for the shallowest part with a stick, but even so the water was up to the doors, and they were afraid the engine would stall. So they came back the other way, but at the top of the first steep hill, Doug accidentally killed the engine and they started sliding backwards, praying the brakes (notoriously bad) would hold. They did, and miraculously made it out OK.

Things are still a tad unsettled on the personal safety front. Doug and Jan's house was robbed a couple weekends ago, while they were all out at church. They lost their camera and stereo, some shoes and clothes. One of the other missionary couples was also robbed in Manila a few weeks ago—they weren't there, but their helpers were tied up and the place ransacked. I know it's only a matter of time before our place gets it too. I just hope I'm not there.

I went downtown yesterday to eyeball the damage to the big Mantex Department Store, where one or the other of the fanatic groups had planted a time-bomb the night before. I imagine things are going to heat up again until congress gets this land reform mess straightened out. Well, I better quit babbling and get this in the mail. Say hi to everyone for us. Bye for now, Love, Debb and Art

❦ Journal Entry

Reflections on our short New Zealand vacation: tidy suburbs with clean streets, chocolate cookies, orderly traffic (Art didn't call anyone an idiot once), cozy old houses, giant cooked breakfasts, good tea, mountains with snow, being cold, bathtubs, meat pies, antique and book shops, yogurt, comfy hotels, and not once did I see anybody peeing on anything.

❦ Journal Entry

Today was supposed to be a total eclipse of the sun, so I was really disappointed when morning came and the sky was completely cloudy.

As the eclipse started, there was a gradual deeper darkness. Then about ten minutes to total coverage, the clouds peeled back and we could see the last few coverage movements. There was the darker circle and the corona, just like all my old science textbooks, then the sun sloooowly came back until it was 1/4 there. At that point, the clouds closed up again into darkness. The whole thing was very eerie. As it got darker, the entire town became quieter until it was dead silent: no traffic, no horns, no radios, nothing. Not even any people on the streets—all stayed in their houses. Marcey shut herself in her room and wouldn't come out until it was all over. Art said the cloudiness was probably a gift of God to keep thousands of clueless people from staring straight at the sun and damaging their eyes. He could have something there. It was the last eclipse here until 2054. Hope I am not still here.

❦ Journal Entry

Slingshots are proliferating among the neighborhood kids—they're trying to shoot the ripe mangoes out of the trees by our house, but they've got no aim. Rocks were crashing on our tin roof all day.

Hi Tim and Mindy,

I'm sitting here in the aircon, for the few minutes it's going to last until the power goes out again, because it's about a million degrees outside, with humidity to match. This is now hot/wet season—as opposed to hot/dry, hot/windy, hot/cloudy, etc. The evenings still cool down real nice for sleeping though—mid-80s. Typical March to June.

Life continues moderately unboring over here. Holy Week was kind of quiet and restful. The whole country closes down from Thursday through Sunday—even the TV stations go off the air. I stayed at home Good Friday and watched people drag their life-size wooden crosses up the hill to the shrine. Tired me out. Art took the truck across town for a free oil change and checkup—this one car company had the bishop approve their giving free car service during Holy Week as their penance.

Easter was a real experience. The church had a 6 a.m. sunrise service but of course it was after 7:30 before folks started trickling in and they got started. Afterwards, everyone that wanted to (about 40 people) piled into our and Doug's and Tinong's trucks and headed off to visit the Philippine Eagle Conservation Center up on Mount Apo. OK, we were out of our minds to even think of going: the road was a dirt track and it's a known NPA stronghold up there. So we went anyway. Left the highway, started up the track. 2/3 of the way there, with about 5 km to go, had to abandon both 2-wheel-drive trucks and stuffed everyone into ours and had a few hike. Kept on going. 1 km from the end, had to abandon our truck too—steep mud downhill with a creek at the bottom roaring fast from heavy rains. Kept going (these folks were nuts—my mountain-climbing brothers would love them). They formed a human chain and passed each other across the river. Steep uphill on the other side and they're finally there. But the clouds were moving back in fast. It started pouring so hard you couldn't even see through it and our road back (red clay) turned into a river. Everyone trooped back from the eagle center looking wetter than drowned rats, back across the roaring creek and stuffed into the truck. We skated back down the track, totally out of control because there's no way to steer on wet clay—it's just like driving on ice, which, as you know, is just my favorite thing in the world. Arrived back at the other trucks (thank you, Lord) where it wasn't even raining. Everyone said they had a terrific time but I think it was just the thrill of still being alive.

The guys went off for another pastors' conference in the boonies, so Jan and I decided it was high time we had a break ourselves. We pooled our resources and got the cheapest room at the Insular Hotel, but still, what a place—right on the beach, pool, outside buffet, lovely gardens. Only one tiny hitch in this paradise—we had to bring along the Terror Twins. So there we were, relaxing, while keeping the kids from falling into the goldfish ponds, diving off the balcony, or mashing the baby chicks in the Easter display. Dinner wasn't too bad—we could get a few mouthfuls while the kids stood in front of the lobster tank thumping on the glass, went from table to table checking out what everyone else was eating, or followed the strolling musicians around the room. We did get in some great swimming though, and because it's a private beach, none of the coral had been dynamited by fishermen, so there were some excellent tropical fish. I found lots of giant starfish—the kind that look like huge, multi-legged chocolate chip cookies—for the kids, and we all built sand things together.

Before I run out of room I should mention that this morning I finally mailed off to you that package of durian candy you asked for. There is a warning however. Pay attention to this. Look at the candy, give it out for Halloween, put it in your scrapbook, but do NOT attempt to eat it. People here love it, but even Darcy the Dog would reject it. OK, my conscience is clear. Let me know if you're lucky enough not to receive it. Bye for now, Love, Debb & Art

❧ Journal Entry

Went to the grocery store for bread. I ran in, left Art to park. Came out—our truck was in the middle of the street with its door caved in, glass everywhere, a big crowd gawking, no sign of Art. I'm screaming around in circles like a chicken without a head, trying to get words out like "What happened? Where's the driver?" Of course nobody knew, or more likely had no idea what language I was speaking. Turns out he'd gone in to call the police. Another truck had run straight into him as he was turning—probably had no brakes. About half the vehicles here have no brakes – or windows, handles, lights, little stuff like that. Forty-five minutes later a cop came by to write a report. Had to tie the door shut to get home.

❧ Journal Entry

To the post office and got all the mail we've been missing for weeks with that stupid registry system. Received a doctor's report from our Manila physicals. Art is OK but I turned out to be carrying amoeba—the doc outlined a program of medicines I was to start taking right away so it wouldn't turn into full-blown amoebiasis. The letter was postmarked almost a month ago, so it's been sitting in post office never-never land while I could've been taking the meds I needed. I'll probably be dead in a week. To town to get pills and leave the truck at the repair place. We're going to have to order the window glass from Japan, and it'll take forever.

❧ Journal Entry

It rained a lot during the night. Around 12, Art sat up and said he was being dripped on. We moved the bed. Half an hour later, he woke me up again—the leak was spreading, so we moved the bed again. The ceiling panel is now warped and hanging down. Pretty soon the whole thing will come through. Got up and left before 6, made great time to Malungon. Stopped by Rey's place (he knows Asterio) and talked with his wife, Pilar, who teaches at the Malungon High School. There are 372 students there, but only seven rooms, with one of those being used as an office. Some rooms are concrete block, but most have woven nipa walls, dirt floors, and no windows. There's no library, in fact few books of any kind—the kids learn by what's on the blackboard. There is some English usage, which is the official language of high schools and colleges around the country, but here it's at about a third grade level. Having no books is ridiculous. I'm going to get them some. Maybe lots.

❧ Journal Entry

Back to Davao for supplies. I tried to have a nap with a relaxation tape of woodland birds, but the chickens next door didn't fit in. So we decided to try swimming at the pool at Gap Farm, just outside Davao. It's pretty expensive and not too crowded but we got stared at the whole time. One girl even took our picture. I felt like a circus event. Home. Found my first grey hair—I'm not surprised.

❧ Journal Entry

We've pretty well decided to move to Malungon until our house is
ready back in the mountains. From Malungon, if we drive over the
river and on the rough track to San Roque to leave our truck there, it's
then about a 7-mile hike over the mountains and through the rivers
to Lumabat. Do-able. Met up with Rey to go see a Malungon house
he found we could rent, but could only see the outside. There's no
running water in the house—only a pipe with a faucet out in the side
yard that the whole neighborhood shares. Bring your buckets and line
up. The landlord wants 500 pesos a month ($25) rent, which sounds
OK. It's a crowded neighborhood, as everyplace is. There's another
tiny concrete place next door, but all the others are bamboo houses
with tin or straw roofs. The place in front of us, about the same size
as ours but made of bamboo, is a boarding house for high school kids
that come in from out of the mountains—there must be about 50 kids
in there. Drove back to Davao. The 'highway' is falling apart rapidly
now, and is almost back to being a dirt track. I think all the fillings are
starting to come out of my teeth.

❧ Journal Entry

Met Jan and had a nice lunch together. Told me she's pretty sure she's
pregnant again. Terror Triplets! She and Doug want to move over to the
Davao mission house in about a month, so Art and I better get moving
over permanently to the Malungon house.

4

Edging In
Testing the Waters: Malungon
Spring 1988 (continued)

Dear Tim and Mindy,

We're here in Davao, a paradise of electricity, for a few days and had better take advantage of that to get a letter off to you. We've sort of moved again and, as always, it has not been boring. We heard of a house for rent in Malungon, which is the small village on the highway closest to our mountain tribal area, so decided to live there most of the time. This way we can oversee the on-again, off-again (mostly off-again) construction of our house and get all our projects started. We'll come back to Davao once in a while to breathe fumes, enjoy the roar of the jeepneys, and pick up all our building supplies.

At first glance, this house we're going to rent looks pretty good. It's concrete and wood, instead of bamboo, so it stands out like the Taj Mahal among all the neighbors. It's got two microscopic cubicle bedrooms upstairs, and a downstairs living space that's the size of a smallish one-car garage—with about the same atmosphere. But there are just a couple of tiny drawbacks to my decadent, American way of thinking. No running water, for one thing, which also means no sinks, drains, showers, tubs, flush pots, etc. The so-called bathroom is a little addition tacked on the back with a concrete water-gravity toilet (pour bucket of water down it to flush). To wash, you crouch on the floor, get the same dipper bucket of water and pour it over yourself until desired cleanliness has been reached, realizing you have to haul in every drop of said water by yourself, which tends to drastically modify your cleanliness standards. The water eventually runs out a hole someone knocked in the side of the wall, or else just dries up. This 'bathroom' used to be open to the sky and have waist-high walls, but I made the owner put some roof tin up and I've got a curtain up until he fixes the wall sometime in the next decade.

For the kitchen, there's one room inside with a tile counter for preparing your dried fish, live chickens, eels, fruit bats, whatever, and then another attachment on the back with a concrete slab for building your charcoal fire to cook the stuff. This is a high-class step up from the three rocks in a circle in the back yard that everyone uses up in the hills. However, I closed off the back part and got a little 2-burner bottled-gas hotplate. No refrigerator, of course, but I guess sardines don't need to be kept cold. There is electricity but I'd say it's more of an optimistic dream than a reality, as it only works a few hours of the day, and is about half the strength it is in Davao. That's OK, there's only one outlet in the whole house anyway. We were sitting there last week eating some sort of pseudo-Spam hotdish by the light of a candle stuck in a Coke bottle when the thought flashed briefly across my mind that I at one time actually owned a microwave oven.

Actually, we get along there just fine. There is one thing that'll tip me over the edge though, unless I can win the current war: giant bugs. I used to hate all bugs, and I've become so acclimatized I don't even notice things under three inches, but here there aren't many of those. When we moved in, this place was filthier than the Black Hole of Calcutta—Art did a nice job scrubbing the brown tobacco juice stains off the kitchen walls, but we still had to haul out a lot of the landlord's rotten food left to mold away in cabinets—so I knew there were going to be a lot of bugs.

The first day, I sprayed everything pretty good with Drelanox. Thank heavens for lethal banned chemicals the U.S. dumps on foreign markets like the Philippines—Raid wouldn't say boo to this place. We then went to bed, after setting up our little mosquito net. Middle of the night, in my sleep, I felt something crawling on me and instinctively brushed it off. It must've registered in my brain that it was a pretty big something, because I instantly woke up, shook Art awake, and told him to get the flashlight and see what it was. It was a giant cockroach! But then in the light of the flashlight, we could see the whole room was crawling with cockroaches! Several inside the mosquito net, fifteen or twenty scurrying all around the walls and floor. After a brief panic attack (I was going to commit suicide but I can never get the blades open on Art's Swiss Army knife) I bailed out of bed, turned on the light and got my shoes on. So there I am in my nightie, socks and sneakers, directing Art where to whap the big ones while he ran around the room mashing bugs with his flip-flops. The poor neighbors either thought there was a war going on or that Americans' late-night habits are even stranger than they show in the movies. Finally we got the last of them, brushed most of the cockroach body parts out of the bed, tucked in the mosquito net all around the mattress (which makes it impossible to get out, but something had to be sacrificed) and left the light on all night. We figure they came from the parts of the house that had been sprayed to those that hadn't, so the next day it was war. No gross-looking germ with legs was going to kick me around. I got my second bottle of Drelanox and sprayed so much of it around that the place probably glows at night and can be seen from outer space. I'm doubtless mutated for life but I don't care.

And that wasn't the end of it. The day after the big revenge spray, I came down to the kitchen to find the biggest millipede ever observed by a human being, crawling on the kitchen door. Remember the one Bill awed us with from his foreign bug collection? This one made his look like a midget from Munchkinville. I went to get Art. He came down with his shoe and went into the kitchen while I waited at a safe, very far distance. He said wow, and several other things, came back out, put his shoe down, and went outside to get a board. Loud whackings. He wanted to tell me how long it was fully stretched out but I didn't feel like talking about it. I found my first grey hair a couple weeks ago, and now there are several. By the time I get back to the States my head will be snow white.

Well, enough of all this. Glad to hear you got your package. I *told* you not to eat that durian candy, but you had to go and do it, didn't you. Well, I cannot be held liable in a court of law—I did my part. We're not immune either. We had lunch with a family in Malungon last week and had some kind of seaweed with little round bubbles that pop when you chew them. I thought it was pretty good, especially with palm vinegar. I better end before the paper does. Bye for now, Love, Debb and Art

❧ Journal Entry

Pilar has been helping us get settled into Malungon. She found us a great new helper, as Marcey is terrified of tribal life and thinks everyone is out to poison her. So Marcey will stay in Davao, and keep up the house there. Our new kid is Leksa. She's about 16, finished high school, and is related to the pastor of a tiny Baptist church in Malungon (who has no interest in going into the hills but likes to hear our plans.)

❧ Journal Entry

We heard that Viktor (who has helped to 'divert' most of our money and lumber so far) had what they call a high-blood attack—a stroke. He's still a young man, can't be more than mid-30s. The attack isn't surprising, though, when the national diet revolves around pork fat, coconut oil and layers of salt on everything. He's also high-strung, excitable, drinks like a fish, and chain-smokes. But the villagers are all saying it's a curse from God because he's a thief and a liar. Veeeeery interesting.

❧ Journal Entry

Back to Davao for roofing steel to haul in. We passed a jeep that was so loaded with people on the roof, back, hood and sides, you couldn't see the structure of the vehicle—only the tires. I couldn't figure how the driver saw out, or the people stayed on. At the post office, we got three big boxes of books and National Geographics that I'd asked Wayne to collect and send me. Great start for the High School library.

Summer 1988

Hi Mindy and Tim,

I am the delegated faithful correspondent this time, so with my trusty Kleenex box at my side (I hab a code id da head because I was up in Badibba) I will get started. We had an interesting few days up there. After a meeting at the mission office, we had to catch a cab back to where we were staying, and got to enjoy what they like to call a Monsoon Rain. All the taxis just quit when it rains. This is either because they all have bald tires, or else they have to drive with the windows wide open to keep them from fogging up, and then the driver gets all wet. So we stood there for over half an hour. And I thought you could only drown in lakes and rivers. But I love to watch folks in the rain. Everyone is paranoid about getting their head wet, because then they're sure they'll get sick. So they'll be drenched to the skin in a downpour, wading around in filthy water up to their knees, but will have a plastic bag or little hankie on top of their head.

Our tough-stuff truck is all repaired and back in action; they even put back the stupid-looking stripe. On our way back from Malungon a couple weeks ago, about eight military guys flagged us down for a ride. We're nice, and besides, we always stop for people with automatic weapons. So we let them all pile into the back and ride a few miles. I'd look back once in a while to see them resting their rifles on their knees—all pointed straight at my head as we crashed through the potholes. And I was sort of hoping they wouldn't meet who they were looking for while they were still in our truck. Finally they knocked on the roof to get off, and all faded into the woods.

We're still struggling on with the house. Most days Art loads up the above-mentioned tough-stuff truck with cement block, steel re-rod, tin roofing sheets, sand, cement and all kinds of et cetera. Drives about 7 miles straight up and down over the clay trails and six rivers. After unloading, he likes to hang around and talk with the village guys—they all sit around shelling corn off the cobs with their thumbs (no machinery, remember?) and has the giant blisters to prove it. Then he drives back out with the 20 or so people who've been lying in wait for him with their massive bags of corn, rice and bat guano, their bamboo, bananas, live goats and chickens, and their 475 children. He mostly tries to get everyone to ride back in the truck bed as a lot of them (especially the kids) have never ridden in any vehicle in their lives and– as sure as God made little green papayas—are going to throw up everywhere. I collect all the barf bags I can gather when we fly, but that's a lost cause. Oh well, what with all the goat, chicken and bat crap, how could the truck smell worse anyway.

Bad news last time we went back to Davao. Our favorite hotel—which had a nice band, our favorite restaurant, and the only decent public bathroom in town—burned right down to the ground. The fire truck was still there Sunday morning when we passed by, and from the water gushing out onto the ground from the holes in the hoses, you could tell why it burned. Peg, up in Manila, was also telling me about the giant Shoe-Mart department store that burned down. It was a huge place, all enclosed, with no windows—or sprinklers either. The fire started after hours, and at first didn't look so bad. The firemen entered through the ground floor, and that's where all the fancy imported clothes are. So the firemen started stealing all the jeans, until the security guards stopped them, and kept them outside until the police came. Meanwhile the building burned down. I don't try to make sense out of this. I just live here.

Well, I better be ending. It's getting dark and I don't feel like getting up and turning the light on. I get cranky when I hab a code. Keep enjoying those lazy, hazy, crazy days of summer! Hot season is finally done here, thank heavens, and it was a delight-fully cool 93 degrees today. Bye for now, Love, Debb and Art

P.S. Has Art quit smoking yet? What a question. Has hell frozen over yet? Perhaps something to do with every guy in this country smoking like a chimney, and cigarettes costing about a penny apiece. In our tribe they even measure distance by cigarettes. A journey can take "one stick" or "three sticks" – i.e., the time it takes to walk and smoke that many cigarettes. To be honest, he still does quit most Mondays, though.

❦ Journal Entry

Drove back to Davao for Doug and Jan's graduation from language school. We picked up a nice ripe durian as a graduation gift and went on to Maryknoll. They had changed the start time, of course, so we arrived in the middle of Doug's speech, but got to meet new students from everywhere: Japan, Holland, Ireland, Spain. We chatted with the teachers in Cebuano. Wow.

Stayed on a day. I bought some odds n' ends like covered soap dishes because the mice and cockroaches keep eating our soap in Malungon. In the evening, Art and Doug waited up to see the big boxing match in Manila live on TV. Three and a half hours of hoopla and commercials, and then one guy gets knocked out in one minute. Big deal.

❦ Journal Entry

Headed back to Malungon and arrived just as the Founder's Day parade was starting—we were the last vehicle through. They had an honor guard, local dignitaries, several bands, a few tribal groups in costume and every school kid for miles around. I chatted with a few of the 6th graders and was soon surrounded by hordes. We met up with Doug, Jan and the kids and were mobbed again, this time on account of Kerry and Danny. Local kids, even adults, are always trying to touch or pat them because of their blue eyes and blond hair. For being the Terror Twins, they are remarkably patient with it. I lit my new kerosene lamp and blacked up the glass chimney but good. Can't get the hang of it.

❦ Journal Entry

It absolutely poured for hours in the night. I came down to find huge puddles in the living room. Also a big scorpion (first I'd ever seen) just standing there so I dropped the big Readers Digest Fix-It book on him and waited for Art to clean it up.

✤ Journal Entry

Doug, Jan and Tinong came over for a meeting with lots of initial planning and assignments. Art and Doug will do the Bible classes, teaching, training leaders, arranging farm seminars, well drilling, garden planting, community betterment, etc. Jan has a medical interest, so will start the medical programs and clinic. I love education and have a bit of background, so will set up adult literacy classes, get primers started, work with existing schools (where there are any), gather materials, etc. We've already started large parts of it but now will get more organized, start looking for grants, etc.

Dear Tim and Mindy,

Just a quickie to let you know of the safe arrival of the *Victoria* magazines (both of them, no less!) Now that the post office and all their friends, and the friends of *their* friends are done reading them, it's my turn, but at least I actually got them. I read an article in the local paper the other day that says there's a new and lucrative post office racket: you can take out a secret paid subscription with your mailman for the magazine of your choice, he will sort of 'relocate' that copy to you from its originally intended owner, and nobody knows how it got lost in the mail like that, but isn't it a shame. No, I'm not making this up.

Doug and Jan finally graduated from language school in a blaze of glory and the usual but wonderful over-abundance of snacks. Instead of moving over to the Davao mission house, like they'd originally planned, something addled their brains and they're now thinking of moving straight to Malungon, like we did. Trouble is, there seems to be only one remaining rentable house in the whole place which has those little amenities we've learned to treasure—like an indoor so-called bathroom, nearby water, and a few hours of random electricity. So why don't they move right into this palace, you ask? Because the deal is being arranged by the guy fondly known to us all as Larry the Liar, who is one of the ones finding more creative, personal uses for all our construction funds rather than boring old building supplies. No doubt Larry is more than willing to rent this place to them, but the terms and details are going to be interesting. Watch this space for further news.

Art had a pretty good adventure. We were in Davao gathering building supplies, so he and Tinong took off for a couple days to deliver them to Malungon. I stayed behind in Davao to watch the house, as Marcey was on vacation. I was doing laundry out back in a bucket under the faucet tap with a bar of soap, when I heard big booms of thunder and hurried to finish—but then I noticed the sun was blazing and there were no clouds. Next day at suppertime Art pulls in and says he and Tinong had gotten stopped by a war. They had gotten as far as Baracatan, where some soldiers told them they might not want to go on. There was apparently fighting on Mount Apo, and a truck of military reinforcements had been ambushed on the highway. But Art and Tinong saw traffic coming from the other way so continued on (and you thought only Bantay was brainless). Near Santa Cruz all traffic stopped again, and this time they could hear up close all the mortar and machine gun fire (the thunder I heard miles away), so they turned around and went back to Baracatan. They chatted with the soldiers there again for about an hour until a bus came through from the other side, so they finally made it to Malungon.

One final food thrill for you and then I better quit and get this in the mail. Wayne was down from Manila a couple weeks ago and always likes a new taste sensation, so we took him out to Barrio Gaisano's, the traditional natibo foods place. Their specialty is grilled tuna eyeballs, which Wayne was anxious to try, but I stuck with the kinilaw (a sort of marinated raw fish salad which is reeeeeeeeally good), and the puso (banana-heart) salad. It might not be Kraft Mac n' Cheese, which, as we know, is God's most perfect food, but it comes close.

OK, that's all for now—will write a longer letter later. Keep those cards and letters coming. Bye for now, Love, Debb and Art

❦ Journal Entry

Doug and Jan arrived in Malungon about 10 a.m. and went to the tiny power company office, which we finally discovered in some obscure alley. As expected, Larry owes a huge back bill—P3,300, which must be paid before the electricity can be turned back on. Doug and Jan were discouraged, as they wanted to move down right away, and went back to Davao about 5. But excitement—we can now get the "Voice of America" on the shortwave radio for the first time!

❦ Journal Entry

Doug and Jan still haven't returned. It turns out Jan had a rash, got some medicine, had a terrible reaction—hives, and eyes swollen shut. The doctor put her in the hospital, where student nurses trooped in all the time to study her case, giggle at her, and feed her nothing but strong fish for every meal til she wanted to heave. When I visited, her face was still very puffy, with scabs from the hives. Now she has a big list of restricted foods due to allergies—probably chocolate and ice cream, knowing her luck. Worse, she thinks the itchiness is coming back.

❦ Journal Entry

It's raining again—I've never seen such a downpour. We were playing Trivial Pursuit and had to call the game on account of getting drenched in our own living room. There's no place to sit without being under a hole in the roof. Doug finally arranged to pay Larry's electric bill in lieu of rent, and they can at last move in—if they can get out all the squatters and bugs.

Fall 1988

Hi Tim and Mindy,

Art is up in Manila, so I will be the current correspondent. He was called up a couple days ago to write some project proposals for the literacy and medical projects, and they're supposedly under a tight deadline . . . at least that was his so-called story. But *I* know he's up there watching the Olympics and eating jelly donuts.

Things are moving right along here under the motto "hinay, hinay, basta kanunay" which means slowly, slowly, even if it takes forever. Tinong, his son Rollie and I hauled 225 floorboards into Malungon yesterday, where they're now stacked all over our rental house. It was too wet again to even consider getting into the mountains. We wouldn't even have made the first river. Davao was flooded out again Sunday night—a lot of streets knee-deep and you can imagine what the water's like with people throwing their garbage everywhere and spitting all over the streets, and worse. Now the radio says cholera is starting. We haven't been boiling our water, but I guess we ought to start.

Great excitement, I now know how to drive our big mean tough-stuff truck, instead of the wimpy blue Beav. I had to take Marcey home, so I was forced to drive it. Actually not so bad. I didn't even kill anyone (that I know of). I *told* Marcey to put her seatbelt on but she didn't want to so is it my fault I almost put her through the windshield three times? Power brakes. For awhile there, we didn't have any horn, which is absolutely fatal. The horn is the most important part of any vehicle. Now it's fixed again so I can express myself: "Go ahead, Bubba, pull out in front of me and I'll rip your fenders clean off." I notice I get a lot more respect driving this truck. Maybe it's the terror-stricken way I clutch the steering wheel.

The boys at church built a wooden rack on the back so we can haul lumber, and it sticks up above the cab of the truck. So when I brought the truck home yesterday, I didn't know if I could get it in the garage or not. Marcey was directing and said go ahead, go ahead, plenty of room. Of course it didn't fit and I got it jammed up but good on the top frame of the garage door. It was probably her revenge for my putting her through the windshield.

Doug and Jan's experiences, as they come along behind us, are mirroring our own, but so far they haven't packed up and gone back to the States. They finally moved down to Malungon, to their own rental house, a few weeks ago. Jan doesn't douse the place in as much Drelanox as I do, so they've been having the usual giant spiders and scorpions in the bathroom. Doug was even bitten on the face while sleeping a few nights ago, and he thinks it was one of those big centipedes. OK, I'm not even going to let that picture enter my mind.

Last week Jan woke up in the middle of the night to hear this scratching noise, which she thought was someone trying to get in the back door. So she's punching Doug, trying to wake him up (I guess he's like Art—will sleep through Gabriel's trumpet blast) when there's this big crash. Turns out it was a rat trying to get into a covered metal pan of cookies she had on top of the stove, until it knocked it to the floor. Doug never did wake up, but the crash scared off the rat and woke up the kids. So they were out of bed and running around until she finally had to get up to get them back in bed—and stepped on a big slug on the floor in her bare feet. Now I know why the buses don't run at night. We'd all be sitting there at the airport at first light waiting for the early bird special out of here.

A couple of nights later, the rat came back (it lives in the ceiling) but this time got into their helper's room. She wasn't too pleased about having a rat running around her room at 4 a.m., so took after it with a machete. She never did get the rat, but she did, in the process, create some rather interesting home fix-it projects for Doug to do so he's not just lying around in his hammock all the time.

Well, I'm not in the mood to think about any more troubles. The sun is shining, the breeze is wafting—in fact, I think I'll go out there and get me a fried banana on a stick from a street vendor. Bye for now, Love, Debb and Art

❦ Journal Entry

Back in Davao for supplies. Jan stopped by to say her rash is better—it's an allergy to citrus and molds. That's the worst news, as there's always mold growing on everything; we have to keep wiping green stuff off our books. I went to town to get my watch fixed: it's stamped Made in the Philippines but no one has parts. I finally handed it to some guy with a little sidewalk stand over near the post office; he took it apart, fixed it, works fine, charged 5 pesos (25 cents).

❦ Journal Entry

Picked up Flora at the airport. She's down from Manila to look at our medical administrator job. We took her out to Malungon, and she'd never seen a Skylab—a motorcycle with the big board balanced across the back to hold three extra riders per side. Decided to go on to Lumabat, so we loaded our truck with us, Tinong, Flora, Doug, Jan and both kids, Viktor and two kids, the 2nd wife, various endless relatives, sacks, rifles, on and on. Made it in fine. Had coffee with Raymundo and other friends. We could see rain just across the valley, so packed up the whole load again, including more vigilantes with rifles who saw us going in and waited for a ride.

❦ Journal Entry

I finally fixed the typewriter; then, when I plugged the transformer back in, flames shot out, scorched the socket, fried the plug and blew a fuse. We're also out of cooking gas, so Art went out to look for some while Marcey started preparing the rice for lunch. There was no cooking gas anywhere in town. *None,* in a town of over 800,000 people? Yup. Threw out the rice, looked about ten other places for gas, but none was promised until Tuesday. Bought some crackers. Marcey took her rice over to a friend's house to cook.

Hi, it's Me.

Just a quick one here. I even have to handwrite my part because Art thinks he's coming down with something and has planted himself in front of the big fan, so I can't use the transformer to run the typewriter, but why am I explaining all this anyway, who really cares?

Getting on with it, we're still plodding along. Several months ago we decided to ditch Larry the Liar and buy all our remaining house lumber at a lumber yard and haul it in on our truck. Terrific idea on paper. The kids at church built this big rack on the back of our truck, we loaded it with umpteen 14-foot two by two's, and started out for Malungon. Not even out of town, we found our regular road was blocked by a landslide. So we took another one—which was so bad that it started a severe bouncing in all the loaded lumber. Back to the house, unloaded half of it. Continued on. Got as far as the first mountain when the rack just started to literally disintegrate—the load was shifting and nails snapping off right and left. So every few miles we'd stop to rebuild it, and slow down more. We ended up crawling into town hours later, with visions of strewing lumber all over the highway.

First thing we did was run into Doug, who had just had a meeting with the local military officials. They told him there were currently a lot of armed NPA groups up in Kawayan and Lumabat, and if they were to ever stop us and demand our truck, to just give it to them. OK, that's just fine by me. I wonder how I can contact them. They can have the whole shebang, as far as I'm concerned, and the sooner the better. Doug says he's thinking of getting a horse.

We've been getting most of our food now from the market in Malungon, which is just a series of big open sheds. Jan and I went over the other day, along with the Terror Twins, to pick up some meat. They butcher one pig a day, but we never seem to get there early enough. When we arrived, all that was left was the head. Little Kerry studied it over pretty good and the gal at the stall used it to help her learn Cebuano words for all the parts: eyes, teeth, ears, nose, etc. The kids are picking up the language fast.

Will write more later. Bye for now, Love, Debb and Art

❧ Journal Entry

We went back to Davao to pack for the Manila mission conference. At the post office, I would've parked in my usual space but a car's engine was on fire there so I parked around the corner. I got a whole box of Reader's Digests for the High School! That's good because "Word Power" is where they get the words for the national test. A woman came by the house to ask about buying our coconuts from the trees in front. I finally said OK but bargained on the price.

❧ Journal Entry

Manila. It started raining hard and poured all night, so Peg and I couldn't go for our usual stroll. When the paper came, we learned there was a typhoon down at Cagayan de Oro, which washed out their big new bridge. The guys headed north for their mission conference in Baguio. The rain continued all day with the typhoon coming north, signal 2. Finally in mid-afternoon, it was raised to storm signal 3 (most serious). About 7 p.m., the wind started to rise and stayed strong. It seemed to peak about 2 a.m., with rain pouring down sideways, steady screaming winds, trees bent double, stuff crashing. I had the worst headache, with sinuses draining, probably from low pressure, so I got up every half hour all night. At least I could keep track of the storm.

❧ Journal Entry

Reports were starting to come in—the Marikina area was flooded, people were being airlifted off their roofs by helicopter. There was a huge power failure around 5, so we ate supper by candlelight.

❧ Journal Entry

The guys got back from Baguio around 1:00. Bad news: all the wrong people were elected to top positions in the leadership. Accusations were flying of graft, money stolen, all the usual. But worse: a huge fight and big coup attempt in our own mission group! A couple of the guys up north hate the administrator in Manila and tried to get him booted. Sides taken. Graham and Art were snubbed, our mission criticized. Calls for it to be cancelled. Very bad feelings all around—no one talking to anyone else. Sigh.

🍂 Journal Entry

Left for the airport. We saw that the Bacolod flight returned to the gate and was cancelled, but all the passengers still wanted it to go anyway. They staged an uproar and refused to get off the plane. The police were on their way. Our flight was rescheduled too, and we knew we'd be way late. While waiting, I got to pondering: if our mission gets closed, I wonder what they will do with a 3/4-built house in the mountains. They could turn it into a giant chicken coop, or no—it would be a great place to store all the bags of bat guano. How appropriate.

5

Hanging On
Battling the Obstacles: Malungon
Fall 1988 (continued)

Dear Tim and Mindy,

Just got up and did my daily morning routine down here in Malungon: get dressed (first check shoes and clothes for insects—shook a massive spider out of my hanging-up skirt the other morning), light the mosquito coils, haul water, put the lantern away, make coffee, start the rice, get Art up. With all that energy going, I figured I better get a letter off to you before the first disaster of the day interferes.

Speaking of disasters, we flew up to Manila a couple weeks ago for that big mission planning conference we told you about. There was so much fighting I figured we were back in the States there for awhile. Everyone was jockeying for their own position and it ended up with no one talking to anyone else. Logistically, that's hard to do, but I think they pulled it off. There was big talk about firings and closings and lots of pouting. Sounded like a raging case of mass PMS to me, but unfortunately for that theory, they're all guys. Well, everyone finally cooled down and now they're all tiptoeing around each other. Which is good; maybe we can finally get some work done.

So the guys all went up north to Baguio for the conference, but I stayed in Manila with my friend Peg . . . and we had a typhoon (what you'd call a hurricane)! I've always wanted to see one but it wasn't at all what I expected. Sure we had torrential rains, and winds that built up to a sustained scream and stayed there for hours, and lashing trees, and floods and power outages. But we just didn't deal with it properly. I've seen that old Humphrey Bogart classic, "Key Largo," and I know what you're supposed to do. But we didn't board up the windows or fill all the bathtubs, or slug back whiskey and chain smoke, or casually stand around talking cool in the face of certain death. I felt like we sort of wimped out. Art said up in Baguio it was pretty much the same. They were staying in a school dormitory and had to keep moving to interior rooms at night because every few minutes another window would blow in and go crashing on the floor, with glass everywhere. Interesting as it was, it might be good that they never have these things down in our area of Mindanao.

The rest of the week I tagged along with Peg to some of her women's meetings (their congregation is for all the expats in Manila) and it was something like being on "Lifestyles of the Rich and Famous." These women, who are all political or corporate wives, with half of them being rich Filipinas, live in houses posher than the Biltmore Mansion, and more massive than Buckingham Palace. You sit on elegant cushioned lounges and strain to see the people way off on the far side of the room. The air conditioners hum quietly—not just to keep us all dainty, but to keep the humidity from the lily ponds and swimming pool out back from making mold on all the original oils and artworks scattered around. After a while, the uniformed servants come out and hike quietly across vast tracts of Persian (real) rug to offer us iced drinks and little designer snacks, which do not include fried banana on a stick or chicken feet. I concentrated real hard on not letting my mouth hang open, not staring at everybody's diamond jewelry, and not spilling anything on myself. I tell you.

Now that we're back, we can get into all our projects again, including the ongoing saga of building our house. You might not want to read this part—it only gets worse. The 'road' to Lumabat has fast been washing out as we continue to get constant downpours. It acts as a natural river, with the water rushing down it, carving a big channel in the middle. The truck has to straddle or get around this trench, get over the big rocks and continue to pull the hills while not falling over the edge. So there are Art and Tinong with their big load of lumber, 500 Tagakaulos clinging on, Art driving, Tinong directing. Well, it finally happened—a wheel slipped into the trench and Art says the next thing he saw out his side window was the ground, right next to his face. The lumber shifted and the whole thing was teetering right on the edge of the ravine. The 500 Kaulos bailed out pronto, but Tinong went rushing around to the *down* side, and started bracing himself against the truck as if he was going to keep it and tons of lumber from rolling off into the ravine. Art, who finally managed to lever himself out of the truck, was having a little chat with the Lord about how it's OK if the whole truck rolls down the hill but *please* get Tinong out of there before he's crushed to death. Finally they managed to talk him out, the 500 Kaulos pulled against the *up* side, and they slowly eased it out of the trench. Even with the lumber intact! Looks like it's back to the horses.

And Art finally got to meet Charlie, the rather mysterious missionary who's building something way over on the far side of the mountains. No one knows anything about him, not even his church affiliation or who he represents. He's older, and supposedly has a family back in the States. The usual rumors are flying about how he's CIA (*every* American is CIA until proved otherwise). Art only got to talk to him about three minutes in passing but in the process discovered that they're both from Missouri. So naturally they started tawkin' 'bout they vee-hickles, and crossin' the crick, and other unintelligible stuff. Good thing it was only three minutes or they probably would've started singing Johnny Cash songs.

OK, time to get this in the mail, so you'll receive it in the next month or so. Keep writing! Bye for now, Debb and Art

❦ Journal Entry

Flora is back again, this time for good—hurray! She decided to take leadership of our mission medical project, but first has to attend language school. I didn't realize Manila Tagalog-speakers need to learn Cebuano just like we did. She'll live in the Davao mission house with Marcey for a few months until she's done with school. I told her not to worry about school—the snacks are great.

❦ Journal Entry

I packed up more donated books, after I finally finished with the cards, pockets and covers, and took them over to Pilar for the High School. I learned that the last batch I gave them (67 books) is already completely checked out. The most popular are those Sweet Valley High romances that Jayne sent us from Australia. Art said he spotted a few of the secretaries down at city hall secretly reading them.

Then I asked Pilar about further needs, and she said they could use a sewing machine for Home Ec. The classes are trying to learn machine sewing, but they don't have an actual sewing machine—they do it all by looking at pictures! What next—learning to type by looking at pictures of keyboard charts? I shouldn't laugh—I bet that's exactly what they *are* doing. I think I will write to the banner-making ladies at Dad's church for the sewing machine funds, and ask Tinong's wife to start checking local prices in Davao. I thought I saw a stock of Singer treadle machines there.

❦ Journal Entry

Art and Doug went to Dadiangas for more lumber. They loaded it up, had Cokes at the coffin factory across the street, then came back . . . after fixing their latest flat tire (16 and counting). I took the truck over to Banate to get the flat vulcanized. When they charged me 30 pesos, I told them the price was 10 pesos, but gave them 15 to be nice. I now have a new working phrase to use in most transactions (in Cebuano of course): "I might be white, but I'm not stupid." It makes them laugh—but not quit overcharging.

🦋 Journal Entry

Up, started fixing breakfast. I watched ants dragging a whole big spider body, with its various unattached limbs and the parts we had whomped last night, up the wall and into their nest in the ceiling. It was a pretty impressive display of organizational skills.

🦋 Journal Entry

We made a lightning trip to Manila to fix the big fight. Graham is now the new mission administrator, so he'll have to stay on another term. Peg is very sad—she had wanted to go home so badly. Flora called from Davao to say one of the huge mango trees collapsed, broke the wall, and is now blocking the road. She also reported Marcey is gone a lot, not doing anything and trying to borrow money all the time. Uh oh, trouble on the horizon.

Dear Mindy and Tim,

Art is upstairs, trying to fix the bathroom sink for the 4 billionth time. After saluting him, and encouraging him to come home with his shield or on it, I have wisely left the field of battle and am downstairs as far away as an extension cord will get me. Some screams and strange words still come floating down, but so far no blood.

By the fact that I mention we have a sink (which *used* to have running water, but never mind about that now) you can tell we are here in Davao City catching up on all the fun fix-it chores that have been piling up. Later in the day I will go up on the upper roof and try to nail down a sheet of roofing steel to cover a hole the size of a softball we found up there (I figure it was a meteor but Art swears the whole place is demon-possessed), and try to stop the various leaks in the bedroom, most of which are still directly over our bed. Then maybe later we'll try to fix both toilets, change the latest flat tire and fix the ignition wire on the Suzuki Beaver, and finally get rid of the huge piles of wood which came from one of our mango trees which collapsed in its entirety one calm night several weeks ago. Then in the evening, for our grand finale, we'll douse the whole place with gasoline, toss a match on it, stand out in the street and watch it BURN.

We're still staying down in Malungon most of the time. I like it down there in the boonies a lot better than the hassle of Davao. My garden is really booming. Already I've got little green tomatoes, although in putting in about 20 plants, Leks might've gone overboard just a little bit. My kang kong and camote tops (your basic roadside ditch plants) are taking over the yard and I put them in everything. This is just a small garden though. I'm saving my big effort—plus the chickens, horse, fruit trees, cacao, coffee, etc.—until we get into the hills. Be ready for some laughs. The tribal folks are still waiting for us to show up like you'd wait for the curtain to go up on a vaudeville act. They think it's a riot we're going to get electricity from the sun. And they might be right—I don't believe in it either. It'll be cheaper than Malungon, though. Our electric bill for last month was 14 pesos (about 70 cents). We're going to have to cut back and stop burning the light bulb so long. Maybe go to bed at 8 instead of 8:30.

Now that I know Pilar at the High School and was fool enough to give them books and materials, we're big-wigs whenever they need a handy dignitary. I lately got to pin the sash on "Miss Intramurals," be a judge in the cheering/yelling contest, and listen to endless droning speeches. The recent fiesta at one of the elementary schools was better. All the kids had great costumes (one grade stapled leaves all over their T-shirts and shorts to be trees) and did dances—or milled around in confusion—while the teachers beat the gong. Good stuff.

How's the election coming along? I bet it's way less dramatic than the one we had over here. I wrote to the County/City Building there in Point and asked for our absentee ballots for President *only*. Due to tax and residence factors, we cannot vote in any state or local elections. So back in the mail come these big official envelopes stuffed with ballots for *all* the state and local races, and *no* presidential ballots. Tell you what, why don't you each vote twice, once for us. It's a time-honored American tradition and you are from Chicago, aren't you Mindy?

I better quit and go eat supper. We're having some kind of weird garbanzo bean casserole and, of course, rice. Write back soon. Bye for now, Love, Debb and Art

Winter 1988-1989

❦ Journal Entry

We were unable to get into the mountains due to big downpours overnight, so came back to Davao to get the mail. In family letters, I read that Dad has a damaged lung due to asbestos, and Art's mom has ulcers. Vickie wrote to say that Chet, one of our students at the Junior High, died suddenly of an apparent heart attack at a school ball game—I had just been thinking about all those kids lately. So the sad year continues, after Grandma and Aunt Olga's deaths earlier. Art put the plastic tree together and I put on the Christmas decorations. During that, Flora came downstairs and told us she discovered she's pregnant and will be going back to her family in Manila. She'll be leaving soon and it's back to square one to find a new medical person.

❦ Journal Entry

I went on a great errand run today: I badgered the administrator at USIS into giving us five boxes of books, and went to see a good sewing machine that Tinong's wife discovered at the Singer store. She even bargained a discount for us, so it cost P3,900 (about $195). It's a treadle machine, perfect for the usually-no-electricity of Malungon High School, and exactly like the one we kids used to play on in the basement at Grandma's.

🦋 Journal Entry

The two lizards behind the pot in the bathroom started having an all-out fight, screeching and clicking. Art went to town but that was a big mistake. He was blocked from going across Claveria by a huge parade crowd from the Davao festival, with traffic jams everywhere. He finally just left the truck in the middle of the road like everyone else, and went to watch the parade. He met Tinong there, who said the church had been broken into and all his truck tools stolen.

🦋 Journal Entry

Art was up and out by 7 to take the Tribal Council to Bansalan. I went to market for a few items plus some pork, and was early enough this time that there was more left than just the face. Chatted with Viktor on my way back. We discussed the proposal for the Lumabat water system but he doesn't want engineers brought in as he says they'd only steal the money. Really? Talk about the pot calling the kettle black. Art got back, and said it was a pretty good trip, with about 28 leaders. They made a bench in the back of his truck which broke going over the first bump.

Hi Mindy and Tim,

How's the skiing this year? No snow here yet, but I'm keeping an eye out for it. So far we've just had to be content with sliding around on the mud.

Speaking of which, the road (or the lack of it), has still been giving us our biggest adventures. It washed out entirely way back around the end of October and now has crevasses in some parts about 5 feet deep. Doug hiked it about a month ago, but couldn't get to the place he was trying to survey. Going in, the water in the river was knee deep; coming back out it was chest deep. It was market day and all the hill people were squatting along the edge waiting for the water to go back down so they could cross to market. But Doug's a big American, he's not going to wait, so he gets in there and wades across. Unfortunately, that gave some little Tagakaulo guy, who was about two feet shorter and 60 lbs lighter, the idea he could do the same thing.

The current grabbed him and he was half a mile downstream before he could even say oops. He managed to crawl out and the people on the bank thought it was great entertainment.

So we can get our materials and supplies in at least a couple miles, but then have to make arrangements for them to be hauled the rest of the way to Lumabat by water buffalo and sledge. That'll be interesting, seeing our solar panels dragged in by water buffalo.

We were kind of discouraged there for awhile. We lost our medical administrator (she came down, started language school, discovered she was pregnant and headed back), and then our promised language translator for the literacy program backed out. So Graham, who is now our new boss, came down to look things over and hand out some encouragement. Although he's been in the Philippines about 5 years, it's always been in Manila, so the trip was going to be an experience for him too. The first morning after he'd stayed with us in Malungon, I came downstairs to find him roaring with laughter. He said he'd been back in the little bathroom for his morning sitdown, accomplished everything to his satisfaction, got his dipper-bucket of water to flush the pot, when out jumps this frog from the pot and indignantly hops out the hole in the side of the wall. We all figured we could identify with the kind of day the frog was having. Then Graham was kind enough to kill two scorpions in the bathroom for me with his killer flip-flops, and he and Art spent their evenings in the time-honored Malungon way: listening to the Junior Science program in simple English on the Voice of America, while lying on their backs on the little couches, watching the lizards stalk bugs on the ceiling around the light bulb. Hey, you just have to be here to appreciate it.

Doug and Jan finally packed up, left Malungon and returned to Davao for a couple months, all because Jan is too culturally chicken to have her baby delivered by some toothless village crone muttering incantations. They loaded *all* their stuff (including stove, refrigerator, clothes, dishes, you name it) into their truck, along with themselves, their two kids, two helpers, and huge German Shepherd puppy, and set off. Five miles down the road, their spiffy, bring-it-from-the-States car-top carrier collapsed the roof of their truck with its weight, so Doug had to get out, repack the entire truck, and say a few things they don't teach you in Seminary. They finally got home, which made their dog so happy he scared the chicken out of the yard never to return, chased the cat down the sewer where it got bit by something and died, and ate all the hamsters their helper had been raising as a project to sell at the market. It's hard to believe these days are generally the norm around here.

Well, Christmas is almost here and I hope we live through it. In Malungon we're close to the little Catholic church which, from Dec. 15 to Dec. 25, celebrates what they call Midnight Mass, but which actually takes place about 4 a.m. And they want all the Catholics to attend. So the morning of the 15th, at *3 a.m.*, we sit bolt upright in bed as Christmas carols start blaring out of the loudspeakers on the Catholic church and somebody starts banging the old metal truck wheel which serves as a bell. This continues for one solid hour, to make sure everyone's awake, and then the hour-long mass starts, accompanied by amplified guitar via the same loudspeaker. This goes on *every day* until Christmas. Apart from that, and the urchins that show up at the gate every night bellowing carols to earn some pocket change, and the already constantly-exploding firecrackers, everything is peaceful.

Well this is a novel, so I better end and get it in the mail so you'll receive it at least by the end of January. Hope your Christmas is (was) extra specially happy. Bye for now, Debb and Art

6

Still Hanging
Battling the Obstacles: Malungon, Part 2
Winter 1988-1989 (continued)

🦋 Journal Entry

Got a Texas fruitcake from Jayne. Yum—how can people not love fruitcake? Of course, I also eat pig blood stew and seaweed. Anyway, the best part is that it comes in a great rat-proof can. Plastic containers are a complete joke—rats gnaw through them like they're butter.

🦋 Journal Entry

Dolores, now a good friend, and Migo came in from Lumabat today. Dolores will help me plant a demo garden out there. I don't know why the hill folks don't plant and eat vegetables. They only grow scrawny field corn that they try to sell for rice in the market. They have a lot of papayas in the village, but call them pig food. Migo, who is 11 years old, is helping Art learn Kaulo—we now have to use our Cebuano to learn the tribal dialect. That ought to be culturally interesting: one glottal stop turns the word 'boss-man' into 'monkey.' Wonder how much tolerance they have for insults.

🦋 Journal Entry

We went back to Davao for errands. There was a big wreck near the bridge: an army truck had rear-ended a pickup truck, snarling traffic, and causing massive gridlock. The traffic cop was blowing his lungs out on the whistle, but being completely ignored as usual. The windshield on the troop truck was pretty interesting, though—full of bullet holes. Came home and I tried to rest, but first the garbagemen came banging on the gate looking for a 'Christmas present,' and then a roving band of carol singers, ditto. I went to bed early but woke for good at 2 a.m. when some drunken bozo called and wanted to be my phone friend.

❧ Journal Entry

We both tried to catch up on writing letters. We still owe 29, not including the whole newsletter that has to go out this week. The last time we were in Manila, Graham showed me a computer. He says it can save and reuse parts of letters so you don't have to type them all individually. Also, you can make changes or corrections, which it saves in some kind of memory until you want to print up your final perfect copy at the end. No more erasers? No more white-out? Wow. This idea could save years off my life. Why didn't they dream up this thing sooner? Wait— I bet it uses electricity.

Dear Tim and Mindy,

It's been kind of a slow morning, perfect for writing letters. I got up, had my cup of coffee, and sang through the national anthem a couple of times. I'm trying to learn it so I don't just stand there on the platform like a tree stump at events and graduations, but with words like nagniningning, it's a lost cause. Made fried rice for breakfast, and got Art on his way. He's negotiating to rent a weapons carrier for a couple of days. He only wants it to take more wood into the hills but I myself could occasionally find some good uses for a grenade launcher.

Oh boy, presents! Our favorite way to spend a day—tearing wrapping paper off packages—thanks a ton! We also just received your letter about the Christmas party, and everyone that came back for it. We sure missed being there—especially for your stuffed grape leaves. Art even has a brand-new special outfit he could've worn. One of the missionaries from up north gave him a wildly bright, tribal woven loin cloth common to the Igorot tribe. So now except for the beard, the big nose, the grey hair, being white and way too tall, he looks completely natibo.

New Year's was the usual ordeal. People start at least a week ahead of time, shooting off fireworks. Since all fireworks are supposedly illegal, everyone brews up their own in their garage, and they tend to get carried away. Our neighbor was constantly blowing off stuff that was stronger than what they use to blast quarries. But New Year's Eve itself was the worst. About 7 p.m. we locked Bantay the Brainless in the garage so he wouldn't get hit by stray bullets. Then we shut ourselves up in the bedroom, closed the windows and planned to run our little air conditioner to drown out the noise. Of course the air con chose that moment to break (it's older than God) so we got to enjoy every boom plus the thick pall of black smoke (they also like to burn tires out in the streets). Oh well.

And finally! Doug and Jan's Terror Twins have at long last become the Terror Triplets. The doctor told Jan she was due Dec. 27, but that the baby could come as early as mid-December. It finally arrived January 6—Epiphany—when Doug was almost completely out of his mind with the waiting. If it had come on Christmas, they were going to name it Nicholas, so with its arrival on Epiphany, they should logically have named it Balthazar. Unfortunately for that plan, she was a girl, so they named her Karen.

Doug said going to the hospital to have the baby was a somewhat interesting experience for both of them. They had to look all over town for a hospital that would allow him in the delivery room in the first place. Everyone in there wore their rubber flip-flops, and when he stepped out of the delivery room for a break, he almost tripped over a cat, many of which were just roaming the halls—probably to keep the rat population down.

Big news! We've just decided to head back to the U.S. of A. No, not for good. We're not that sane. We're hearing that my dad and Art's mom are not doing so well health-wise, and as Art says—they're not spring chickens anymore. Plus we haven't seen them for well over two years. Our official furlough, where we trek around to 500 churches to present our dog and pony show, doesn't come up until the middle of next year. So this one will just be a lightning trip, over and back. We'll keep you posted as we wrestle out the details. I'm already dreaming of sitting around talking smart in your driveway with the bratwurst on the grill, your honeysuckle hedge in full bloom, strolling down to Belt's for ice cream . . . Sorry. Got carried away. Better get this to the post office. Now besides the mango stall and the gas-stove repair stand that I have to weave through to get to my mailbox, the gas man has his fighting chicken staked out there too, so I'm generally in peril of falling on my head. Bye for now, Love, Debb and Art

🦋 Journal Entry

We loaded up the new Singer treadle sewing machine, took it down to the high school and handed it over. I thought the sewing teacher was going to burst into tears. She just kept looking at the machine and every once in a while she'd touch it, to be sure it was real. After many speeches (and snacks, of course), they gave us a handwoven purse and hat that the kids made for us themselves. I will send them on to the banner-sewing group (all of Mom's old buddies—she would be so proud) at Dad's church, who provided the money for the machine.

🦋 Journal Entry

The little hut stores on the corner, and actually all over Malungon, are completely out of ice as the power is off way more than on. The Muslim rebels up in the hills are doubtless blowing up the transformers again as they like to do every Christmas season. Dependable, just like clockwork. Guess we'll have to throw out everything in our cooler. I went to Dadiangas with Art and got a good American Coleman cooler at Gaisano's for $65. It's exactly the same as the one I sold at my garage sale in Stevens Point for $2.

🦋 Journal Entry

We were heading back to Malungon from Davao and stopped at the gas station in Digos, as usual. I came out of the bathroom, standing with Art outside when I felt something crawling around inside my shirt. After jumping around and swatting at myself, I went back in, took the shirt off, and out came a giant (mad) cockroach. Gross. Arrived in Malungon, and Art, Doug and Tinong headed off to San Roque, where Doug finally got land to build his house. They hiked out and gathered at our place for supper. We listened to the Voice of America news, and Tinong napped on the pile of wood. Had a small earthquake—the walls pinged and creaked a little but no big deal. Then some mouse came out of the locked storeroom and tried to crawl up Doug's leg. Lots of activity at that point. I see that the mice are making holes in the back of the couch. Must be a whole bunch of them living in there.

🦋 Journal Entry

A bunch of the Hill Tribes members cadged a ride into Dadiangas with us. They wanted to see some big-wig politician's wife to get project funding. Too bad, she was at her coconut plantation "at the edge of town, very near" and why didn't we just drop them there? Set off. Two hours later, over torture roads that probably ruptured my spleen, we finally arrived. Talk, more talk, endless talk, on the theme of "we need money" (Hill Tribes), and "no dice" (politician's wife). Finally, in late afternoon, we loaded ourselves back on the truck, turned the key, nothing happened. Discovered that the battery clamp had broken on the rough road, so the battery just jounced around in the engine, breaking it and spilling acid everywhere. The guys finally push-started the truck and we drove to the first battery-repair place in Dadiangas. The riders all bailed out, leaving us to take their stuff back. Drove back in total darkness, arriving just as the rain turned into a major downpour.

🦋 Journal Entry

We got our new computer in Davao! I've been taking classes and tearing my hair out about equally. There sure is a lot to remember, and you have to hit exactly the right key in the right order or it refuses to work. That little blinking line even mocks me in my sleep. We loaded it up on blankets and pillows, like the fragile princess it is, and set off for Malungon. We went super slow so we wouldn't jounce it, but still hit some huge holes. The road looks like it's been bombed. Maybe it has. I assembled the computer and it works perfectly – a real miracle! Then Doug and Jan came by, all depressed. Rudy, their neighbor's hell-born brat of a son, had been tormenting Buck, their new German Shepherd puppy, slingshotting rocks and nails at him. Buck finally broke his chain and bit Rudy, so they had to take Rudy to Dadiangas for stitches. Also, one of Larry's relatives had stripped the outside of their house of all lights and wiring last week while they were away.

🦋 Journal Entry

Art got up early to pack up and head to Lumabat. He had his backpack, stuffed with the new Easter pamphlets, his cap, water jug, and his big bamboo walking stick. He looked like Moses, getting ready to cross the Red Sea. It poured rain all afternoon, so if he's unable to part the waters of the seven creeks, he'll stay in Lumabat again overnight. I had supper with Jan and the kids, and borrowed Doug's National Inquirer that he just got in the mail from home, so I could read about slightly different aliens.

Spring 1989

Dear Tim and Mindy,

Just got our copy of your party invitation for our big homecoming. Sounds like everybody and his dog will be there, and we are counting the days! Now that mostly everyone has graduated and scattered, it was a good plan to divide us all up into four quadrants to determine what we'll all bring to the Big Feed. We're having a tad bit of trouble with our own geographical assignment, though. I say we're Southwest, and I have a nice stewed fruit bat recipe in mind. But Art says no, we're closer to Southeast and he wants to bring halo-halo for dessert, which is frozen coconut milk, ice cream made out of this purple root vegetable, munggo beans, corn, gelatin squares, plus other mystery ingredients. Maybe you'll have to decide.

Yes, we would be honored to stay in the guest suite. I hope it won't bother you too much when I get up at 2 a.m., wander around, watch TV, fix breakfast, run the faucets, flip the light switches on and off, go to the all-night grocery store, make several phone calls to strangers (just to use a phone that works), and then go to bed at 10:30 a.m. Look at it as an adventure.

Well, it's been a quiet week here in Lake Malungon. We haven't had electricity for the past three days. You wouldn't think that's so bad because there isn't that much to use electricity *for*, plus my neighbors can't play the Cebuano radio soaps (slap and sob extravaganzas) into my window at top volume. But I kind of like it—electricity, that is. Without the ice from down the street, all the food in my ice chest gave up the ghost, and HOT hot season decided to arrive while I couldn't even run the fan. Whine, whine, whine. Do you think I get a little crabby when the temp won't come down under 100 degrees? The part that really bugs me though (sorry about the pun) is that at night, with no lights, all the giant Creatures think we're not here and move into the house. I already booted some poor toad halfway across the back kitchen because I couldn't see to step around him in the dark—that's a real tactile sensation, booting a big toad in your flip flops. Plus some gigantic spider jumped on my foot and I woke to find a granddaddy cockroach waltzing across my mosquito net six inches from my nose.

Well, enough of this pleasant chit chat. I still haven't heard back as to whether the family could get us tickets for Wisconsin. But that's OK because we're probably not going to be allowed out of this country: we need to have an exit permit, a re-entry permit, our alien certificate of registration, five pictures each, a booklet of our fingerprints, lots of money, and some more money to 'facilitate' things. If I were dreaming big, I'd say we'd call you from Kansas City to confirm our arrival info, but in reality it would be a nice gesture if all of you at the party sent us a telegram telling us what a nice time you're having. Send it to the Manila airport. Bye for now, Love, Debb and Art

✿ Journal Entry

I went over to Dadiangas with Jan to get Ernesto's baby released from the hospital—she's all well again. Ernesto and his wife had gone over to Doug's place several days ago to have Doug baptize their baby, who was dying, and then just quietly sat there, waiting for her to die. So Doug drove them to the hospital instead. We almost couldn't get the baby back today either—didn't have enough cash with us and they wouldn't let her go. After arguing for two hours, we finally got them to take a check. Art and Doug are back out of the hills, and had an excellent trip. They're being welcomed everywhere now, plied with coffee, and urged to hang around and chat. I still remember when all the people would run into their houses and hide when we'd come through the villages.

✿ Journal Entry

Went over to Doug and Jan's. Ernesto was there, and a woman from one of the other villages who wanted help paying a hospital bill—word is getting around. Uh oh. This could get very complicated. I then went to Vita-Rich in Dadiangas for baby chicks—it's time to start my big chicken project. When I told them I only wanted four or five, they thought I meant four or five hundred (they only sell wholesale). Came home chickenless. There's been no power since late morning. Jan came over in the afternoon to learn to use the computer, forgetting that might be just a tad tough without electricity.

✿ Journal Entry

I'm spending all my time now doing literacy work: plans, consultations, materials. Leks is still on vacation so I'm also doing all the dishes, water hauling, and garbage disposal (burn the paper, throw the rest down the ravine). I dragged in about eight buckets of water this morning to stock up.

Diwata, the wife of some distant relation of Viktor's, came over to chat. We talked awhile, and she 'borrowed' 50P off me. It must run in the family. Viktor has been trying to recommend a carpenter friend of his to replace Franco, our best worker. And Nilda, younger sister of another of his relations, wants me to fire Leks and hire her as my helper instead. Sure, when hell freezes over.

✤ Journal Entry

Art got back about 11, said our house is looking good. He stays there long stretches of time now when he's out working in the hills. He tore up his knee again, wrecked one shoe and lost a flip-flop in the creek. The crossings are really rough lately with the rains. Right at siesta time, a whole delegation came over to complain that Carmelo had cheated them out of their rightful pay, and yelled for about an hour. I whacked a scorpion in the bathroom.

✤ Journal Entry

It's been raining steadily so we decided to go back to Davao for a couple days before heading out to Manila and on to the States. Packed and loaded the truck in the rain. It's a miracle we got out to the highway, since the alley is solid mud. It poured all the way back, and it's impossible to tell whether the potholes are little puddles or massive tire-swallowing craters. We stopped by the post office. Emma, our elderly penpal from a South Dakota church, sent us Sunday School stuff and real lime Kool-Aid. Love it! She's a real sweetie. Got a message from Babs down the street. She and her neighbors want us to bring them four bags of bat guano for their gardens next time we come back.

✤ Journal Entry

While Art was filling out reports at home, I headed off to town for last-minute errands. I went to Aldevinco and bargained for a few souvenir gifts. Then I started walking to the post office up San Pedro St. when there was a loud noise right next to me in the mouth of an alley. At first I just thought it was kids with firecrackers, but turned to see some guy shooting another one in the face at point blank range, right next to me on the sidewalk. As soon as I saw the gun I dove for the nearest cover, down off the curb into the gutter behind a parked truck. I hunkered down under the bumper, best I could. But almost immediately a cop appeared and more guys with guns, and general shooting started, so I was trapped. All up and down the street, shopkeepers were slamming down the metal grates over their windows and doors, and the street was deserted except for the shooters. Then I saw that the folks in the appliance store across the sidewalk had seen me, held off barring their door, and were frantically waving at me to come in. So I made a run for it. We all hid behind the refrigerators in the back whenever more armed men appeared or we heard more shooting (the killer had apparently either run behind the store or upstairs). After about half an hour, it seemed OK enough to go. The shops opened back up, and the cops took the body away.

7

Interim I
Touching Home: U.S.A.
Spring 1989 (continued)

❧ ❧ ❧

Last minute rushing around, frantically grabbing gifts and mashing stuff into suitcases. The hopefully reliable-looking cab I bargained with in the street yesterday arrived early, and we were off to Davao airport. We could see our plane come in on time but then they towed it to a different area of the runway, probably to slap duct tape on whatever part was acting up, and jury-rig the wiring so we could take off. Finally boarded. They've crammed in more seats again but the rows were tiny Filipino-width to start with, so we got to fly with our knees up around our ears. It's always interesting to see the pilots thread their way around the massively tall thunderheads. We squeaked by, not through, them all, thereby keeping breakfast intact.

We're staying with Peg and Graham in Manila for a few days before flying out to the States. Lucky us—there are all kinds of finger-printing, immigration papers and various other fine bribery opportunities to go through for the pleasure of being able to get back in again. It's also a nice little reorientation seminar for civilization. For example, we can relearn how to eat with real silverware, rather than using the bare-handed three-finger scoop method to shovel in our rice. And we can practice dinner table topics that do not include diarrhea, exotic diseases, chicken butchering or rats.

Finally! The big day! Noy drove us to the airport. We arrived way early but spent all of it in lines (no, make that shoving, wrestling clumps) for immigration, airport fees, etc. Arrived in Tokyo for the shortest layover on record. We barely had time to laugh at what the kids were wearing and look for a bag of squid chips, then it was back up into the air again. Art bought the headset for the two or three bad movies they use to sedate the restless crowd, and I wadded myself up into as close to a prone position as I could get and tried for a nap. Art woke me up over Alaska to see the awesome mountains and glaciers.

Arrived in Chicago about two hours before we left Tokyo. I love crossing the dateline. I told Art that if we just kept flying forward at this pace we could be young(ish) forever. Had to sprint through the airport to make our next connection. I started to go comatose at this point - had no idea what planet I was on or what language to speak. Another flight and there we were in Kansas City. Total time door to door: over thirty hours. Mary, Leonard and Diane were there to meet us and take us through the dark to their house. We'll have to wait til tomorrow to see if America looks any different after all this time.

❧ ❧ ❧

A new day! And there I was all bouncy and alert at 2 a.m.—isn't jet lag great? After only many hours of trying to be very, very quiet, I could finally get a clear look at things. They seemed sort of the same, but then again, not. I began to realize this at breakfast, where there wasn't a sardine in sight. We had some kind of strange non-cornflakes cereal that seemed mostly made of twigs and other pieces of tree, and tasted like bark smells. Wet bark. I learned that this is supposed to be very healthy. The milk was good though—not made out of powder but real stuff in a big jug and miraculously cold.

Diane is very generously lending us her car and this could be interesting. Art and I are way out of touch with how to drive here. Even in rush hour on the freeway, people apparently don't lean on the horn to issue death threats to each other every thirty seconds, or jam their fenders in front if a six-inch gap opens up, or even make the exciting (but professional level) instant right hand turn from five lanes away on the left. Pretty boring stuff, especially since folks here don't seem to feel a need to spread out their crops to dry on the highway, or tether their goats on a long rope at the very edge of the road.

Made it alive into downtown to see Art's mom, and then across town to see my dad—for the first time in two and a half years. Neither of them likes talking on the phone. From their generation, the phone is what you use to report stuff like getting drafted, breaking your arm, or announcing some distant relative's funeral. So finally seeing them after all that time was a little tear-inspiring. Both look so much older, and frail now. But we had great visits. We'll be staying with Dad for a few days.

❦ ❦ ❦

Dad had a list and sent us out to pick up a few things at the new grocery store. We walked in and stopped dead, almost causing a multiple shopping-cart chain reaction pile-up. The place was mind-boggling— and completely terrifying. First, it was enormous. Comparisons to multiples of football fields are inadequate. The whole village of Lumabat could fit in there, including the entire Malungon market plus the carabao wallow down by the river. If the hill folks had this much space, they could probably afford to sell two pigs a day, and I'd get something better than the face.

Next, the decision dilemma. We were completely paralyzed. First thing on the list was mustard, and there were about five shelves full of nothing but mustards. Not just lots of the same jar either. Different kinds. Different textures. Different flavors. How can mustard have flavors? What if I pick the wrong kind? They all come in vat-sized jars. We will be eating the detestably wrong kind of mustard for twelve years, and now we need to choose potato chips. Had to get out of there.

Not all shopping experiences are that harrowing, thank God. Here, there are still . . . yard sales! How I have missed them! Who can resist milling around in strangers' garages, pawing through mounds of out-of-style clothing, groovy lava lamps and eight-track tapes, macramé toilet paper holders, jello molds and unused wedding presents from twenty years ago, like lime-green three-tiered candy dishes. I used to live for this stuff. Well, at least until it was time to move away, and have my own garage sale, to try unloading all my own tapes and candy dishes on other unsuspecting junk addicts.

But now I have an actual purpose, and this could be good. I've already found some sports equipment, tons of good kids' books, a couple of those blow-up world globes, even the ultimate prize: a working student microscope set with slides. The Malungon high school especially asked for some of those. Also, amazingly, I found an antique cast-iron corn shelling machine and wouldn't they love that back in the hills. But it weighs at least a million pounds and we'd never be able to get it over. Also found tons of reading books for Art and me and perhaps got a little carried away. Now I have to mail all this junk to myself . . .

❧ ❧ ❧

Time to battle it out with the post office. First, I went to the liquor store. No, not for liquid courage, but booze boxes are the sturdiest for challenging all the big-foot Neanderthals and the gorilla-type crushers who seem to be assigned to my packages. I loaded up all the boxes and taped them down so even a direct-hit mortar couldn't blow them open. Hauled everything to the post office and got ready for the crush. Something was wrong. People were all just standing there. In a line. Taking turns. I played along with this, and in way under an hour it was our turn. The post office guy just took the boxes and paperwork, and the posted fee. Apparently, he didn't want a bribe, didn't want a couple items out of each box. Maybe he wasn't feeling well. He was kind of a humorist, though. Said the boxes should arrive over in Davao in about two weeks. Funny man.

❧ ❧ ❧

Finally it was time to head up to Wisconsin to visit Tim and Mindy! We had to keep going through smaller and smaller airports, getting planes that were formerly used as crop-dusters, until we finally arrived at mighty Mosinee International. And there was Tim. He's always hated to say goodbye. So the day we left, two and a half years ago, he said, "Come on over for supper tomorrow night. We'll have bratwurst, and pie, and sit around talking smart." And we said, "sure!" instead of "goodbye." We got off the plane. And Tim said, "You're late for supper." We said, "Sorry about that. Unavoidably delayed. . . " So we went over for supper, and pie, and talking smart, and it was like we'd never gone.

What a reunion! All our friends from the olden days, a big get-together out in the country, enough food to stuff the proverbial Chinese army. We stopped by the new grocery to stock up (another massive food palace). Mesquite Grill potato chips, fudge-covered Oreos, chocolate-cherry soda, I've never heard of any of this stuff. Best of all, we caught up on everyone's news, new spouses, new babies, new lives.

I got up my courage and went by to see my old house. The porch swing was still there in the sunshine, lilies of the valley were blooming next to the garage. We told Tim and Mindy we'd be over for supper tomorrow night, and flew back to Kansas City.

❦ ❦ ❦

More family visits. So few days left, but we were cramming in celebrations, reunions, dinners, everything. Peter and Elinor flew in from Delaware along with little El, who is now a motion-machine toddler who wants Aunt Debbie to watch her go up and down the stairs 500 times. Peter, the outdoor-living guru, brought us some new sandals called River Walkers, that attach to the feet with velcro straps. This is a big deal—could keep us from getting stuck in the rocks like we usually do on the six crossings into Lumabat. Less amusement for the villagers, though, as we no longer take the big dive, with our flip-flops floating gently away.

We're frequently visiting Art's mom, too. We've had good chats, except for the sacred hour when she's watching (still) the sainted Lawrence Welk and his bubble machine. Art continues to give her grief about it, like the whole family did decades ago. Some things never change. Well, except maybe for TV itself. I've watched some recently and cannot believe the stuff they are able to say—and show—on programs now. Land sakes, Emma, what's the world coming to? Maybe this is the hell in a handbasket we've all been going to, as predicted.

❦ ❦ ❦

One last little errand before I returned was to get a bit of real medical attention. Apparently they still have mammogram machines here which aren't broken, and aren't waiting for ordered parts ("come back next year"). Unfortunately, my results were abnormal, and they suggested a biopsy. Gave me names of a couple surgeons. I looked into the timing (would have to change our flight) and cost (wow, are they kidding?) I talked to one of the surgeons and it might be OK to wait til next year after all. It'll give me something to occupy my mind and worry about, since life is so calm and I never have anything to stew over back in the hills.

❧ ❧ ❧

Time to go. How can that be? Felt like two days. Goodbyes all around, and back on the plane. It was relatively uncrowded, so I could nap a little bit on the endless flight back. The last leg, the flight to Manila, was jam-packed. Got rice and fish for supper. Toto, I think we're on our way home. Late arrival, but Noy was still waiting for us, thank God, and drove us to Peg and Graham's. Peg showed us up to our room and Graham stomped a huge cockroach for me on the way up the stairs. Welcome home.

8

Here and There
Final Steps: Malungon, Lumabat
Summer 1989

Dear Tim and Mindy,

Being as we're out in the boonies again, I haven't been to the mailbox in weeks, and thought I'd start our time-hono(u)red tradition of having our letters cross in the mail. So how was your trip to Merrye Olde Englande? (You know how we uncultured Yankees have to put an e at the end of every worde to make it real English.) Tell me all about it, especially the cream teas. I bet you came back looking nice and fat. That's all I'm hearing around here: "Welcome back, Mum Debb—you look so fat now!" Actually, it's supposed to be a polite compliment, meaning you're rich enough to be able to pork out at your every whim. I guess they're right.

We made it back OK through 4 airports, 3 movies, 5 full meals, countless snacks—over 30 hours' worth. We started out lucky by being on the maiden voyage of our airline's direct flight between Minneapolis and Tokyo. Got to the lounge and there were Japanese dancers waving fans around (I still think all their music sounds like cats fighting in a sack), a big free spread of sushi, free saki, the works. Then, just because everything was going so wonderfully, they lost all our luggage in Manila. There we were, after 30 hours, propped up by the luggage carousel, staring with zombie eyes as 5,785 giant cardboard boxes tied up with twine went round and round, and no Art/Debb luggage. After making irate noises (at that point more like plaintive whimpers) we finally left and spent the whole next day on the phone trying to get our stuff back. Now that's a real treat. Manila phones don't work when it rains, and when they finally do, nobody you talk to knows anything, and cares even less. We finally had to slog all the way back to the airport, but miraculously it was all there.

So we're down in the backwoods again where they've been having a worse run of disasters than usual while we were gone. Some torrential downpours caused the Lumabat 'It Never Floods' River to flood. Doug and Jan managed to get in once and check on everybody for us. Jan said the trail was solid mud—she fell three times, and saw a loaded horse go down. The water had come up to the path right in front of our house, and the village lost several horses and carabao, but fortunately, no people. When your tank-sized water buffalo gets swept away, that's no drizzle. Even the main highway from Davao was the worst I'd ever seen. There were many places where one whole lane just fell off the cliff. I didn't look to see if there were any buses down there under the rubble, but it happens.

Now I figure we're going to have typhoid for awhile. We're racing to get wells dug back in Lumabat—one right in front of the little school, one near our house—and get a couple old long-broken ones by the central field back in working order. Our only available well-driller, from Dadiangas, refuses to go in because no vehicle can make it back here. It would be no problem to haul the repair equipment in on horseback, but he would have to hike in and he's way too important for that. Sigh.

One bright and happy note though . . . the mailbags came!! Such jubilation, such dancing in the streets, such broken backs as we staggered down the post office stairs and way down the block with all those wonderful goodies. I have to say, this is by far the biggest and best batch of stuff we've ever received and is exactly what we were looking for: easy dictionaries, kiddie books, picture magazines, globes, equipment. Where did you come up with all of it? I've been working like a dervish to get it all processed and will send it out to the hill schools via horseback in a couple weeks. I wish you could see the end result where the kids each clutch a book like it's solid gold, and the teachers' eyes light up, and the parents grab you and cry all over you, but you'll just have to imagine it.

Well I think the paper is ending, so I better, too. I have the group picture of us all at the Reunion Party up on my bulletin board right here by the computer. It's next to my little cardboard sign that has the Bible verse: "I can do all things through Him who strengthens me." Both picture and verse are now liberally spotted with lizard poop, which seems an appropriate background for real life here, but they—and possibly some potato chips—will get me by. Keep writing! Bye for now, Love, Debb and Art

❦ Journal Entry

Art and I headed for Dadiangas to see the new Kimball's store addition, which is finally open. It's an immense grocery store (well, maybe 1/4 of a U.S. store) with lots of stock, but nothing new—just many cans of the same stuff. Two entire aisles of sardines. But there are *escalators* to the upper floors, the first that people around here have ever seen. Clerks in uniform are posted at the top and bottom to show people how to use them and keep kids from joyriding up and down all day. Most folks are terrified to even step on.

❦ Journal Entry

We loaded the Beav with all the bathroom stuff and took it to Binugawan. Coming back, the Beav broke a culvert and fell through, bumping everyone severely but it didn't roll, thank God. All the guys in the back had shotguns and luckily they didn't go off either. Jan and I went to Dadiangas but there's still no cooking gas anywhere—over a week now.

❦ Journal Entry

I'm back to working on the adult literacy primer, as new classes are all set to start soon. I finally finished another consonant—intense headwork. Made myself a salad for lunch and then plugged in my radio to listen to a soothing tape for siesta. Heard a loud pop. I had forgotten, and plugged it straight into 220 without the transformer. So much for that machine. Went to haul some more water and ended up talking with Bebe next door for a couple hours—she was plucking a duck for their supper. And we cut down a jackfruit. The thing is bigger than a watermelon but grows in a tree. Over people's heads.

❧ Journal Entry

Still no cooking gas. Tried to make ramen noodle soup in the crockpot for lunch but the electricity today is so low, it only got sort of lukewarm and the noodles were still crunchy. Then I noticed it was *full* of floating dead ants. I scooped most of them out, ate it anyway. I got my electric skillet back from the sidewalk stall at the market. They rewired it to 220 and it works fine, but they won't even try fixing the tape player. I worked in the garden all afternoon. The seeds I brought back from the States are coming up nicely but now are being attacked by all kinds of insects. Back to the market to get an insecticide. I rejected one that looked like it would lay waste to the ecosystem for centuries and got a milder one. When this one doesn't work, I will go back and get the first one.

Dear Mindy and Tim,

I need a good excuse to come in from weeding the swamp cabbage out in the garden and sit in front of the fan for awhile. Looks like time for a letter.

Well, how are things going around here, you are almost afraid to ask. And you should be afraid because the answer is—as usual. Having had our fill of frustration and flat tires, we decided to go back to Davao and pick up some plumbing supplies. The next morning, the tire which had been fixed the day before was again flat as a pancake. Art, in an extremely non-cheerful mood, got it repaired once again and drove off to do errands. Right in the middle of the main bridge into town, which is only two lanes and always jammed with traffic, he noticed the guy behind him honking wildly. Stopped on the spot, saw that all six of his lug nuts had come off and the whole wheel was about to fall off any minute. Jacked up the truck and did a temporary fix, right there in the middle of the bridge, thereby having the satisfaction of for once being the cause of the daily gridlock madness, complete with screeching brakes, wild horn honking, fist shaking, yells, the works.

Jan finally got a horse—now that's the way to go. She's been searching a long time for one that was better than the usual dog meat on the hoof. She got a 1½-year-old that had never been ridden so she could train it herself and then use it to haul the kids around. It's your typical mountain pony, tough and low to the ground. I doubt she'll be able to ride it without her feet dragging. We walked it home—about a six-mile jaunt. Not a bad walk as it was rainy and cool, but this was the first time the horse had been away from Mommy, and threw a major fit at every bridge and motorcycle, of which there were plenty along the way. I hope Jan has better luck with this horse than with the rest of their animals. They just lost their fourth dog. It got hit by a bus last week, and as soon as it did, the neighbors came over and asked if they could "have it." Come on, I don't make these things up, I just live here.

Speaking of food, remember when you and I got food poisoning in Austria, Mindy? A few nights ago, it was the same delightful symptoms all over again: the all-night splitting headache, and not knowing which end of the body to hang over the pot first, with the upchucking and trots lasting for hours (see, you do remember). Except this time, all I had was a semi-outside bathroom shared with large bugs, a non-flushing toilet and a candle. Gads. It was probably something I ate in Dadiangas, or maybe even at the high school the day before. That was when I got to be one of the 'honored guests' for their ceremonies to dedicate their new building. Last year the government gave some local official the funds to build several new classrooms, and that was the last anybody ever saw of that money. So the parents got together and donated bamboo and nipa (woven grass) for a new little three-room building. They can sure use it—their enrollment is up over 500 this year and they only had seven small rooms. Anyway, after the usual endlessly droning speeches, we all got a big plate and toured the rooms, where the kids had set up tables full of different foods—heavy on the dried fish, munggo beans, gabi (taro root), kangkong (swamp cabbage), cooking bananas, unknown weird things, and, of course, enough rice to feed the entire island and have leftovers.

Allow me to try and retype the last three paragraphs I hadn't saved when we had one of our usual surprise power outages. Since we have two or three every day, you'd think I'd learn. And Art should be back any minute from his latest trip so I better quit. He's been staying in Lumabat almost constantly lately as he and the tribal leaders have projects going, while I stay out here in Malungon for the computer to work on the literacy stuff. Bye for now, Love, Debb and Art

❧ Journal Entry

Jan brought Faith, their new horse, over to my yard again this morning as we have grass and they've only got mud. We used to tie her in the alley but the motorcycles couldn't get by and the little kids were scared, so we keep her inside the fence. But now my neighbor is mad as fire. Faith ate all his beans which were growing on the fence. Actually, she only ate the ones growing on the inside (my side) of the fence, but I don't think he would appreciate a civics lesson on property boundaries at this point. I'm laying low.

❧ Journal Entry

One of Viktor's relatives came over again to pointedly blab on and on about how they have no money. I don't know why not, after all they lifted from us in the last couple of years. They should've invested some of it in a money management course. I didn't have any cash in the house so gave her some rice, eggs and mangoes. I've started giving Leks typing lessons—she's doing really well. She said she'd gone to a Baptist Crusade in one of the bigger villages down the highway. Apparently two Americans had come to speak, but they were from somewhere way in the deep South and nobody (not even their translator) could figure out they-all's English.

🦋 Journal Entry

A couple of days ago, Emilio, who is our new carpenter boss after Franco died while we were in the States, came to tell us he lost all the plans we gave him for the interior shelves and cabinets. So after hours of redrawing them all, we gave him a new set and some money so he could head back in to Lumabat and finish the project. Now we hear he didn't go in at all, but he and Drigo were arrested for getting into a big drunken fight and slugging a cop. Great.

Dear Tim and Mindy,

The lovely peace and quiet calls me to write you a letter. The power is out again of course (hence the trusty manual typewriter) but at least the neighborhood radios can't blare into my window at the usual eardrum-cracking volume. There's a new wildly popular radio program: little pre-school kiddies call in and try to belt out popular rock songs, karaoke-style, with their parents urging them on in the background. It is excruciating.

I figure there's plenty of drama without the radio. In our last installment, our truck wheel almost fell off on the bridge, so we had to order all new bolts. They came, we drove to Malungon, and the wheel almost fell off again. What a comforting feeling, driving through craters and trenches, knowing your wheel is going to come off at any moment, probably as you are edging around the latest landslide on the highway. Art decided he better get a whole new wheel, so it was back to Davao City. First, we got a jump-start for our dead battery, which might've been due to its being tied with wire to the engine compartment, or there might've been a short. The horn doesn't honk except when you put on the left blinker, and then it honks in rhythm with the turn signal.

After stopping about three times to re-tie the battery down, we arrived in Davao and I'm humming little songs—oh boy, a mini-vacation. I'm going to have a big glass of cold water, pop on the air con, finish the ice cream we left in the freezer and just mellow out. Wrong-o. First of all, no cold anything. The refrigerator was not only warm but empty and cleaned out. No lights, no nothing. I started looking around and found the little yellow 'power disconnection' notice by the phone, along with a note detailing six months of unpaid bills. Since the Manila office is supposed to receive and pay these bills I thought I better call at once. I picked up the phone and above the dial tone was a loud radio station, playing samba music. Impossible to hear anyone talking. Sent poor Art down the street to the hotel to use their phone. To condense this long sad story, the office swore they never got the bills, the power company swore they sent them (into the black hole of the postal system), so after only three days of sweat and candles, we finally got our power back on. Even got the phone company to get the radio off the phone, just in time to head back to Malungon where the power is always out anyway. So much for that vacation.

Now Art is down in Dadiangas picking up more last-minute supplies and then he'll have them hauled into the mountains while he hikes along. When he was in a couple days ago he spent most of the time ripping out the bathroom walls he'd told the carpenters not to put in until the pipes were installed. Remember that Franco, our old foreman, died while we were in the States, so the results thereafter have been kind of unique. The general work plan involves piddling around on one thing until you get tired of it, and then doing something that might be more interesting for awhile, and then having a snack. Sort of like I would do it. Except I don't build houses for a living. Anyway, instead of using the wood Art sent in to hold on all the screens, they used it to build decorative doo-dads on the front porch because that was more fun. Since the usual bathroom in the hills is either a bush or the river, Art is going to have to try and put in all the bathroom plumbing himself. Judging by his previous attempts in Davao, I foresee using the bushes a lot myself.

Wow . . . did my eyes see right? You think you can get the Jaycees to hold a book drive for us? Not only would that be utterly fantastic, but would get me out of a lot of trouble and I could quit wearing my moustache-and-glasses Groucho Marx disguise, so passing teachers won't recognize me. Here, where politeness is everything, some of them from the farther hill schools can't come out and say, "Listen, gringo dog, how come you're giving books to those schools, and MY school, which is just as poor and bookless, isn't getting a thing?" Instead, and with the same effect, they clutch your arm and look at you with sad beagle eyes and say how wonderful it is that those other schools are finally getting books for their students, and maybe someday, with the help of the Lord, they too can have books for their poor and pitifully struggling children, if only someone would come along and recognize their great need. Keep me posted and let me know how I can help out at this end.

I've been teaching Leks how to type, as in: Mag-return kita sa carriage pinaagi sa carriage-release lever, o seguro sa line-space lever, aron sa pag-type . . . She's doing great and wants me to turn it over to her so she can practice, so I better go. Bye for now, Love, Debb and Art

🦋 Journal Entry

Art finally finished building my little chicken cage, including a few re-do's on the design and the feed tray. Jan came over with three young chickens for me, so I have them all tucked away on the porch in their new home under the eave, awaiting tasty breakfast egg results. They're drier out there than in the house. It poured rain again last night, resulting in the usual flood in the living room.

🦋 Journal Entry

We heard on the radio news that CAFGU (Civilian Armed Forces Geographical Units—i.e. the local vigilantes) threw grenades into a beauty contest and dance over in Santa Maria, just on the other side of the mountain from Lumabat. Eight killed, including kids, 56 injured.

❧ Journal Entry

Art got home at noon, still sicker than a dog. He had tried to get back here from Lumabat yesterday, but the rain stopped him. I cooked up some ground beef, then put the bowl in water to cool. Came back into the kitchen a little later to find a cat up on the counter, eating it. I sent the "Vogue" magazines that Jayne mailed to me over to Jan so she could have a laugh too.

Fall 1989

Dear Tim and Mindy,

We just picked up your fine letter in Dadiangas and are glad to hear the school year is starting so well. We're already in the middle of ours here. Summer break was in April and May, when it gets hot enough to fry the scales off a snake. Then the temp gradually comes back down to the mid-90s, where it is most of the time, and we can all breathe again.

I sure have come up in the world since I used to work over at Ben Franklin Jr. High. It's dizzying. Art and I were invited to be big cheese guests again at another High School event— this time Culture and Sports Day. Art couldn't make it, but I headed over. They started with an oration contest (in English) with me, the only native English speaker for miles around that day, as one of the judges. Then I had to rate the English singers and didn't even crack a smile (it was hard) as one of the little 7th graders, who looked more like a 6-year-old, emoted his way through that old seduction stand-by, "Help Me Make It Through the Night."

But the very best part of the program was the folk dancing. A group from each grade had to make their own costumes and do a traditional dance. OK for the first three groups: nice outfits with long dresses, butterfly sleeves, and shawls—very graceful. Then the last group came on—must've been the freshmen. The girls wore flour sack dresses, which were cute, and were all carrying three glasses of orange liquid: one in each hand, and one balanced on their heads. Did a nice job, and then they passed the glasses off to the boys. Well, you know boys of that age. No chance in the world. They were supposed to lower themselves to the ground with the glasses balanced on their heads, and then get up and dance bent over with the glasses balanced in the middle of their backs. After the first ten seconds, they had dumped the glasses all over themselves, were covered in sticky orange liquid, the crowd was roaring (even the teachers were grinning), which made them start laughing and goofing up even more. The girls kept on doing their part with expressions on their faces like they were going to axe-murder the boys out back of the school the minute the dance was over. Everyone had a great time.

Well now, what could've come up to prevent Art from participating in such merriment? Our house in Davao was robbed. We were still storing some stuff there and lost about $800 worth: the TV, my little portable sewing machine, a couple of cameras, all of my jewelry—none of which was valuable but still had sentimental value—and a whole bunch of other stuff. Everything was pulled apart upstairs—a real mess. Art called the police, who arrived a while later and instantly demanded 100 pesos so they could "buy film for their camera to take pictures of the crime scene." So far they haven't recovered anything, probably because they haven't fenced it yet. And at just about the same time, our house in Lumabat was robbed too, of some pieces of plywood and some of Art's wrenches. That ought to be some kind of record—we have three houses and two of them are robbed in the same week. Now there's only the one in Malungon left. When they finally get to it, I hope they take the couch with all the mouse-holes in the back. Maybe I should leave a note on the door.

And I've finally turned farm girl and have started raising chickens. Just call me Ma Kettle. I have three whole chickens in a cage that Art labored days to build. From personal observation, I can now state that if you put together the brains of every chicken on earth, you'd still come up with something dumber than a tree stump. Jan's chickens were sick the other day, and since she and

Doug were gone to Davao, her helper came over to get me. Why, I don't know. I couldn't diagnose a chicken illness if it was printed on the bird in big block letters. We decided to separate out the weaker ones and it was quite a scene: one helper was pointing out the skuzzy-looking ones, the other was holding the door of the cage, a guy from next door was scooping out the birds (getting chicken poop all over his nice shirt in the process), and I was holding back the pig, which, since it couldn't reach anyone else, was trying to eat my pants leg and succeeding pretty well.

It's been about the same with Faith the Horse. I've been riding her once in a while to give both of us a little exercise, but the horse is still in the process of being trained and I'm not exactly an expert myself. The other day we were crossing the highway—at least that was my dream. We got to the middle and the horse started backing up, bucking, then refused to budge. Up roared a bus, following the #1 Filipino public transport rule: never stop. So I was waving one hand to keep the bus from mashing us, trying to control the horse with the other, the bus was almost on top of us and laying on its horn (which really helped) and it calmly crossed my mind that if I was going to die in the Philippines, what better way to go that get run over by a happy yellow bus. Well, I somehow survived and didn't even get hit by the fish truck the next time I decided to cross the highway. I've been walking a lot since then.

I found a bunch of colorful pressed maple leaves in one of the dictionaries you sent over. I have mentioned, haven't I, that the leaves over here never change color or drop off? Anyway, on the first day of fall, I'm going to take these leaves outside, throw them up in the air and watch them fall to earth. After that, I'll rake them up into a nice pile (all five of them) and then burn them. Bye for now, Love, Debb and Art

❧ Journal Entry

I heard a big crash in the bathroom and found one of the neighbor's chickens in there. I finally cornered it in the living room and threw it outside, after it made a lot of messes. We went over to Doug and Jan's to get the remaining bamboo for the fence. They were just back from Davao and reported that, because of the robbery, Marcey and her mother had *nailed* the whole mission house shut, using the wood from what used to be Doug's bed. No stolen articles recovered. What a surprise.

❧ Journal Entry

My birthday. Survived another year. Snuck away to Dadiangas for breakfast, and Art got me some food goodies at Kimballs, including a jar of olives and a can of real Campbell's Cream of Asparagus soup. Doug and Jan brought me chocolate chip cookies. Even the chicken laid another microscopic egg this morning—what production. Guess I can stop chatting about McNuggets and Kentucky Fried every time I pass their cage.

❧ Journal Entry

I set out late afternoon with the truck to get Art on his way back from Lumabat, and see how high the river was. It seemed about the same as yesterday, high and strong, about up to the doors, but I decided to chance the crossing. Made it OK, picked up Art and the others. Art told me that Letecia, one of last year's Lumabat school grads, died this weekend. She had been planning on attending High School in Malungon next year, one of the few. She had severe diarrhea, so they just quit feeding her for 12 days, and nobody knew. They finally tried to take her out on horseback, but she died on the way. How deeply, sadly terrible.

9

The Back of Beyond
Finally: Lumabat
Fall 1989 (continued)

Dear Tim and Mindy,

You better hurry and read this before the power goes out again. Our one and only light bulb has been flickering, so it won't be long now. I've even delayed my beloved breakfast sardines just to get this written for you. Why am I not eating lusciously large egg casseroles for breakfast, you ask, now that I have a whole chicken farm going? These are not exactly your State Fair quality prize hens. I have named them Dopey, Dumbo, and Bob (surely you remember that old Bob Dylan classic, "Lay, Lady, Lay"), and their names about sum them up. Once in a while a microscopic, anemic-looking little egg, about the size of a marble, will roll out and we'll all celebrate, but it's going to take weeks before I have enough for an omelet.

Well, would you believe it, our house is done! More or less. Art took me in a couple weeks ago and it was memorable. Once there I figured out what I'd need for basic furniture, arranged with the carpenters to chink the biggest cracks (which cats and chickens, much less the rats, lizards and various other wildlife can waltz through at will) and we turned around to head back. Of course the sky instantly blacked up and it started to pour. We bumped our way through the six rivers, which were rising fast, and almost made it to Kiabol but, even in super-low 4-wheel drive, the truck couldn't pull the final hill and we were stuck.

Now this was a tiny bit of a problem because the mud was making the truck slide backwards and soon it was going to be back in the river—which was rising fast enough to wash it about five counties down and smash it into the rocks. Not good. But here comes the happy part. I actually got to see a real miracle! I've always wanted to see one, like getting lunch out of nothing, a big impossible healing, or striding around on top of water. The men in Kiabol came rushing down to help Art, and I posted myself over to the side and started praying. The guys were all floundering around and falling in that red clay mud that was slippery as ice, and I thought they were going to get squashed under the truck. But inch by inch, even as the mud got worse, they (I include the Help) shoved that truck up the hill until they finally reached the top, and level ground! It couldn't possibly have happened, but it was quite a sight anyway.

That's where we left it, and hiked back to Lumabat in the downpour, looking like drowned rats. Reginia and Dolores rushed over with a dry dress for me and some coffee and bed mats. It gets dark about six, and we had run out of fuel for the lamp (I think there's something ominously Biblical in that) so we went to bed real early. I slept about two hours total all night. At one point I woke to hear scurrying feet and saw this huge mouse racing down the closet post, just about to jump on my face. Thankfully he gathered himself in one last heroic effort and managed to vault clear behind my head and out the back of the closet somewhere. We hiked back out the next morning but had to leave the truck in Kiabol for days until things dried up. Looks like I better get me a horse.

Once he got the truck back, Art kept plenty busy. He had to get supplies in Dadiangas, so agreed to haul down a load of native dancers who wanted to compete at a festival. Mistake. There were about 15 tiny natibo dancers, their huge wooden drum, a long rack of gongs, and about 500 relatives clinging on to every available surface of the truck. I think Art got up to third gear once, but most of the way roared along under 20 mph. Trashed the truck (what's new) but at least the dancers won first prize.

Don't forget to write again soon! I always hate to wrestle my way to the mailbox for nothing, and your letters are our favorites. Bye for now, Love, Debb and Art

🌿 Journal Entry

Attended a tribal missionaries' conference in Bansalan. The literacy session, which I came for, was a real disappointment—just a trainee reading a paper. Oh well, our room was nice. It had an actual bathroom with a flush toilet and real toilet paper. Wow. I ordered my rabbits for next year but they didn't have Jan's goat. I drove back with her and had noodles with the Terror Triplets. Then we tried to listen to the radio, even though the Chinese are heavily jamming the Voice of America short-wave channel again. But we thought we picked up something about a big earthquake in San Francisco. I hate it when we get little snippets of news and can't find out what's happening.

🌿 Journal Entry

I heard around town that Rudy, Malungon's monster brat, was seen throwing rocks at Faith, Jan's horse. This is the same charming child who used to shoot nails at their dog. On getting hit by one of the rocks, Faith reared up and came down on a bamboo spike, a pretty deep wound. Doug and Jan are now furious at the neighbors and their whole clan, who immediately started lying about it, saying it was some other kid. Things are pretty tense.

🌿 Journal Entry

We picked up a load of simple bamboo couches, benches, and tables in Davao. Art managed to jam it all in the back of the truck and we headed for Malungon—we looked like a bunch of dust bowl Okies on the move with all that furniture strapped on. I felt like I ought to be playing the harmonica and looking for a breadline to stand in.

🌿 Journal Entry

Art went out to invite everyone and his dog to our upcoming house blessing. Now the mayor wants to come in and stay overnight. We're starting to gather all the food supplies we'll need for the big bash, especially the rice. We've got 350 lbs. so far. It's shaping up to be quite a party.

Dear Tim and Mindy,

Exciting news here—we had our super-duper house blessing and party last week. Naturally, since I was in on the planning, food featured high on the list of activities. We got our very own first pig—for about five days—and then he took that long, slow walk down to the river from which no pig returns alive. Mighty tasty, though. We hauled in four sacks (40 kilos each for about 350 lbs.) of rice, tons of noodles, vegetables, sauces, spices . . . and we ate it all! I used to think the college kids were champion eaters, but these guys make them look like anorexics nibbling at a carrot stick. The way the mountain folks pile a plate is awesome. Of course, their usual standard is 'one day, one eat' and think we Americans are rich and wasteful because we have 'one day, three eats.' I've never had the heart to tell them that for myself and most Americans, it's 'one day, five (or six, or seven) eats.'

Leks and I had been house cleaning for days, including scraping off most of the chicken poop from the front porch. Art tightened all the pipes and slapped vulcaseal everywhere which dried up (temporarily) the festive waterfalls that occurred whenever a tap was turned on. The women arrived in their best outfits with the incredibly beaded tops, the ankle bells, and their horsehair headdresses. The guys came armed to the teeth with machetes, rifles and ammo belts, and we all drifted over to the big meeting area in the central field. We had prayers and the blessing and then, of course, loooong speeches by every official and their relatives, friends, chance acquaintances, total strangers and livestock. I think it took three days. Finally, we were able to head home. Vijay had brought over our new bamboo bed. And we even got to wash off in our very own new bath enclosure, with the uphill drain.

The well drillers have come and gone again, for about the millionth time. They went down around 20 feet, found water right away, but when we had it tested, it was undrinkable. So they kept drilling, down to about 70 feet, and still no additional water. They were getting close to rioting, so we had them pull out and go away. Now we have this lovely running water in our house (pumped up by hand into a tank, and then down into the pipes), but we can't drink it. I think we'll borrow the well-drilling outfit from the Baptists and try again later but for now it'll have to be rainwater (but hey, there's plenty of that, isn't there).

A few more odds and ends of things happened. We had several earthquakes, one of them a pretty good shaker. We rushed outside because all the walls were pinging and creaking. The ground looks really stupid in an earthquake—it ripples, and all the bushes and trees bob up and down, which are like the special effects in a grade-Z Japanese monster movie. We also had another mouse infestation upstairs in the Davao house— most of them concentrated in our dresser drawers. I discovered this *after* I tossed in a bunch of money, like I usually do, and they chewed up a bunch of 100-peso bills. We won't go into my saga of going to the Central Bank, which prints the stuff, and trying to get them to exchange my gnawed bills for new ones.

That's about it from here. Think of us, as those snowflakes drift down on your house, and you stumble over the Ice Melt and the snow shovels to get to the front door, where you keep your boots and parkas and triple-insulated mittens, and the door is frozen shut again . . . We do have a guest room, you know, and it's always 93 degrees. Bye for now, Love, Debb and Art

🐛 Journal Entries

I felt queasy this morning. Dolores came over—everyone is trying to sell me a horse. I brought out donuts but didn't eat any—must be getting sick. Rested, had crackers for supper.

🐛 I woke, feeling terrible, in the middle of the night. Trudged down to the bathroom, lit a lot of candles (of course the power is out when I'm sick). Tossed and turned in there a few hours. I felt so bad I didn't even care about the scorpions. Had an extreme headache and terrible nausea. Finally in the morning I couldn't stand it anymore. With a splitting head and stiff neck, I didn't want it to be something serious so Art drove me to the little cottage hospital in Dadiangas. I tottered into the ER, which was just a bare concrete waiting room, where they poked, stabbed, took samples, then admitted me. I got a private room, which was a small concrete square with a plain metal bed and chair, but no air con. Art went back to Malungon at dusk and I had a rough night—still a severe headache and lots of attempted vomiting.

❧ The next day the doctor finally saw me for the first time. He said it might be amoebic dysentery or typhoid. Then they wanted a stool sample. Ha. They'd already stuffed me so full of anti-diarrheals there was no chance I'd go til next February. Doug and Jan brought Art—our truck was broken again; the battery was jouncing and almost tore off the whole fender. The hospital system here is interesting: a doctor will see you and prescribe stuff, but the family has to go out and buy it, and also provide all your food, utensils, towels, etc. So they went and got me some crackers, fruit and baby food. No good. Still spent most of my time trying to throw up.

❧ Got pretty discouraged. They next guessed it might be gastritis or an ulcer. So they were giving me every pill ever invented in a random shot-gun approach. The place was deserted in the afternoon—I had to wander around the hallways, stepping over cats and rice pots, to find help getting my mango sliced. It was Election Day, so everyone was probably back in the province voting or shooting candidates. The guy down the hall finally died so everyone could quit wandering past my window asking, "Dead yet?" The carpenter came and rumbled by with the coffin.

❧ The Doc finally said I could go home—no amoeba!—although they were out of guesses as to what it was. Art came and paid the huge bill of P2,000, or $100, for five days, and I was a free, although not exactly well, person.

Dear Tim and Mindy,

I've been a tad sick lately so am resting up a bit in Malungon, that civilized lap of luxury. Some days we even have electricity, but it's getting close to Christmas, so that won't last long.

Art is out in Lumabat and his classes are going great. Only an hour or so after they're supposed to start, people gradually wander in until the place is packed. Now he's going to take a bunch of guys over to the ag research station to learn terrace planting. I can't wait to see Mr. Ghetto Kid from inner Kansas City start acting Farmer. In keeping with my own country image, I have learned how to butcher a chicken. It's a pain in the neck, for both the chopper and the choppee, so I would still rather buy the little plastic-covered trays of chicken at the grocery store. Trouble is, there aren't any.

Otherwise, things are sailing right along—I purposely use the nautical talk. You guessed it: more rain. What else is new? But this has given rise to some great sea-faring adventures as we try to get Moby Truck across the rivers. When Art hikes out of Lumabat, I my very own self have actually learned how to drive the truck across the first river to pick him up, which saves over 45 minutes of steep hill climbing. No wonder I'm getting grey hair. . . and tremors, sweats, a tic, etc. My worst nightmares will forever feature my last attempt, with water actually rushing across the hood of the truck (remember this is a jacked up in the air 4-wheel-drive monster), with visions of me becoming just another piece of flotsam rolling down to the sea. Now we have water in the headlights. It's real cute. I'd put goldfish in there if I could find any.

At least I'm not alone. Jan brought in a bunch of city nurses to see our area. They only had to hike in from the top of Lumabat hill, but Jan still had to get them singing the whole way (200+ choruses of "This is the Day") to keep their spirits up. Then driving out, they got stuck but good in the Lumabat River. First, she had to talk the men who were riding along out of trying to get it unstuck by jacking it up, thereby sending the jack straight down into the center of the earth. Finally they had to get a water buffalo to pull them out. Now they have water in their headlights too.

With all that rain, you'd think the last problem in the world we'd have would be the water supply, but here we can make a problem out of anything. Some pipe or the other broke up by the spring in Malungon so we're often without water for three-day stretches. I can now take a complete bath in less than two pints of water. What an accomplishment. The laundry suffers a bit, though. Whenever the rain starts, we dash around the house grabbing dirty shirts and underwear—even if it's 2 a.m.—to wash in the runoff from our tin roof. It's an automatic reaction to the sound of rain. This could look interesting to the neighbors if we ever get back to the real world.

Actually I think the real world is overrated—we've been enjoying life out in the boonies. It can even be somewhat peaceful, although maybe I'm just hallucinating again. Leks made the well-meaning but tactical error of waxing the floorboards on the front porch. Try to imagine the sound a roving band of chickens make as they come in for a landing on a highly waxed floor. No brakes. And living in a house on stilts also takes some getting used to. A few weeks ago I was having one of my rare but treasured afternoon naps, and delightful it was too, when all hell broke loose right underneath my bed, with yapping, snarling, screeching and various other noises to wake the dead. Art, who was outside painting boards, saw the whole thing. He said two dogs got stuck together under the house in the process of creating more village mutts, and started yipping, whereupon every other dog in town raced over to get into one of the world's largest and loudest dogfights, right under me, of course. He thought it was a riot, but we, like Victoria, were not amused.

Enough of these fond reminiscences. I see folks lining up in the alley so maybe, miracle of miracles, the water is back on again. I better get a bucket and go find out. Bye for now, Love, Debb and Art

❦ Journal Entry

Art was taking me up to Manila for a checkup. Got up real early and drove to Davao airport, but found that all flights were cancelled because of a new coup attempt in Manila, with the fighting still going on. So we headed back to the Davao mission house to watch the coup news on TV. Once again the streets were crowded with spectators who scattered and hid behind the solid safety of their bicycles whenever the shooting got too close. And the army can't aim with those howitzers. Of course there were lots of civilian dead and wounded again.

❦ Journal Entry

We finally abandoned the whole Manila idea, and maybe we'll go in January, if it's still there. Headed back down to Malungon, and as soon as we arrived, Ernesto dropped by to ask us for a ride to the Dadiangas hospital. He had taken a Lumabat baby there yesterday with tetanus (as usual they had cut the umbilical cord with old, rusty scissors, hence the tetanus) but he heard the baby had died in the night. So Art drove him over to pick up the body. The power clicked off about midnight, and we heard later it's another power station blown up, with repairs expected to take months.

❦ Journal Entry

Made an errand run to Dadiangas. Grocery prices are all now double or triple their everyday level, as the store owners know folks want to put on a spread for Christmas. Back and had a literacy meeting with Asterio, firming up plans to start more literacy groups next year.

❦ Journal Entry

Over to Doug and Jan's. Thanks to the night's rain, their water tank is finally full and Jan didn't have to go down to the river to wash off like she did yesterday. Her luck, of course, it was the morning all the bathers discovered a snake in the river, with much screaming and bashing at it.

Winter 1989-1990

Dear Tim and Mindy,

At long, long last you get another letter from us—we are still alive (more or less). I was going to write to you weeks ago, but a lizard bit our computer and we had to take it in to be fixed. Try that excuse at the office next time. Actually, it's true. When they opened it up to take a look, they discovered a couple of wires bitten through. I know that cockroaches get in there, giving new meaning to the problem of computer bugs, but they don't have big enough teeth. Not to discount the rat population, either— we've been having a plague of them lately. I've become expert at mixing tasty treats doused all over with the blue poison powder. Last time we hiked back from the mountains, we arrived in Malungon, flung open the door ready to crash on the couch, and discovered (and smelled) one of the world's most gigantic rats dead behind the front door. Gross.

Life continues to be interesting back in the boonies. Leks and I started up our Sunday School over at the village school while Art jammed the house again with his adults' class. The first week I didn't think any kids would show up, but as soon as we banged the truck-wheel bell, they started pouring in. Leks taught them songs and since they're used to learning by listening (remember they've never had any books, bulletin boards, filmstrips, show & tell, etc.) they could belt them out after one hearing. Art said he could hear them hollering all the way down at the house. Everyone's favorite was the coloring, after we had a little talk about how no, they look tasty but you don't eat the crayons, you rub them on the picture to make colors. Had to break all the crayons in half to have enough. It was a huge hit.

We had to hike out for a couple days right at Christmas, and as I was slogging along the trail I have to admit I was getting plenty maudlin about yet another Christmas away, no family, no get-togethers with friends, no Christmas cookies (really reaching for it there), boo-hoo, etc., when the most wonderful thing happened: we came up out of the river toward the little coffee plantation, and all the trees were blooming white along their branches! The whole place looked like it was covered in snow—just like a Christmas postcard snowstorm in Wisconsin. What a lovely present—I felt a lot better after that. Possibly because I knew I got to admire it, but didn't have to shovel it.

We were going to go up to Manila last month for a physical checkup, but our flight was cancelled due to another war. Even if we had waited out the coup, the hospitals were too busy treating bozo spectators who stood around the street watching the fighting like it was a movie or a pinball game, forgetting about little details like bullets.

So we traded in our tickets and went up the first part of January. I sat and waited outside doctors' offices most of the time (they've really taken to American ways there). They finally decided on allergy testing and determined I'm allergic to everything I love in life, starting with chocolate, eggs and cheese. Why live? They also pinpointed dust and smoke. What a laugh. Out in the boonies they farm by 'kaingan' - they burn off all their fields in rotation the three or four times a year they want to plant. *I* think I'm allergic to rice and sardines, but when has anybody ever listened to me?

Anyway, we had a nice week in Manila, gorging ourselves on McDonald's breakfast biscuits, donuts and esoteric grocery store items like cheese (see above forbidden foods list) and lettuce. We even strolled the shopping area, admiring the bullet holes all over the buildings, and buying whatever was left from the looting. Our friends Peg and Graham are heading back to the States for good soon—they've been here two terms now and are finally going back. First they'll visit our friend Jayne in Australia. Jayne keeps inviting us to come and visit too, but I'm sticking to my rule of not visiting anywhere I would refuse to come back from.

Thanks again for the terrific box of goodies—it sure cheered up our lives. Hope your own Christmas and New Year's (and probably Valentine's and St. Patrick's, by the time you get this) were good times. Bye for now, Love, Debb and Art

❦ Journal Entry

Went over to Doug and Jan's, and gave them their presents, including the great knitted-with-sparkly bangles, violent green "God Bless our Trip" sunshade for their truck. Doug had been on a hospital run to get Hernan's brother—no one knew what he had but guessed it was just his usual huge hangover. At the hospital, they met the guy from Banate who had been badly burned trying to pull his three kids out of his burning house (he didn't succeed, and they all died). The notoriously lazy city doctor, who hadn't wanted to come in in the first place, was trying to discharge him early so he didn't have to treat him.

❦ Journal Entry

Stopped by Maning's but he's out harvesting—only getting a half yield on his yellow corn due to no rain. It's hard to believe that now a drought is starting. His family came to get the new lantern I picked up for them in trade for horse hauling. We were all awakened about 3 a.m. by a pretty strong earthquake. Mice are still running around all over the place.

❦ Journal Entry

Art put chicken wire in front of the screen door so the kids who lean on it while staring in all the time won't tear the screen. I just sat down to supper, had the fork halfway to my mouth, when the same singing group came by, even though it's way after Christmas, doing the song with the 300 verses. Just got them on their way when Maning came by to get us to fix his new, but now broken, lantern.

🦋 Journal Entry

Art was at a big tribal meeting back in the mountains, so Leks and I headed to Malungon, got ice for the little cooler and hit the road. Drove to Malalag Cogon, waited forever for the vet to get washed and dressed, then sent him in by horseback (his first time into the hills) while Leks and I hiked. Arrived to find a huge crowd at the house. The vet went around vaccinating all the pigs for cholera (massive squealing) then left vaccine and instructions for all the chickens. Art was back from the hills and said we'd just missed the big carabao fight—Vijay's big one went after another and everyone had to head them off at the river.

🦋 Journal Entry

Got mission news from Manila: now that Peg and Graham are leaving for the States, the office wants Art to move to Manila and take over Graham's expatriate church. They'd probably just abandon Lumabat, since it's so off the beaten track they'd have an impossible time finding anyone else to go back in that far. After all the work, connections and friends we've made in the last three years.

Over our dead bodies. Which is, of course, always an option.

10

Digging In
Getting Established: Lumabat
Winter 1989-1990 (continued)

Dear Tim and Mindy,

I think I'm still alive but since I somehow forgot to put any mirrors in the Lumabat house, I can't check to find out for certain. I'd guess my chances are about 50-50. *Now* what's going on, you ask.

Things started out calmly enough. We dashed out to Malungon to pick up mega-tons of rice n stuff for the giant Founders' Day celebration in Lumabat. Big doings, on a par with the Fourth of July parade there in Point but no polka bands, beer floats, or kids dressed up as potatoes. In Malungon, Art came down with a fever, so decided that he better stay in bed, and I could represent the family and head back with the girls to Lumabat for the big festivities. I mean, he said, how hard could it be? Show up, deliver the food, and watch all the merriment from my front porch.

I negotiated for some extra pack horses, loaded them down til they were on their knees, and sent them in. By the way, I have my very own horse now. She's a scrawny old nag, tough as nails, who would just as soon bite your arm off as look at you, but she goes the distance. I felt a kindred spirit. Horsemanship is a little different over here. No saddle, just a sort of pad made of old rice bags and lumpy kapok, and a rope bridle. I've discovered a horse knows where its own body parts are at all times, but truly doesn't care about anything else up there. So when it comes to edging around the landslides or staying in tight to the cliff and away from the ravine, you can pretty well count on having your leg torn off. Usually I send Leks and Riza (our second helper) in on the horse while Art and I hike. Art is not a horse person. He says anyone that's idiot enough to get up on the back of a dumb animal and let it take them wherever it wants to go, is stupider than the animal. I don't think he gets the concept. Anyway, since Jan called her horse Faith, I call mine Hope. Mostly because I hope I don't fall off too often. But I digress.

So the girls and I got out there on the trail. I had my umbrella (no, not for rain, for sun—it keeps it from frying your head), my red backpack with my river sandals, and my gallon water jug. We made it in in three hours. I'm getting so tough I'm about as fast as the locals, but in fairness I have to admit they've still got me beat—I'm not carrying 50 lbs. of rice on my head. We'd just climbed out of the last river, I could see my house, we were almost there . . . when Reginia spotted me from the school. From that point on it was a lost cause. I was handed a large banner and got to march in an honored spot in the school parade—in a long line of drums and gongs and kiddies snaking around the village about three thousand times.

Then it was up on the platform for . . . you guessed it, the endless speeches! My favorite part. I was sitting right next to the mayor, which I always hate to do on account of political figures usually getting assassinated while on speaking platforms, but his buddy behind us with the grenade launcher looked like he was protecting us pretty well. I gave a bunch of off-the-cuff prayers, cut the ribbon for the new school classroom, who knows what else and then, time for lunch! Don't ask, just eat it, and then could it be time for a nap?

Nope. Hiked around town delivering all the stuff I brought in, especially the medicines, then over to the school to arrange the toothbrush clinic tomorrow. I brought all the big gas lanterns, and when evening came, it was queen pageant time! I got to pin on all the sashes and corsages and then—what endurance—there were more speeches by all the officials, except this time they were ramblingly maudlin from drinking coconut wine all afternoon and being three sheets to the wind. Stumbled home about 11 and enjoyed the cranked-up battery-operated disco music outside my back window most of the night.

Early the next day, Jan's new midwives, Nita and Fe, arrived for the toothbrush seminar. We've had fantastic response getting in those toothbrushes—some dentists' offices have sent hundreds! I wish they could see how much they're needed: most kids' baby teeth rot out before their adult ones are even in. And every adult has mostly rotting teeth. Anyway, we rounded up kids until we had tons of them, and went over to the school. Leks led off with songs, and then Nita and Fe showed what a toothbrush is, how to use it with charcoal or salt to clean your teeth (of course there is no toothpaste), and what *not* to do with it, like scrub the dirt out of your toenails or clean the ears of your pig. The kids were excited to death and ran home clutching their new prizes. Great time.

I figured at that point I better hike out and see if poor Art was still alive. Ended up in Malungon three hours later to find he was not only well again, but out in Dadiangas with the hill tribes guys, probably eating donuts and not pinning corsages, listening to speeches or marching in parades. Try to remember him fondly. Bye for now, Love, Debb and Art

🦋 Journal Entry

Today Art had two baptisms, and our Lumabat front room was jammed with folks. Kids are gathering on the porch by 1 o'clock now, waiting for us to start Sunday School. Headed over to the school in a big parade at 2. New record today: 56 kids! Had the story, blackboard stuff, lots of loud songs. Games afterwards—I taught them freeze tag and I was the WakWak (witch). Lots of delighted screaming and running. But then they wouldn't play unless I was *always* the WakWak. Thought I was going to pass out from all that running.

🦋 Journal Entry

Made a fast trip back to Davao to solve the mission house caretaker problem. After consulting everyone, and on mounting advice, we finally had to let Marcey go—she was having big parties while we were gone, was forever out with boyfriends, leaving the house empty a lot. We've had enough robberies. We were desperate enough to take Neilda back—the one with the 5,000 relatives that trashed the place right before we moved in. Then Tinong told us her husband is on the run from the military over stealing a lot of money. Great, let's set the mission house up as a hideout. Manolito and Marisol, from church, came over to ask about the caretaking, and they look like the best bet.

🦋 Journal Entry

Called Manila to check on our literacy primer money. Graham said the U.S. Embassy contacted him to warn all of us that the NPA is threatening to kill five Americans soon. Guess we will have to pretend to be French. But I can't remember how to say anything in French except "where is the bathroom?" Maybe we can just talk through our noses and look supercilious.

Dear Tim and Mindy,

What a lovely morning. The breeze is gently wafting, the 100 people on my front porch all have a nice cup of coffee and are chatting with each other, Leks and Riza are on their way back from Dolores's with homemade donuts, I got the keys unjammed on the portable typewriter and I will write you a letter. Maybe I am also spacey this morning because of our bamboo bed. It was being tunneled to the point of collapse by termites, so yesterday I painted it all over with industrial strength bug killer, and all night long it smelled like I had my head stuck inside a bug specimen jar.

Doug and Jan are finally back and brought our mail. They were over in Hawaii, where they met Jan's family for a little vacation. Jan said the beaches there were OK—they even hired some snorkeling equipment and an underwater camera, but then were disappointed. She says our beach in Davao is lots better for tropical fish and even shells. But I bet the one in Hawaii didn't have pigs and goats wandering around on it, like ours does.

They sure needed the vacation. Shortly before they left, the brakes went out on their truck, and they had to drive it all the way to Dadiangas with their heads stuck out the window hollering "No brakes! No brakes!" and everybody ignoring them like they all do. Then to get to the airport in Manila, they had to take two cabs. Doug put Jan and the Terror Triplets in the first one, which looked newer, and took the second one and all the luggage for himself. He almost made it to the entrance of the airport when the cab's rear axle broke and both rear wheels collapsed. Since it had front wheel drive, the driver tried to continue to the airport entrance, dragging the rear of the cab along the ground with sparks flying everywhere (including around the gas tank) and Doug hollering at him to stop, he'd really rather walk the last bit.

And then Jan, who had been fantasizing about K-Mart for two years, gets to Hawaii and discovers that they don't *have* K-Marts. How can a place that calls itself the United States not have a K-Mart?

One more great story Doug told us from the news in Davao. A jeepney driver was finishing up his last run late at night and just had a few remaining passengers on board. Almost to the market, one of the passengers got up, pulled out his gun and told the driver to hand over the cash. But at the same split second, another passenger showed his gun and demanded that the driver hand *him* the cash, or else. Whereupon the two robbers started screaming at each other about who was there first, whose robbery was this anyway, and probably graphic speculation about each other's mothers. The driver and passengers took the opportunity to bail out and dive into the market (with all their cash intact). The last they saw of the robbers, one was chasing the other down the street, firing shots. I sure miss big city living.

Speaking of which, we were afraid we might have to do just that (live in the city, not rob jeeps). Peg and Graham are heading back to the States for good, and the powers that be up in Manila were really pressuring Art to move up there and take over Graham's church. Well it was sure enticing, what with the colorful brown air, the coup attempts and interesting bullet holes in all the buildings, the gladiator-style traffic, street flooding with fun floating sewage, and, best of all, a church made up of rich businesspeople. We regretfully declined and have elected to stay out in the boondocks.

But thinking about choices meant we finally had to come to some decisions about our future here. Since we're just barely getting started, it looks like we will come back for another stretch, but the second term is only a little over two years this time. Did I say we're coming back? That insecticide must've laid waste to my brain more than I thought. Before the next round starts, though, we head back to the States for our official furlough—the Art and Debb Traveling Missionary Show, now appearing in half a gazillion churches. That's a long ways away yet so I'll get more details to you as they come up. Start stockpiling Twinkies! Bye for now, Love, Debb and Art

❦ Journal Entry

We heard Rafi was in the hospital so we went over with his wife. Turns out he doesn't have TB after all (although it's rampant back in the hills), just a bronchial illness and malnutrition from alcoholism. Then on to meet with Asterio re literacy. The revised primers are almost ready to go, and he's setting up a week-long training seminar for the new teachers. We've decided to officially hire Rolando as the head literacy coordinator—he's very smart and dedicated.

❦ Journal Entry

Peg's friend Sylvia left us a big donation check for materials, so we went to the National Book Store in Dadiangas and selected tons of Tagalog books for the schools, plus some cassette tapes. Got to the checkout and found they had to write each title out by hand to fulfill a gift certificate. I thought I was going to grow into the floor. Wayne is getting us hand-crank tape players.

❦ Journal Entry

We hiked to Kiabol to deliver the antibiotics for the kid with the giant
ear infection—his brother had poked a stick in there, and the poor kid's
head was swollen like a basketball. Art looked like a druggie, cutting
up the capsules into equal kiddie portions. We left instructions and the
meds with the mom.

❦ Journal Entry

Art and Orlando went to Digos to talk with Telesforo about the guano
project, and he proceeded to read them the riot act because he'd already
dealt with Viktor in the past, and said all his money had been stolen.
What a surprise. Then on to Bansalan to see about setting up an
agricultural radio program in the Tagakaulo language.

Spring 1990

Dear Tim and Mindy,

It's about 6 a.m. and this is going to be a quickie because
we're supposed to be heading off to Dadiangas in about half an
hour, which is my only shot at the post office.

Now we're in the middle of a big drought. I never thought I'd
see the day I'd actually pray for rain. Haven't had any to speak of
since the beginning of December. Everything is yellow, the ground
is all cracked, and pretty soon the people back in the mountains
are going to start dropping like flies, starting with the kids and
the old folks. They're supposed to harvest their corn in March,
but of course none has grown. I'm already handing out rice daily,
and there's a steady stream of people stopping by and offering to
sell me necklaces or horses or anything that will get them money
for rice. A couple women have already offered me their children!
We've started trying to come up with plans to set up some feeding
centers in the next few months. This is getting very, very tough.

And more bad news. Let's get it all out of the way at once. Bantay the Brainless, wizard watchdog beyond compare, is no more. He was killed when thieves broke into the Davao yard recently to steal the radio and tools out of Doug's truck. Old Bants was just too good a watchdog, I guess, and was buried with great honor and immense sadness under the mango tree. I knew this would happen some day and shouldn't have gotten attached to him so much, but I did anyway. I can picture him up in heaven now, annoying St. Peter no end by barking his head off and hurling himself against the Golden Gates to keep out the riffraff. Atta boy.

There are still a lot of bright spots. We had another huge bunch of kids at Sunday School—almost 80. There are getting to be almost too many now for one class. We had the Holy Week story this week, where Jesus gets arrested and then dies. None of the kids had ever heard it before, so they were sitting there with huge eyes, glued to their benches, wanting to know what was going to happen next. I tell you, it was a good thing the story had a happy ending and we got Jesus out of the tomb alive on the last page. Otherwise, I think they would've rushed home to get their dads (complete with machetes, ammo belts, grenades or their handy household weaponry of choice) and gone scouring the hills for Pontius Pilate and the Romans.

The new adult literacy classes are also about to get started, and we've had so many requests (over 200 students in seven villages!) we've had to wait-list enrollees. I was amazed. I thought we'd have to beat the bushes for students. But I guess there is a real history of fast-talking scam artists coming in from the outside, making a lot of big promises to the farmers, and getting them to put their X on a document they can't read. Of course said document hands over their land to the scammer, but since they'd signed it, that's that. Well, no more getting picked on. We're going to learn how to read signs, and add up purchases, and make change, and decipher documents, and follow written instructions, and write official signatures, and quit getting kicked around. Stand back.

Will write more later. Bye for now, Love, Debb and Art

❦ Journal Entry

Now that we, at long last, got down deep enough for decent water, we've been improving the pump. The concrete pad we put around it finally dried, so we rigged up shade with roof steel for the girls to do the laundry out there. Vijay came by early with his water buffalo, dragging the kitchen table and the bunk beds for the girls. We contracted with him again to build more porch benches for the daily crowds, and the guys came to dig up the front yard. Art built some shelves for me in the back room for all the medicines. Guess I should contact Better Homes & Gardens for our photo spread.

❦ Journal Entry

We arrived at the Malungon house to find someone had been in there— our stuff was all pawed over. It turned out to only be Tito trying to fix the roof (fat chance) so while we were dreaming, we told him to fix the fence too, as the yard is being really trashed by kids. He said he cleaned 10 dead rats out of his locked storeroom (the room right under our bedroom). I was going to tell him if he wouldn't leave old sacks of rotten grain in there, there wouldn't be any rats, but figured what's the use.

❦ Journal Entry

We're getting just tidbits of radio news on how the rest of the world is going, on the rare times when the Voice of America program can break through the Chinese jamming. I still remember when they put the Berlin Wall up—never did think it would come down again in my lifetime.

Dear Tim and Mindy,
    I am writing this to you in sign language because I am now totally deaf. And all because of my noble participation in graduation days. Yes, it's that time again. Now that hot season is really rolling, the schools are all closing for vacation. And since

some non-forward-thinking, foolish gringess has scattered books, supplies, equipment, toothbrushes, etc. to all the schools, she has been invited as honored guest to all the graduations. That would be me. I've already had two of them this week, so I'm getting into the drill.

The graduation exercises at the Lumabat school were supposed to start at 8 a.m. sharp, so long about 9:30 or so I wandered over there and joined the few earliest folks who were starting to trickle in. Another big-wig official from Malungon was supposed to come in and take part but he never showed up, so things finally got started about 11. Remember this is hot season, with the sun blazing away on a platform, but we're all sitting there under our umbrellas and we all have a nice cup of coffee and a tasty sticky-rice snack. Since Mr. Important from Malungon wasn't there, every part of the program he was supposed to have (recognition of the graduates, inspirational speech, handing out of diplomas, awarding of medals) I now 'got' to do. Everybody and his dog has to get a ribbon for something, or else it's rude, so the program stretched on to eternity. Speaking of dogs, there was one sleeping behind the awards table, and various little kids running around on the stage the whole time, to keep it interesting.

Oh yes, about the deafness: to make the ceremony more high class, they got the car-battery-operated loudspeaker system, located right behind my head on the platform, and played Pomp and Circumstance for the entire hundred hours it took to award all the diplomas and prizes. I spent the rest of the day with this loud buzzing in my head, going "What?" "Huh?" and then the very next day it was the same thing all over again at the graduation in Upper Mainit. Except this time, since it was much closer to the road, the Malungon mayor managed to arrive at the very last moment - after the whole ceremony was done, but just in time for the rice n stuff luncheon. How timely. I bet he isn't deaf.

Last week we headed back to Davao, and Leks and Riza wanted to come along to see the Big City. Well, that was fine, but we forgot that Riza is mostly a tribal kid, unused to riding in a vehicle so yes, she threw up the entire trip there. It seemed to be worth it to both of them, though, when they encountered that highest miracle of the modern age . . . TV! Their eyeballs almost fell out, and remained glued to the set most of their waking hours. I felt kind of guilty, exposing them to that trash, but I bet TV will even reach Malungon in the next few years.

Art enjoyed his Big City vacation by taking the truck out to get the fender rewelded for the millionth time, and then trying to fix all the broken faucets around the house. The national motto of "push it until it snaps" is hard on plumbing. I finally broke down and took the literacy primers to a printing company. I had actually been insane enough to try and do them myself on a mimeograph machine, but you remember my relationship with machinery. I'd rather polka with the devil. In the first five minutes, my laboriously prepared stencils were shredding, crumpled wads of paper were being spit out, and giant ink blobs were everywhere, mostly on my head as I tried to tear my hair out. The Biblical phrase "weeping and gnashing of teeth" was coined by one of the authors who first tried to run off his book on a mimeograph machine. Possibly Jeremiah. Anyone who writes a book titled "Lamentations" must have had experience with a mimeograph machine. . . . Sorry, got a little carried away there. I'm alright now.

The time for our furlough is crashing upon us like a steamroller. Art has to write a million reports, and we're putting the finishing touches on our traveling dog and pony show. I can't wait to meet the folks who have been writing to us all this time and sending supplies. Now all we have to do is hook together a traveling route to churches in about eight states and relearn some of the little things, like eating with a fork. Will contact you as soon as we get in. Bye for now, Love, Debb and Art

🦋 Journal Entry

We loaded up and took off for Davao. The new fence is finished at the mission house, now that everything's already been stolen. Drove to the pharmacy where, wonderfully, we never need a prescription—they just hand me the big drugs, so long as I have the cash. They had most of what we needed for the mountains, for once, and we left everything for Jan to take in.

❦ Journal Entry

Awakened by gunfire at 3 a.m. (just me—I still say Art will sleep through the Second Coming). They were single shots, across the street, probably from the security guard for one of the houses over there. I heard voices about half an hour later so looked out—a police jeep with a dead body tied to the fender was heading off for the police station.

❦ Journal Entry

Finally in Manila, and all ready to head out on our furlough. Got up at 4 a.m. and assembled the bags. I'm afraid I overpacked the big suitcase a tad, so Art got it as far as the front sidewalk when the handle tore clear off it, without hope of repair. He was not exactly Mr. Happy Wanderer at this point. Finally found something to tie it shut. We got Mrs. Reyes up to open the gate, and their dog came over and peed on the suitcase. At least we were able to get a cab, but there was a big traffic jam around Shaw already at 5 a.m. because the underpass was closed. Through the usual airport exit hassle and then our first flight was over two hours late. But they held the connecting plane for us in Seoul, thank heavens. Got into Detroit with just enough time to call Jan's mom to say hi. On to Kansas City—and home once more.

11

Interim II
Furlough: U.S.A.
Summer 1990

Dear Prospective Traveler:

So, you're thinking of leaving the golden (more or less) shores of the Philippines to travel to the United States. Well, before you sell all your household goods to pay the travel tax, maybe you better stop and think if you will be able to adapt to the culture there. To help you out, we have prepared the following quiz.

MULTIPLE CHOICE

1. It's time to go! When you get on the plane, you have with you:

   a) one carry-on bag
   b) one carry-on bag and a purse
   c) one carry-on bag, a purse, several duty-frees, three big boxes of donuts, and a collapsible luggage cart with fifteen various-sized packages to cram into the overheads

2. The flight attendant comes around with coffee. You take yours:
   a) black
   b) with a little cream
   c) with a lot of cream and 15 packets of sugar

3. You finally arrive and pick up your rental car. At the first red light, you:

   a) stop
   b) wait for it to turn green
   c) drive straight through it or swing wide to the right to make a left-hand turn in front of all the stopped cars

4. Uh-oh, now you've got a flat tire. To fix it, you:

   a) pull into the nearest parking lot
   b) pull over onto the shoulder
   c) stop in the middle of the street, pull out the back seat and throw it behind the car, tear down a branch and put it in front of the car, and start working on your tire

5. Back in the car again, you've been driving for quite a while and have to go to the bathroom. You:

   a) look for a park with a public restroom
   b) pull into the nearest gas station
   c) pull over anywhere, get out and pee on your tire

6. It would be fun to go to the movies with your family. You select:

   a) The Teddy Bears' Picnic
   b) the latest Disney feature
   c) Ninja Kung Fu Warriors Meet Commander Death in the Killing Fields

7. You drive to the mall and find a space in the parking lot. You:

   a) lock your door and go inside
   b) remember what aisle you parked in
   c) toss a quarter to the nearest kid and say, "Just guard it, but no washing."

8. While you're in the department store, you see a nice shirt. The sales clerk tells you it costs $40. You:

   a) hand her your credit card
   b) say, "OK, I'll take it."
   c) say, "Wow, expensive! They have this same shirt for $17 down at the other store and look, there's a flaw on the pocket. I'll give you $15 for it, best price."

9. You go to the post office to buy stamps for your postcards. You:

   a) buy them at the stamp machine
   b) wait your turn in line
   c) crowd up to the window, wedge your body half in front of the lead person, get one arm in front of her, and put your postcards down on top of her letters

10. You've finally gotten used to the time change and it's 5 a.m. You:

   a) roll over and get some more sleep
   b) go out for some early-morning jogging
   c) take your radio outside with you, turn it on full blast, and start sweeping your yard with a broom

11. It's a lovely day and you're going to the beach with your friends. You:

   a) lie out in the sun and get a great tan
   b) frolic in the waves with your beach ball
   c) find a table, set out the rum and Cokes and the dried fish snacks, get the rice started, put the six food bags up out of reach of the goats, and stretch out in the shade for a nice nap

12. Vacation's over and it's time to head back home again, but you bought too much stuff at K-Mart. You:

   a) buy another suitcase
   b) mail it back
   c) stuff everything into twelve gigantic cardboard boxes, tie them up with twine, and haul them all on the plane with you

ORAL SECTION

Everyone should have the ability to carry on an interesting conversation. Which of the following topics do you find yourself chatting about most often:

the stock market   your water supply

the latest recipes   recipes for rat poison

TV shows   beggars

what's new at the mall   earthquakes

designer clothes   electricity

ice cream flavors   diarrhea

your favorite restaurant   cockroach control

So, that's it for the test. We'll close with just one more short multiple choice question:

When do you expect to receive your test results?
a) tomorrow morning
b) at the end of the week
c) next year at this time, if all goes well

Thank you for your cooperation. Please pay your $75 non-refundable fee when you turn in your papers. An envelope is enclosed for any additional gift you may wish to include.

12

Second Verse, Same as the First
Back to Work: Lumabat
Fall 1990

Dear Tim and Mindy,

I'll attempt an actual handwritten epistle this time, since we're way out in the ultra-boonies, where computers and electricity are but a faint memory. Our flight back from furlough was fairly uneventful in that we didn't crash or anything, but the Tokyo layover was a tad rough. I should've guessed something was amiss when we stepped out of the plane—you still have to go down stairs to the runway there, hike across the tarmac, and get on a bus for the terminal. Well, the rain was pounding down like a waterfall, except it was straight sideways in the wind, which was about to knock us off our feet, and in a second we were all drenched. It's hard to enjoy your bag of squid chips in the lounge when you're soaked, and we weren't even dry yet when we had to reboard and got tossed all over the sky taking off. The pilot said it was a typhoon.

A few days in Manila adjusted us to being back again. There was actually water coming out of the faucets, but a main line somewhere had been broken so it all had to be boiled before drinking. Roy and Sandy arrived (they're from Wisconsin, too!) to take over Graham and Peg's place, and they're nice folks. Poor Doug was still in Manila too—he'd come up for a meeting days earlier and was still trying to get back to Davao. On his first try, a Thai plane had fallen off the runway so all flights were cancelled. Second day, some senator bumped half the plane (including Doug's part) for her entourage. The next day he actually got on a flight, approached Davao, even *saw* its runway, when all the lights in town, including the runway's, clicked off in a power outage—plane went back to Manila. He finally made it on the fourth day.

It felt great finally being back in Lumabat, but getting in was a little dicey. The drought is now well over and the heavy rains have started again. There doesn't seem to be any middle climate—the switch is either on full blast or totally off, sort of like our oven in Davao. Which means the trail is all mud wallows and landslides. Walking on it is fun. The clay builds up on the bottom of your shoes (or bare feet) to about 4 or 5 inches, and feels like you've got bags of potatoes tied to your feet. This is between the slipping and desperately trying to keep from falling. Believe me, you don't want to land on your face on a trail which horses use regularly. In one place, 2/3 of the trail just fell into the ravine and gets narrower with each rain. The horses won't even attempt it anymore so I send them in by the back (steeper) route.

The rain has been great for our new gardens all over town, though. Leks and some of the other women kept mine up, and it is gorgeous. I've got long beans, talong, upo, calabasa, ampalaya, and the detestable okra. I *hate* okra, so naturally it's the healthiest thing in there. I don't know what those other veg are called in real life, but they're good. They make up the 'and stuff' in the famous rice n stuff that we eat every day. I brought some Big Boy tomato seeds back with me from the States and we'll see if they grow.

And we finally got a little refrigerator! Oh boy, popsicles and ice cubes and chilled lemonade! Well, not quite. When it first arrived in Malungon, I plugged it in and . . . nothing happened. Hours of tinkering later (even went so far as to read the manual) we determined the electricity level was just too low to operate it. We then hooked it up to a gas canister where it now keeps things just slightly cooler than room temperature, if you've got a good imagination, and runs through an entire canister of gas in a couple days. The plan was to bring it in to Lumabat, mostly for perishables like vaccines and medicines, and hook it up to our coming solar power. The solar equipment finally also arrived in Malungon—minus one crate with, of course, the stuff we need the most: deep-cycle batteries, battery protectors, etc. Not that it matters anymore, with the trails so bad. Art thinks they're going to haul it all in here slung on poles or dragged in by carabao. You know what I think? Remember all those rusted-out cars we saw at the bottom of the ravines in the Appalachians?

Well, enough of this rambling. If we ever manage to slog our way out of here, I'll get this in the mail to you. Bye for now, Love, Debb and Art

🐛 Journal Entry

Changes and readjustments: the post office in Davao is holding three of my packages hostage. There are new guys in the package room and I haven't had time to establish a good bribery relationship with them yet. On to Gaisano's for groceries and I saw a huge rat run across the floor by the meat counter. Usually I don't see them in person—just their teeth marks on the meat and produce. I couldn't find my old pharmacy on San Pedro—it looks like the entire shopping arcade burned out. Lastly, I got my hair cut—finally a decent job with a nice head massage, unlike the butchering I got in the States. Went to bed early but had to get up for a phone wrong number, which was long distance from Japan.

🐛 Journal Entry

The hike back in was really muddy but we finally made it to the house. Art strolled around and told everyone I now had medicines, so before they were even unpacked I had mothers and kids cramming the porch: fevers, cough, face wounds, body blisters, various creatively-oozing infections. Leks helped me treat everybody.

🐛 Journal Entry

We set up for a new baptism, and people started arriving about 9:30 a.m. There were eight sponsors! Best news of all: they could *all* sign their names on the baptismal certificate, instead of just making their mark, because of our adult literacy program in Balobo. Wow! Rolando came by, then headed off to Angus to talk to their leaders about setting up literacy. The Datu (Chief) up there is one of my favorites—he brings his kids over to the porch all the time and stays to chat. One of his four wives (the third one, I think) will be a good literacy teacher.

❧ Journal Entry

The church youth group kids from Davao drove over and hiked in for the All Saints holiday. They finally got themselves together for a basketball match-up with the local Lumabat kids. I don't know why basketball is so madly popular over here where everyone is so short, but it is—they even have pro teams in Manila. Our best shooter for the Lumabat kids was playing with only one flip flop, and most of the rest of them were barefoot—on a muddy, rough surface. Our Lumabat guys lost by only 4 points (96-100). We served lunch for all. Doug and Jan came over for the day. The Terror Triplets are now speaking only Cebuano, no English.

Dear Tim and Mindy,

There's a lull in the action—the screaming kids have all left the front porch, the chickens are going to their favorite roosts in the trees, the sun is gently sinking behind the mountains, and the giant fruit bats are flapping their way out across the twilight. How idyllic. Before some new disaster strikes, I will quickly write you a letter.

It's been a pretty interesting week here in Lake Lumabat. Art decided to visit the neighboring village of Pantang—an extremely steep trail where they had to scramble up waterfalls to get back out. I was too smart to go along, but I doubt Art was Mr. Cheerful Hiker on that occasion. I went over to Balobo to visit one of my literacy classes. It's pretty close—only a 45-minute hike on a good day. But of course it was *not* a good day. To get there, you follow the river, crossing back and forth over a dozen times and wading down the middle of it for long stretches. It looks just like a Tarzan movie, with big cliffs and vines, but no stampeding elephants. Since it had rained most of the night, the river was fast and deep, and you *know* how much I love water. We made it OK but didn't stop to think that since it had just quit raining, the river was going to keep rising all morning. Sure enough, after we had our guest lunch of rice n stuff, it was too deep to go back. So we had to hike out the alternate way—2 1/2 hours straight up into the sky (nice views of the ocean 40 miles away) and back down again. I think the literacy administrator ought to be a person who sits behind a desk and receives reports from the field.

When I'm not killing myself on the trail, I continue on in my new career in doctoring. My medical knowledge remains at about zero, which gets interesting every afternoon when my porch gets jammed with all the sick people in the village and they all expect me to *do* something about it. Most of the time it's fairly easy like bronchitis, flu, worms, or giant cuts with infection. I read "Where There Is No Doctor" but it can still get beyond me pretty fast. Last week a woman came running over to tell me that Nico, her 7-year-old, had a high fever, and then she went into a panic on my porch when they hollered over that Nico's hands and feet were turning cold. So I packed up my plastic bag of goodies (thermometer, kids' Tylenol, cloths, giant beer bottle full of my good water) and went to see what gives. Sure enough he had a fever of 104, so first I got them to take off the shirt and thick blanket they had him wrapped up in, quit burning the wood chips under his feet, give him his first drink of water that day, and start the wet-cloths-on-the-body routine. That and the Tylenol brought the fever down a degree but then it started to climb again, up to 105. At that point, I quit messing with the Tylenol, went for the aspirin and prayed a lot. That broke the fever, to where he could be taken to the clinic in Malungon to find out what was really wrong. But then they didn't want to go to the clinic—they wanted to go to the 'healer,' the guy who bangs on the drum and rings bells over you to drive out the evil spirits. I thought I had them talked into the clinic but now I hear they took Nico to the healer after all and he's doing poorly again. Sometimes you just want to sit down and tear all your hair out.

Well, I better quit before my hand falls off (who writes letters by hand these days?) or before you fall asleep, if you haven't already. Bye for now, Love, Debb and Art

🌱 Journal Entry

Headed to Dadiangas early to get to the phone company (the nearest
telephone), to call the Manila office about flying up to this conference Art
has to go to. Even so, we had to wait in the jam-packed waiting room a
full 2 1/2 hours for our turn, then more waiting for the call to go through.
What an incredible hassle to make one phone call. Finally, we went out to
the little airport to pick up Roy and Frank, who came down from Manila
to check out our mission.

🌱 Journal Entry

Took Roy and Frank into Lumabat. First we stayed overnight with Doug
and Jan in San Roque to shorten tomorrow's hike. Got up about 5, but
not as many chickens were sitting on the water tank this time, crowing
into our room, even though Doug said he woke up when one fell off. We
sent the girls and the cargo horses ahead, and started hiking. The trail
was extremely muddy, as usual. Had to take lots of rests for Frank—a
Manila softie, not used to hiking. It took us *five* hours to get in—a world
record, and even then I thought Frank was going to pass out about a
dozen times. Arrived, and I had to go outside immediately and pump
up the water tank, as the midwives had used the house last week and
the tank was bone dry. The guys stayed up discussing their idea for a
5-year plan, training seminars, etc., then all to their various beds. There
was a pretty good earthquake about 10:30, making the whole house
sway for awhile and waking us all up, but no damage.

🌱 Journal Entry

Drove Roy and Frank to the Davao airport—and took Leks and Riza
along so I could get them to the dentist. Doug's regular guy was closed,
as his drill was broken, so we went to Manolito's recommended dentist.
A real sleaze joint, which looked like a medieval torture chamber minus
the rack and thumb-screw (maybe they were in the back room) but
seemed better than all the others. Leks just needed a cleaning but Riza

needed two teeth pulled and five filled, for a total of about P1,700 ($85). I paid, but she got the pain of all that drilling, poor kid. Picked up some meds for her on the way home.

🦋 Journal Entry

I'm having a real run of insomnia, these past many days. I was wide awake again about 1:30 a.m. and ran down both flashlights trying to read. I finally dozed but it was time to get up. I had to hike from Lumabat to San Roque to present a literacy seminar but it had rained and the rivers were high, so I climbed out the steep way. The trail was incredibly bad—I fell a couple of times, especially on Vida's new shortcut—it was ultra steep, and I had to pull myself up with my hands. I finally arrived at Doug and Jan's, gave myself a couple minutes, then led the literacy meeting with all the teachers, Asterio and Rolando. We discussed all the new plans, I announced their new pay and bonus, and met a couple new applicants. I finally went on to Malungon. The fence still isn't done and there was an immense spider on the living room window—with Art not there to squash it. I carefully snuck by it and sat in the kitchen with the rat, who is at least invisible behind the wall.

Dear Mindy and Tim,

How was your Thanksgiving? Ours was great – we went over to Doug and Jan's for the Big Feed. Of their two turkeys, I think it was Stovetop who went to the chopping block for the cause. His brother, Butterball, lives to fatten up another day. We had stuffing, made from some ancient cornmeal I had sitting around. Jan made it the day before and it sort of fermented in the heat—an interesting taste sensation. We also had real taters with camote mashed in, and green bean casserole but without the little French-fried onion rings from a can on top. Shucks. Can't have everything.

We can't get out to Dadiangas much anymore to get our mail and supplies. Our letters will probably get later and later as we get to the post office once a month, if that. Sometimes there is no gasoline at all for the truck, and when there is, we still have to wait in line for over an hour to get some. Because of the gas shortage, there have been all sorts of transportation strikes. That ordinarily wouldn't stop us, but the strikers tend to throw rocks at *anything* traveling on the road. The rebels burned a bus on the highway a couple weeks ago. Art fervently hoped it was number A-28 (we see them so often we know them all by number). That's the one that always tries to run us off the road when it passes, and times its ear-splitting horn for our window as it goes by. Art also hopes the driver is tied up to a tree somewhere undergoing indescribable Asian tortures, but probably no such luck.

Now that our house is done, we miss the thrill of building something, so finally decided we better get some fence enclosures made for our truck. We have to leave it behind in San Roque when we hike into the hills, and it is absolutely the biggest fun plaything for miles around. Kids are just the right height to stare at themselves in the chrome bumper, but that gets boring after awhile. So they learned they could get a little stick, and if they poked it just right into this valve on the tire, it would make an exciting hissing sound, just like a snake! Oh boy! . . . until the tire got too flat to hiss anymore. And then they could copy the grownups and push a stick into the door lock, pretending to open the door, except wasn't it too bad the stick kept breaking off in there? So now our Malungon neighbor Mr. Bancod, who drives Art nuts at the best of times, has volunteered to build the fence (for a very cheap price only) if Art would haul 100 coconuts, firewood and a nervous chicken (in *my* seat) way out to Binugawan for him and come back with tons of bamboo. This is after Bancod almost wrecked the existing yard fence last week, trying to cram the wood rack through it. I foresee dead bodies somewhere in this project and just hope mine isn't one of them.

Well, evening is coming on and it's time to light the kerosene lanterns and fire up the mosquito coils, so I better quit. Although I could probably keep writing just by the light of the moon we've had lately—never seen one so bright in my whole life. I guess not having any electricity for miles around really helps. The kids all stay up and play games in the light, especially one called 'bulan-bulan' (moon-moon) which involves hiding, tag, and lots of screaming. It rained briefly last night and afterwards there was a moonbow, first I'd ever seen. Bye for now, Love, Debb and Art

❧ Journal Entry

I finally talked Fidelo into letting us use that little building by the field as our literacy office, but first we have to clean all the wood, moldy garbage and extended rat families out of it. Art gathered up guys to help clean it out by saying he would give them all lunch. Dolores was gone so the literacy students offered to do the cooking. We got a couple of chickens, lots of rice and veg, as the hauling got underway. In the end, they only stacked the wood outside the door instead of taking it over to Jun's place as planned, but at least the building is now empty and usable. A bunch of little kids was hanging around our yard later in the afternoon, so I had them help haul water to the garden. Gave them a giant bag of okra, which they love and I hate (get rid of it!).

❧ Journal Entry

I hauled water again to the garden and got eaten alive by fire ants while watering, especially from one nest I didn't notice I was standing in. Must've had about 50 of them on my legs. I danced around screeching and swatting at myself and ran for the pump. I always like to provide amusement for the neighbors. Rolando came by with the literacy teachers to get paid, and to pick up all the reading glasses I bought in Davao for the classes.

❧ Journal Entry

Despite another transportation strike, Jan and I decided to go to Dadiangas, as we *had* to get food and money. All sorts of rumors about striker violence were going around. We thought if the guys went, they'd probably get attacked, but since we were two women, we figured we could make it through without getting shot. Made it. Also managed to get gas without waiting in line all day, even got some kerosene! What a victory! Got medicines and groceries at Kimball's. Prices are up so high now in the pre-Christmas rip-off, it's outrageous. And Jan says she heard from Manila that they're cutting our salaries again!

❦ Journal Entry

Ha ha, the Catholics in Malungon overslept and the blaring carols for midnight mass didn't start until 3:30 a.m. We loaded the truck and headed off to Davao, preparatory to flying out to the Manila conference. The road was its usual body-buster, but there was actually gas in Digos, our fixed flat tire held up, and we didn't even get ambushed or burned in Santa Cruz, which seems to be happening to travelers through there a lot lately.

Winter 1990-1991

Dear Mindy and Tim,

Just a quick card to wish you Malipayong Pasko! (Happy Christmas!) Yes, I know that even though it is still before Christmas here, you will receive this around mid-February. A tad late, but you wouldn't want to break up the festive Christmas parties, card games, caroling sessions and sticky-rice snacks going on in the post office back room for something as boring as mail delivery, would you? Of course not.

Art and the guys had another agriculture seminar out in Bansalan, and I came back to Davao as it was just about time for Marisol (of Manolito and Marisol, our caretaker couple) to have her baby. They don't have a car and I couldn't picture them cramming themselves onto a jeepney at delivery time. Good thing I came back when I did. About 3:45 a.m. that night, Manolito tapped on my door and said it was time to go. So I threw on my clothes, settled Marisol into the front seat, and off we went. Marisol said her contractions were just barely starting so, fortunately for everyone, I didn't have to do my usual bat-out-of-hell driving routine. We actually arrived at the hospital alive, they hustled Marisol in and I waited in the corridor. The guy mopping the floor and I seemed to be the only ones in the place not actively involved in giving birth. I finally settled into one of the waiting rooms, where the very pregnant woman next to me on the couch kept clutching my arm and groaning "Dios mio!" until they came for her, too. Manolito came out and said Marisol was in a room and prepared for the long haul, so I went back to the house. Some of the church women came by later to say she finally had the baby about 2 p.m.—a boy!

This might be a nice time for us to stay out of Lumabat too. Doug had told us there were reports that the NPA (you remember, the commie insurgents) were supposed to be increasingly active over the Christmas season, so San Roque increased all their defense patrols. Well, of course there *were* no patrols to increase out in Lumabat, so they decided to appoint Norberto, who lives behind us, as our vigilante defense force. Mistake. Reeeeeally big mistake. Norberto generally likes a drop (or several) of the local white lightning—fermented coconut wine. So last week he got good and soused, wandered over to Upper Mainit and had a big drunken fight with a bunch of (real) military guys over there—stole an armalite, strafed the place, shot someone in the chest, and took off. So the commander and a bunch of guys bristling with guns started combing Lumabat, looking for him. They did not seem like the sort to say, "Aw shucks, accidents will happen, let's just forget about it and all get along." I only hope our house doesn't get too shot up in the crossfire—bullet holes will let in all the bugs.

Well, have a terrific Christmas and write soon – we sure miss you! Merry Christmas also to Darcy the Dog, and Cicely and Speedwell the Bunnies, from all our household creatures: Hope, the Horse; Poing, the lizard on the window behind the couch; Ben, the rat in the wall; Fred, the cockroach, with his family of billions; and too many others to fit on the page. Love, Debb and Art

❦ Journal Entry

Finally time to fly out for the big conference. I would much rather stay in Lumabat and get shot than go to another of these boring, nit-picky get-togethers that always end up in a fight. I don't know why I couldn't have been creative enough to come down with malaria or TB—there's plenty of both back in the hills. We got up about 4:30 a.m., the taxi arrived at 5:15 and we roared off for the airport. After the second traffic light, the tailpipe fell off the cab and started to drag, so the driver took the wire he was using to keep his window shut, wrapped it around the pipe, and wedged the wire into his door. Then we actually arrived at the airport. On our way up to the waiting area, we were sent to the express desk and had to fork over an extra P1,000 for a fare increase they apparently just dreamed up. But big miracle—the plane was on time! I had a hyperactive three-year-old behind me who decided to kick my seat the whole way. I can't blame him—he's probably on his way to the same conference.

13

Keep On Keeping On
Carrying On: Lumabat
Winter 1990-1991 (continued)

Dear Tim and Mindy,

The voltage regulator is making bizarre noises as the electrical current (what there is of it) fluctuates wildly. We'll see how long it lasts before it all goes out, so read as fast as you can.

Well, January is turning out to be one of those months. We started out by going up north to this cushy beach resort for a family reunion with the other missionaries, only in typical fashion we spent every morning going over some radical right-wing doctrinal study document, and then all broke into a fight over the Five-Year Plan for the mission. This was interspersed with those obnoxious 'team-building' exercises, one of which was a depressing-as-hell study on what we would do if we only had six months to live. Not attend time-waster, discouraging meetings, for one thing. I mean, what a bunch of turkeys. There we are under the palm trees, wafted by breezes off the South China Sea (in January, no less), have a pool with bar stools in it where you can just swim up and have a cold one, and we're all fighting about the doctrine of the call and the differences in various Bible translations. Good thing I maintain such a respectful, positive attitude about such stuff.

So after that, we headed back to Manila (which makes the Black Hole of Calcutta look like a flower garden) to take our usual charming stroll to the office, sucking in jeep exhaust, stepping over mounds of smoldering garbage, and trying not to get splashed by the open sewers. You can tell my Little

Miss Sunshine personality has turned into the Crabby Queen for awhile. Must not be getting enough donuts. Anyway, Art sprained his foot somehow, and it got worse and worse until he was limping around. I finally dragged him in for an x-ray, and the doctor told him to stay off it for two to three weeks. That makes it a little hard to get back into Lumabat if you can't walk, so Art said we'd stay in Malungon for a couple days (yes, I know that's not three weeks, but *you* tell that to Mr. Stubborn). It turned out perfectly, though, as the sky opened up and dumped on us for days on end, so we couldn't have gotten in if we tried. Isn't there some saying: "Man proposes, but God disposes"? He's on it.

Then Art had the treat of his life, and he's still smiling about it. We had gone over to Dadiangas for some errands and decided to have a quick breakfast at one of the local hotels. We made our way to the restaurant and there, right next to the big tank with the live eels (so you can select which one you want for dinner) was their proudly-displayed, brand new satellite TV. And on it was . . . the Super Bowl! Live! Yes, being played right at that moment (remember the time difference). I thought Art was going to have the Heart Attack of Joy. The staff was about to change the channel because they doubtless would've preferred to watch the local equivalent of Wheel of Fortune, or televised karaoke, but Art convinced them to leave on The Game. Two and a half hours we sat there, but it was a close match-up and he loved every second. Life can be so good.

Well, enough babbling on from me. Don't forget to write! Even Doug and Jan know your return address by now and send in your letters right away. Bye for now, Love, Debb and Art

🦋 Journal Entry

The clutch is acting up again on the truck, so we drove back to Davao for repairs, roaring along in second gear the last few miles, hoping the engine wouldn't blow up. Art walked down the hill to find a sidewalk-stand mechanic, who not only diagnosed the problem, but actually fixed it! Miracles still happen. Since I was in town, I got dolled up and strolled over to the OMF (Overseas Missionary Fellowship) house for the Expat Women's Meeting. Jennifer had the topic today: a seminar on what colors we should wear, and how to dress for our body type, accessorize, etc. I'll remember that next time I'm dredging my way across some muddy river in my baggy culottes, and trying not to slide into the horse plop on the trail.

🦋 Journal Entry

We loaded the truck to return, beginning with our new copy machine which wouldn't fit in the back seat after all, so had to go way back in the cargo bed. We were stopped once by the military for some unknown reason, probably boredom. It started to rain at the top of the mountain and we couldn't get everything, including the copier, covered, so it all got drenched. As we were unloading the truck, we heard the very first news that the U.S. is now actually fighting a war—something they're calling the Gulf War.

🦋 Journal Entry

While in the bathroom, I looked out and noticed a gigantic rat eating the bananas in my banana tree, so asked Art to go out and throw rocks at it—he's a pretty good shot. Listened to war news. Doug and Jan arrived without Leah and Martha, who were supposed to have come down from Manila for a visit, but probably decided not to because of the war, plus this whole area being a Muslim stronghold. I seem to be sleeping OK, so the sickness is abating, except for the hacking cough, but I'm still kind of depressed. January is going by as slowly as molasses in.

Dear Tim and Mindy,
     Here's a change of pace for you. As you well know, I usually start out whining about the neighbors' radios. But way back here in the electricity-less boonies, we don't have radios, we have ... frogs! As a former farm person, Tim, you would think this is

no big deal. But you would be wrong. We now have 500,000 of them, mostly under our house, making a variety of unique, but very loud noises, all night long. What kind of noises? Well, these are not your normal American frogs. Perhaps I'm hallucinating from lack of sleep, but they remind me of being back in Junior High, surrounded by young teenage boys who think it is the height of hilarity to make socially unacceptable bodily function noises. Loudly. Endlessly. Art calls the frogs the Fartso Frogs and thinks it's funny (what did I say about Junior High boys?) but I am very much less than amused.

You can tell from all that frog activity that it's been raining again in ark-building proportions. On our way back into Lumabat this last time the trail was deeply churned-up mud, and I fell down a couple of times. Then we got to the six rivers into Lumabat. The first five were a little tough, with thigh-high water and a strong current, but I made myself into a big triangle so the water wouldn't knock me over, and no problem. Came to the last river, which should've been a snap, as it's usually shallow and wide, to find the whole thing had changed course and dug a deep channel. People were waving us on from the far side. Art went in first, started getting his underwear really wet (river, not fear) and hollered at me to go back. We trotted up and down the bank a bit until we noticed this huge tree that had fallen across the river upstream, with a bunch of carabao tied to it in the river to cool off (they love that). Art went first, didn't die, so I started out, with the water up to my waist. The current was really strong as it rushed under the tree so I was pushing off against the tree, edging across, trying to keep the current from sucking me five counties down. Halfway across, I looked up and there's this massive carabao staring at me, not six inches from my face. This is when I started having a little chat with myself. Here I am, already in my 40s, been working for over 20 years. I ought to have a big house that I'm redecorating with Victorian fabrics, I should be deciding what microwave chocolate dessert to make, I should be trying to pick which video I want to watch tonight. I think I was actually discussing this with the carabao, when Art saved the day. From the bank he said with great patience and concern, "Are you going to stay in there all day, or are you going to get out?" So I hauled myself up the tree and we slogged our way onward.

That same afternoon, after the cargo horses arrived and I could dig out a dry skirt, I had to have this big literacy meeting to discuss our plans for the graduations, with the chief concern of the students being how much food we're going to have (I can identify with that). And then, at the very end of the day, this gross bat started zooming around *inside* the house. We all made a dive for the outside while Leks, now worth her weight in gold (make that double her weight, she's small) just walked right up to it, bashed it with a shoe, and carried it outside.

Sunday School continues to be the usual madhouse crush as more and more kids show up. Even with American donors raining crayons down on me, I still can't keep up. I wish I could buy boxes of only black. I couldn't figure out why every kid had to have a black crayon until Leks explained the logic: for the hair, of course. If you're coloring Bible story pictures, all the people have to have black hair because black is the only hair color there is. Well, obviously.

And then there's the little naked kid. He was back this week. Eighty or more kids screaming around playing games and in the middle of them, one little boy, about five years old, naked as a jaybird. When I asked Leks what was up with that, and why no one else seemed to care, she said, "His older brother is here too, so he gets the shirt." The shirt? Apparently some of the poorer families can only afford one T-shirt for two or three kids, so by rights, the oldest one gets to wear it out in public. Well, that just tipped me over the edge so I put out a newsletter note asking folks to send me some little kids' shorts and shirts. Last time I looked, most American kids had more than one shirt, so hopefully I will get a few responses.

That's about it from the Far Reaches. Hot hot season is just getting underway here, and I'd ask you to send us a giant snowball, but the guys at the post office would probably confiscate it. Bye for how, Love, Debb and Art

❧ Journal Entry

Went over to our new little literacy office where the girls are waxing the furniture that Vijay built. Rafi and the guys were out back digging a five-foot hole for the outhouse—without a shovel. They were using little pointed pieces of bamboo, which will take twelve years, so I went back to the house and found our shovel for them. Art cut apart some plywood to put up more shelves, and had to borrow his own hammer back from Banoy, who asked him how long he was going to use it, and told him to be sure and give it right back.

❧ Journal Entry

Our cargo horses finally arrived. The geniuses who packed the bags to send in had stuffed the kerosene jug into a bag with another box, where it leaked all over the place. Of course the box it leaked on was our food. Asterio came by to tell us the government road equipment had started to bulldoze the trail but was forced to stop about halfway in because they ran out of fuel, and what were we going to do about that? Had beans for supper for about the millionth time in a row.

❧ Journal Entry

Jun stopped by at the crack of dawn to collect the stack of about 40 new colorful church program T-shirts sent to us by the Manila office. It's a great project dreamed up by Rolando to raise money to build benches for the literacy schools, and Jun is taking the shirts out to sell in the villages. I walked with Art to the top of the hill to see him off, remembering when that climb used to kill us. We answered the traditional "where are you going?" question about 500 times by replying "just there" like we're supposed to, and pointing with our lips. Jun came back through in late afternoon. He had given all the shirts away on credit. I think I will tear my hair out.

Art went out to lead his seminar on forming agricultural cooperatives, and had a great turnout. I think we'll ask Maning to plant our yard to corn—he's closest and can maintain the fence, which his own animals seem to be tearing down anyway. The midwives arrived late morning so I went over to the Mothers' Class to watch them prepare various herbal medicines. A huge bunch of mothers showed up. Then Esmie invited me over to her place to try out her puto (steamed cake) made from kamoteng kahoy (cassava). I loved it—it smells and tastes just like the wonderful library paste we kids all loved to eat in kindergarten.

Spring 1991

Hi Mindy and Tim,

I was sitting here entering five million books onto a computer list when, thrill of thrills, your letter arrived! I had sent the girls to Dadiangas to get the mail as I didn't feel like cramming myself on the bus with 185 other sweating bodies and their screaming kids, chickens, dogs, goats, etc. And there's nothing the girls love better than a trip to Shopping Heaven. Anyway, it was great to hear from you again! I will try and write back with only temporary stops to get up and walk around. I still have a large blister on my butt (nobody had better dare laugh) and things like sitting down can still be painful. The blister, and all the other parts of this poor body, are not helped any by being drenched in sweat. It's finally hot season—somewhere over 100 every day. I have a thermometer but I try not to look. The electricity is back on (they shut it off every morning from about 7 to noon to 'conserve energy,' since we've started another drought) and I have the fan blowing on me so hard my hair is sticking straight out and about to be torn off my head, but it doesn't help.

So what's been going on around here? March was hellacious. It's the end of the school year, so I closed down my seven literacy classes in two big graduation ceremonies. I grouped three classes for the first one and held it in a central spot, which happened to be way up on top of one of the tallest mountains around. I rode over on Hope the Horse, accompanied by the midwives Fe and Nita on their horse, Choy-Choy. Two hours, straight up into the air, trying to keep from sliding off the back of the horse the whole way. Fe led the way because she supposedly knew the best trail, but Choy-Choy was ambling along at a snail's pace. So every other minute, Hope would come blasting up from the rear, plant her nose in Choy-Choy's butt, whereupon both horses would proceed to kick the stuffing out of each other with me and Fe trying to separate them with much hollering and bashing with sticks. Are you picturing this?

We finally arrived and had a nice guest snack of boiled camote while everybody from miles around assembled for the big doings. We lucky dignitaries took our places on the rickety makeshift stage out in the broiling sun, and the program got started. It lasted a full three hours, and included dramas written by the students, native songs (which always sound like a goat being disemboweled), the old ladies dancing around the wooden drum, long and boring speeches by every single person there, handing out of the completion certificates, awarding of ribbons and medals (yes, *everybody* has to get something) and I don't know what else—I'm sure I was in a coma by then. We were all revived by the rice n stuff luncheon served to the honored guests, and I was about to get back on my pony and ride when everybody says—you can't leave now, the fun stuff is just starting. Sure enough, it was time for the honorary basketball matchup, the honorary cockfight, the honorary horse fight. This is all made more interesting by the fact that I hadn't drunk anything all day as there are *no* bathrooms in this place—everybody just uses a bush—but people tend to follow me around wherever I go, and it was getting pretty late. Finally we were able to leave (downhill this time, so I was falling over the front of the horse the whole way) and it was dark by the time we got back.

Next morning bright and early we rode out to the next graduation and did the whole thing all over again for the last four classes. Gads. It was actually kind of inspiring. The little old codgers who have never gotten anything in their whole lives except a lot of drudgery, hunger, illness and hard work, finally got their day in the sun. As part of the drama, the Lumabat top honor student—a little old grey-haired great-grandmother in her late 60s—painstakingly wrote her name and her numbers 1-10 on the blackboard. And the entire crowd stood up and cheered for her! All the graduates came off the stage looking a little dazed and clutching their certificates like they'd just been handed gold. Some of the sappier gringos in the audience may even have gotten pretty choked up and wiped away a secret tear or two.

OK, maybe you haven't been waiting all this while to hear why I have a big blister on my rear end but I'll tell you anyway. After all that riding around to graduations, I still had to ride out of the mountains a couple days ago. We were taking the steep trail and it looked like it was going to rain any minute. Toward the end of the trail there's a ravine so steep you have to slide down it. On horseback, this is a whole new experience. If it's dry, you're only fairly sure you're going to die. If it rains and turns to mud, you're absolutely positive you're going to die. So we rode out top speed to beat the rain and now I'm standing a lot. Someday, I'm going to look back and think all of this is funny.

Well the sun is sinking gently into the dust and the temp is finally coming down below 100, so maybe I'll go haul some water. Enjoy life and write back reeeeeal soon. Love, Debb and Art

🦋 Journal Entry

Now we're back in Manila for more endless meetings. The entire day today was devoted to a stress control seminar. According to the presenter's fancy stress chart, Art and I reached terminal burnout a long, long time ago and are now both dead. I knew all this stuff already, but who are they kidding—who has time to do all that serene meditation and getting away to a quiet spot? I don't even have time to go to the bathroom most days.

🐛 Journal Entry

We heard loud crashings-around real early as Doug, Jan, and the Terror Triplets headed off to the airport for their furlough to the U.S. We'll really miss them! We packed up all our own stuff and got a cab to the domestic terminal. We were sitting through one traffic light until Art realized the driver was fast asleep. The flight was delayed—a last-minute passenger had backed out and vanished, so they had to take off all the luggage and reload it, in case of terrorism. We finally took off a couple hours later, and did not blow up over the ocean.

🐛 Journal Entry

People are now coming by to get their water at the pump in our yard as early as 4 a.m. and *singing*. And I used to be so happy about leaving behind the Malungon radios. Got up and washed my hair but ran out of water in the middle of it. Went out and pumped up the tank so I could finish my hair and quit dripping soap everywhere. I looked like Medusa's grandmother—I just love to provide amusement. I started on the end-of-school-year literacy reports and found I had saved enough money so we *can* offer sessions next year after all!

Dear Tim and Mindy,

So you went and did it—signed up for a real live cruise. To Jamaica, no less (be happy, mon). Are you out of your minds? It's *hot* there. They probably have palm trees all over the place with coconuts that fall on your car, you can't walk 50 feet without tripping over pigs and goats, and the best snack you're going to get all day is chicken feet. I can't wait to hear your reports about this one.

Speaking of trips—large disappointment. Our eagerly awaited quick vacation trip to Ireland fell through. Well, not fell through exactly, but I couldn't go on with it when I found out that to use our frequent flyer miles (which is the only way we could afford to get over there) we would have to fly *eastward* to Europe *via the U.S.!* Gads. It already takes about 30 hours to get to the Midwest from here, and I always arrive within five minutes of death. I just can't imagine flying on to the east coast and all the way across the Atlantic too. So now I've come up with some other hare-brained scheme for an alternate vacation (about six months from now). Will send you a postcard from the mystery destination. No, mon, it's not Jamaica.

Life continues to perk along back in the mountains. I short-sightedly donated the materials to the Lumabat grade school so they could make a permanent stage for their graduations and activities, so I then had to be honored guest at the graduation. Apparently I did not also get them enough nails because as I was coming down the stairs at one point to hand out awards or something, one of the risers flipped over and tossed me on my ear. This entertainment at least woke up those who were napping but unfortunately I did not break anything, and had to just pick myself up and continue handing out medals.

And now my two helpers, Leks and Riza, have discovered Love. Every time I ask them to nip across the village and get me a can of sardines or bag of sugar, instead of heading out the door, they dive back into their room for extended splashing and rustling. They emerge about 20 minutes later, dolled up to the nines and enveloped in a fog of perfume. Here I spent all these peaceful years without children, and suddenly I have two teenagers. Life laughs at me.

We finally announced to the proper officials here that we've decided to terminate when this current term is up (well over a year away), and they should begin looking for a replacement for us. They're already starting to put the screws to us to stay on— probably because they realize they won't easily get someone else crazy enough to take over our particular place. I think we'd still like to stay in missions—Art might even look at development work for relief agencies, probably still outside the U.S., but we'll have to wait and see what turns up. I envision being offered someplace easy and relaxing next time—like coastal Bangladesh.

Well, have excellent fun in Jamaica. Be sure and send us pictures of yourselves with those little braids all over your head. Bye for now, Love, Debb and Art

🦋 Journal Entry

Art is still at an agricultural seminar, so I'm waiting in Malungon a few days for him to get back. I went to the big birthday party for MaiMai, the neighbor's little girl, and was enjoying the tasty pig roast until I learned that they had butchered the pig that some foreign aid group had given them, which was supposed to be the breeding stock for a new livestock project for the hill tribes. In the evening, I strained to listen to the shortwave radio through all the static, just to hear some voices speaking English.

🦋 Journal Entry

A challenging night—the power went off at 1:30 a.m. and the heat woke me up as soon as the fan went off. There's a boxful of new puppies next door and they don't like the heat any more than I do, but are louder about it. Even Ben the Rat won't sleep and is chewing his way through the walls again. It's getting so hot now I have to go in the bathroom every afternoon and pour cool(ish) water on myself, to keep from feeling sick.

🦋 Journal Entry

Banoy came by to tell me the jeep driver is demanding 500 extra pesos above the price we all agreed on, or he won't go and bring Art and the guys back from the seminar. Wow, think of the peace and quiet I could have around here if he stranded them all at Bansalan. No, I bet somebody would bring them home. I told him I didn't have any money (which was true) - that he better hash it out with Art when he got there. So he went after all and Art wouldn't give him the money either. But the seminar went real well; all the guys were excited and learned a lot. Art only dropped a tree on his foot, barked a shin and scratched one eye, but now he's an official farmer with a certificate and everything. Just wait until his brother-in-law Clarence, with the massive hog farm in Missouri, sees that.

❦ Journal Entry

We finally got down to Dadiangas to get the mail. Received a letter from a relief agency in Cebu, written 3 1/2 weeks ago, saying we could have all those free medical supplies we needed, but we had to answer within two weeks. So much for that.

Dear Tim and Mindy,

We had a great time reading the mighty saga of your Jamaican Trek to the Tropics. I don't know, though. When you wrote about your trip to England, I read that one over and over. But for some strange reason, I just couldn't seem to whip up the same enthusiasm for this trip. Something about your stories of real live actual palm trees, and hot weather, and riding horses, and shacks with bamboo walls just didn't whip up in me a red-hot urge to run out and buy travel tickets. Actually, the only difference we were able to pick out between there and here is that here, they don't tend to offer you various forms of recreational plant life every time you turn around. But then, since everyone here lives in the far reaches of the Twilight Zone anyway, they don't need to.

Your description of landing over the water on Montego Bay reminds me of our last flight to Manila out of Dadiangas Podunk Airport. All they can handle are Fokker 50 twin-engine prop jobs that wheeze up off the runway straight out over the ocean. This last time, the ticket agent, who is also the baggage handler and flight announcer, came into the waiting room and announced, "Everyone please disregard your seat assignment. We need all the men to sit in the front and the women to sit in the back to balance properly so we can get off the ground." Nobody even laughed or ran screaming from the room, even when he came back twice more to announce that various pieces of luggage had to be left behind because they were too heavy (it was a tad windy that day). Art and I actually discussed whether we wanted to go through with it, but are more or less still alive to tell the tale.

Everything else continues on as normal. A couple weeks ago we had Vacation Bible School for the kids up in this little sitio (village) called Manipis, which means 'thin', because the village is built on a trail on a ridge, and the back half of all the buildings hang down over the edge of the ravine. The only building we could use was an open bamboo hut with benches, sort of like a gazebo, which also hung half out over the edge. The kids started coming, and coming, and pretty soon there were about 60 of them stuffed in there and I figured we and our hut were goners for sure. Then Leks had them all stand up on the benches and sing *action* songs, where they all holler out that they're going to zoom around the room and praise the Lord, while they jump up and down on the benches. I thought we were all going to lie in a crushed heap at the bottom of the ravine and praise the Lord, but by some miracle we survived to sing another day. The kids all made construction paper crowns and were major cute.

So now we have two more VBS's to go. It ought to be interesting to see how that works out as Leks and Riza, my two helpers, are having an all-out fight (one of them called the other one a crazy, and that one called the first one a devil) and now one of them has walked off in a huff. Add to that delight the fact that I have to write to Doug and Jan in the States that their kitchen floor is going to collapse any day now. It always used to sag because of poor drainage and rotten floorboards, but the moment has finally come for it to let loose and dump through. The cabinets have all already pulled loose from the wall and the refrigerator will probably fall in this week. That ought to perk up their furlough.

We're finally getting a little rain after four months without a drop. Everyone is rushing around plowing and planting like crazy, and I finally got my new garden in (*no* okra!). Trouble is, the harvest is still four months away and nobody had a harvest this last time because of the drought, so they're all starting to drop like flies. Art and I are going to bring in and distribute about thirty 50-kilo bags of rice and corn grits, which ought to be a real fairness and administrative nightmare. But I'm getting tired of treating tots for vomiting and diarrhea followed by fever because all they've been eating for weeks is raw bananas.

Speaking of diarrhea (#1 missionary topic), how was the drinking water in Jamaica? Did you escape the dread amoeba? Did you have to get hundreds of hurtful shots before you went over? If you did (get shots, that is) you might as well come over here and visit us next. We might not have any bathrooms, but we have great snorkeling. Also palm trees. Bye for now, Love, Debb and Art

◕❦ Journal Entry

A wide variety of sickies were on the porch today. Inday brought by one ancient crone who wanted medicines for fever and headache, but kept asking if she'd have to pay anything. Most folks used to bring us bananas or beans when they could, which isn't possible these days, so I told her not to worry, it was free. She was wearing more antique gold and silver bracelets than I've ever seen outside a museum.

◕❦ Journal Entry

I got Rafi started on extending the garden. Every time I went out the back door to see how it was going, lizards would fall on my shirt or head. They must like the top of the door. A couple of guys from Balobo sat on the porch for about 45 minutes, trying to get Art to 'lend' them three sacks of rice (which we don't have anyway) until harvest. They won't hear no because they're fighting for their lives, but we can't say yes to some without starting nasty and dangerous fights. How can we possibly feed over 60,000 people? This is really, really hard. How does God stand it?

◕❦ Journal Entry

All the stuff finally arrived to assemble our solar electrical system! Rollie, who is Tinong's son with the electrical engineering courses, hiked in to install it. He and Caloy had already hauled the solar frames up to the roof by the time the rest of us set off for VBS in Angus. We trudged up the mountain and had songs, games, stories, then handed around the crayons for coloring time. I noticed the mothers had all sneaked a picture and some crayons too, had gone over to Rosario's porch and were all coloring away like mad. After juice and cookies, I went back to Lumabat alone. Arrived to see no panels on the roof. They had mounted them on the back of the roof, facing north, because they told Rollie that was south. We then had a bit of a chat about where the sun came up every morning, and had them change all the panels back to south. Not that I think it makes that much difference this close to the equator. Rollie got the fans to work but not the lights yet. He might be able to come back again next month.

✤ Journal Entry

Last day of VBS way up the mountain in Angus. I sent Leks and Vangie in on the horses, and walked up with Kikay. I was exhausted and almost didn't make it—it was super steep and I couldn't catch my breath. But what spectacular views—you could see all the sitios, even Pantang, and what looked to be the last remaining patch of non-logged-out forest for miles around. Two of the Angus Datu's wives played the 4-string guitar for me: one holding the guitar and playing the chords while the other beat on it with a stick. The kids flocked in, belted out the songs; there was lots of action. I talked with the Datu and sitio leaders for a few minutes about maybe starting the trial preschool next year that they've been requesting for so long. Finally headed back. Then I fell on the steepest part of the trail and twisted my knee. Almost couldn't get back up. I kneaded it out so I could keep going, but was stiff and limping. I've fallen several times now—don't know how much longer I can do this.

14

Staying the Course
Persevering: Lumabat, with side trips
Summer 1991

Dear Tim and Mindy,

Big thrills over here! Our solar is finally in! We had it hauled in about two months ago and Tinong's son, Rollie, spent a few visits installing it. It even seems to work fairly well. When evening comes and things get dark, you press this switch thing over by the door, and shazam!—this round device on the ceiling causes light to fill the room, bugs to swarm in from five counties, and every kid in the village to squash his face up against the screen door with his mouth hanging open. Installation of a device dependent on the sun has also caused the heaviest and longest rains in a year.

Thanks to the rain, I also found a new tactile sensation, one which I think will even beat out frog-booting. Slugs! They're all over the place. Mostly they slime their way across the walls and ceiling, but every once in a while, like the lizards, the less coordinated will fall off and plop on the floor. And of course half the time they land upside down, sticky side up. I was rushing around the other day, had a batch of people clamoring for medicines, and was bustling back and forth between the porch and my medicine closet in the storeroom. I even *saw* the slug on the floor earlier and was too lazy to pick it up. Sure enough, barefoot and hands full of medicines, I stepped right on it and it stuck to the bottom of my foot. So there I was, hopping up and down trying to shake it off, which it wouldn't do, then trying to scrape it off on the chair, almost falling over, finally having to drop everything and pull it off. Gross Gross Gross. I got to wondering if things like this ever happened to, say, Albert Schweitzer or even Mr. Missionary himself—St. Paul. Their writings are strangely silent.

We're still having Vacation Bible Schools all over the place, and one was a little more exciting than usual. We had just started the songs and the leaping around, when this procession came up the hill from Lumabat—a bunch of folks carrying a woven mat slung from a big bamboo pole. We call it mountain ambulance: it's how they carry out the sick people who are too bad off to walk or ride a horse. Sure enough, some kid had fallen out of a coconut tree and broken his big thigh-bone with such force that it punched out of his skin. They ran and got Art, who, I have to say, did a great job of dressing the wound and splinting the leg. I guess his Mom dragging him to all those Boy Scout meetings (and Campfire Girls, and Bluebirds, and whatever else she was leading) really paid off. Anyway, they then had to take the kid out, and not just to Malungon, which has no x-ray or bone-setting facilities, but all the way on to Dadiangas. Now how on earth were they going to do that? My goodness, here's Mum Deb, we'll just ask her opinion. So I got on trusty Hope the Horse, rode out to the truck, gently stuffed the kid in the back along with his 500 relatives, drove him to the hospital, ran around to every pharmacy in town to collect his meds, then back in the truck, and back on the horse in a mad rush to get home to Lumabat before dark. This on a horse who was decidedly peeved at having to go out and back in on the same day and was *not* going to go faster than an arthritic turtle, no matter how much the crazy gringess jumped up and down and hollered. As I tried to ease off my large and rather unhappily-placed blister (yes, another one) I thought back to my naïve childhood, when all I wanted out of life was a horse of my very own. But anyway, the kid is going to walk again, with hardly even a limp. If we hadn't gotten him out, he would've been crippled, which, from the many I've seen, is a death sentence back in the hills. So the blister was worth it.

Break time for an ice buko. I have my gas refrigerator hooked up this week because the seminary students are visiting.

Usually I don't run it because it uses up a whole canister of gas in less than two weeks, and that stuff is too heavy to haul in on horseback. One can tilts the poor horse lopsided, and two cans drag him to his knees. Anyway, I let the girls make ice candy: take a small tubular plastic bag and fill it with a mixture of coconut milk, coconut pieces and sugar, then freeze. When frozen, bite off a corner of the bag and eat whatever doesn't drip all over yourself, your clothes, and all over my porch benches. I ought to have my head examined.

Better end now. I mean, I'll be at the post office in only another couple weeks, so I better get this ready to mail out. Now that Doug and Jan are gone, we get our mail only about once a month—twice, if we're lucky. Keep writing anyway! Bye for now, Love, Debb and Art

🦋 Journal Entry

Got up at 4:30 a.m., still painfully itchy, with my skin rash spreading, and my eyes all puffy. I look like a boiled beet with lumps. Got on the trail by 5:30. Jun's kid loaded our cargo, and then some loose horse attacked his, right in front of us, on the edge of the village. We finally got them separated—it's a good thing they're about the size of large dogs. We drove on to Dadiangas to see a skin doctor. He told me it was an allergy from something called PABA in that new sunscreen lotion I had slathered on the other day. He loaded me down with pills, but the itching is now the worst ever.

🦋 Journal Entry

The six visiting pastors-in-training are ready to head back to their seminary north of Manila. It was an interesting week: this is their own country, but they're all city kids. We sent them to various hill villages with Lumabat guides for culture training. We finally got them all back to Davao but now they're stranded, and can't fly up to Manila. Roy and Sandy are stuck, too, in Thailand, on a vacation. There was a big volcano eruption on Luzon and no planes can fly due to all the volcanic ash.

🦋 Journal Entry

Overloaded the truck as usual, and took off for Malungon. When we got close to the Del Sur border, Art noticed bad overheating and pulled over. The radiator hose was leaking, and about to blow. When he took the radiator cap off, the water geysered out, which was jolly fun for all the watching school kids. We managed to limp back to Davao for repairs. Since it was pretty late, we decided to stay over and go see the movie "Dances with Wolves," which I thought was OK, despite dragging on forever. The theater was jammed, so we had to sit on the balcony stairs the whole time. As it was a new release, the balcony was crammed with people illegally taping it on their video recorders, so they can sell copies, like they always do. Half the videos you rent over here are dark, jumpy, balcony-filmed versions with storyline gaps where they had to shove the camera under their seat because the usher was coming.

🦋 Journal Entry

Got to Malungon and started hiking into Lumabat early, but had to stop and mediate a dispute in Caputian on the way in—the literacy class is fighting with the sitio leader's wife. Finally arrived and unloaded the horses. Jun and Banoy came over with news about the greedy cult leader over in Pantang, the one who ripped off Charlie-from-Missouri so badly that he left. Then this cult leader stripped the school, stopped the programs, and has now been bugging us for 'needs.' He's dead. He was climbing that same steep waterfall on the trail that Art had to climb going in, but slipped and fell.

Dear Tim and Mindy,

By some minor miracle, there appears to be electricity this morning (we're in Malungon) so we'll see how much of a letter I can get written. We've been driving back and forth to the police station in Dadiangas for the last couple of days. Yes, another adventure. We were doing innocent errands over there the other day when a jeepney roared up and slammed into our truck. Probably one of the gazillion that drive around without brakes. Anyway, it dented our fender pretty good and tore off the signal light, causing a large crowd to gather, to offer loud advice and give their detailed assessment of the situation. A traffic cop finally bustled up and told us all to go to the police station. Once there, the jeep driver didn't show up, of course, and we were told to come back the next day with all our official truck papers. Truck papers? I mean, who knew where those were. So after tearing the house apart, we went back to the police station, and the jeep driver finally showed up. He was judged to be at fault for the whole thing, but the police decided to just render an 'amicable settlement.' That means it stays out of court, we pay for the damage, and they don't have to write a report. No wonder everybody (else) thinks it's amicable. So, back to Allah Valley Motors for yet another round of repairs. I think they consider us part of the family. At least we're sending all their kids (and grandkids) through college.

The exciting news is that all my literacy classes are starting up again, we've added a few new ones, and have branched out into a couple of requested preschools on a test basis. Our big kick-off was at the literacy office in Lumabat last week. All my teachers were there, Rolando and the other supervisors, all their kids, dogs, chance acquaintances, passing strangers, etc. I lugged all my supplies over in the mud, and had just opened my mouth for the grand speech of welcome and encouragement when the sky opened up and torrential rains began. Have you ever tried hollering over the roar of a downpour on a tin roof, in an alternate language, with rain leaking through the holes in the ceiling and dripping down your neck? Don't. Then someone started the cooking fire right outside the window, whereupon thick smoke began pouring into the room and nobody could breathe. We survived long enough to have lunch (rice n stuff, who would've guessed?) and officially open the school year. A grand time was had by all.

I suppose you've settled into the gentle routine of summer: mow the lawn, trim the bushes, water the petunias and sit in your lawnchairs on the driveway sharing a cold one with the neighbors. Well, no difference—it's exactly the same thing over here! Once a week or so, all the women strap on their babies, find their razor-sharp knives and come over to our yard to walk the rows and weed out Maning's corn. Then we all jam up on my porch and have a nice cup of coffee. Let me digress to explain that a cup of coffee here is one handful of rough-ground coffee, which they grow themselves, and one handful of sugar, thrown into an 8-oz. drinking glass. Pour on boiling water, let settle for about a minute, drink it down and instantly get so buzzed that your hair stands straight up. So—after we finish our tasty coffee on the porch, we're all perked up enough to chat about current events, such as who might've knifed Jun's horse last week, why Vida won't share the volleyball, even though it belongs to the whole village, and whether the gunfire up in Malita was communist rebel activity or just the mayor getting drunk again. See? Things are pretty much the same the world over.

One good thing about those endless trips to Dadiangas: we picked up several packages which turned out to be kids' clothes! Folks in the States have really responded well to my anti-naked-kid campaign. I'm getting a lot of shirts out to the villages; the Moms are delighted and the kids are so proud. Brother-in-law Clarence even sent over a whole bag of farmer caps (like baseball caps but with seed corn logos on them). It startles me a bit now to see local guys sporting their Funks G or DeKalb seed corn caps as they plow a field behind their water buffalo. Back to the post office and I'll get this in the mail to you. Bye for now, Love, Debb and Art

🌱 Journal Entry

We were just getting to sleep about 9:30 when Maning came banging on the door because Esmie had gotten bitten by a snake. I ran over to check it out, but it wasn't poisonous.

❦ Journal Entry

Hiked out, and when we arrived in San Roque, I decided to hash it out with Dodong about how skinny and sick Hope the Horse was looking. Leks and others had told me how Dodong was taking my money for board and grain, feeding his own animals, and not giving anything to Hope. We both managed to stay calm at first, then he started giving lame excuses, and finally began threatening Leks, and that's when I lost it. It was the first (and only) time I ever completely lost my temper, but I knew I needed to protect Leks. I got kind of carried away, pounded on the fence, started hollering and told him if Leks was hurt in any way I would have him hunted down no matter how far he ran. He knew I could do it too. Uneasy truce. We'll see what happens.

❦ Journal Entry

Headed back to Davao, and took Leks along. Went with her over to the Baptist Bible College that her brother recommended, to check out the enrollment requirements, etc. It's a very nice place and looks like a real possibility. If Leks still wants to go for the business degree like she's been talking about, we'll send her there when we leave next year. Packed for our trip to Manila and then on to Hong Kong for my referral. Thank heavens someplace in the fairly-nearby known world has a real, functioning mammogram machine and can tell me what's going on. I'm a tad worried.

Dear Tim and Mindy,

It was a treat to get your latest letter and hear that, despite being forced to spend time in Colorado, you managed to survive. Your trip to the Rocky Mountains with the teens sounded, like, way out, man. I can picture the whole groovy scene: everyone mellowed out around the campfire, passing around the pipe marshmallows, someone strumming a guitar and singing "Rocky Mountain High." No? Well, maybe that was another generation ago. More likely another century.

Speaking of another century, Art and I crashed into another milestone a couple weeks ago—our anniversary: twenty (hundred) years of wedded adventure. It was a fairly interesting celebration: both of us in a little apartment in Hong Kong, Art working crossword puzzles and keeping half an eye on me, who was whacked out on happy pills after having large bits of my right breast cut away the day before by a fiendish Chinese doctor. No, it's not another Twilight Zone episode—just another typical Art/Debb scenario.

We had this meeting in Manila last month and since I was already that far north, thought I might as well run up to Hong Kong for a follow-up mammogram, as strongly recommended by my doctor in the States last year. So we got some doctor names, some fellow mission folks in HK said we could use their apartment, and away we went. It started out being pretty impressive. The medical equipment looked like the cockpit of a spaceship, and makes the U.S. stuff look stone age. Anyway, when the results came back, the doctor said, "You've got a pretty large cyst in there and it's only going to get bigger so we'll just cut it out . . . right now!" I didn't even get a chance to make a bolt for the door. Like Frankenstein, he had his own operating room right on the premises, and before I could even get to the front of my backwards Chinese magazine, they had me strapped down on the table.

Here's some good advice to memorize: *never* let a doctor operate on you after giving you only a local anesthetic. It gives him the chance to chat at you the whole time. Besides that, you get to watch all the fun. They put up this little screen so I couldn't see much, but since he was cauterizing out the bad parts, smoke kept pouring over the screen and he kept rambling on about, "Wow, this is bigger than I thought, and *all* the tissue in here is abnormal, but I better quit cutting it away now or there won't be anything left (ha, ha)." I'm recovering pretty well, although I guess my goal of someday being a topless dancer in a sleazy bar will now never be realized. That's age for you—your dreams go, one by one. I imagine you're just thrilled to read all the details and gore of my medical experience but I won't apologize. This gives you the perfect opportunity to write back and say you knew someone who had the very same operation, but they died suddenly six months later.

The other, non-hacking, non-cutting parts of the Hong Kong trip were nice. We gawked at all the neon lights, rode the ferry, went out to see the junks in the harbor, even went up north as far as the border so we could look over into China—the real one—across all the duck farms. Our favorite was to get up super early and go out to see folks do their Tai Chi in the park. Some people would even bring along their birds in cages, and hang them up on a branch to sing and get some fresh air while their owners were exercising. Now Art is all gung ho for Tai Chi, and is going to try it to achieve ultimate tranquility. He's already learned the Eagle Stance, the Bear Stance and the Duck Stance (although it looks more like the Turkey Stance to me).

We actually did celebrate our anniversary while over there. Art took me to the lobby of the Hong Kong Peninsula Hotel (they always write about this place in novels) for Afternoon Tea. Big Persian carpet underfoot, huge rococo pillars with gold leaf everywhere, string quartet in the balcony, the international set wandering by in their designer outfits—pretty impressive for two local yokels from a tribal village who eat rice with their fingers. We had our choice of teas, and then they came on with all the silver dishes of tiny sandwiches, scones with clotted cream and jam, fruit breads, selections of the world's most sinfully decadent creations from the sweets trolley. I tried not to disgrace myself, but it was hard. Oh, and before we left, I of course had to go upstairs and check out the bathroom—probably the best I've ever researched—all marble and dark wood paneling, with a wide variety of lotions and perfumes on the counter. As soon as you come out of your own little 'room' (we don't do stalls) the attendant rushes over to turn on and adjust the water, and then stands by with a linen towel. All of Hong Kong is like that. There are so many Rolls Royces they might as well be taxis. In fact, I think that's what the Peninsula Hotel uses as shuttles to pick up folks at the airport. Sure will be interesting to see what the Chinese do with Hong Kong when it gets handed back to them in 1997.

Well, this letter is a volume and a half, and by now you're fast asleep so I will tiptoe gently away. Write back when you wake up. Bye for now, Love, Debb and Art

❧ Journal Entry

I'm still in Davao, recuperating a bit. Doug is back from furlough! He
brought Kerry so she could start classes at the International School here
in Davao. Jan, along with Danny and Karen, is still in the States a little
longer, as she's recovering from knee surgery. Kerry and I, along with
Manolito and Marisol, will stay in the mission house while Art and
Doug head back to the mountains. Kerry helped me glue book cards
and pockets this afternoon, and I read her her bedtime story.

❧ Journal Entry

Roy called from Manila to say there's a new warning out: the NPA are
threatening to kill Americans again. This time they want the foreign
military bases (all of which are American) to pack up and get out by
the middle of next month. Great. Art and Doug are alone out in the
hills. Most American wives worry about their husbands getting fat or
stopping off for too many beers on the way home—not about them
getting bumped off by radical political factions.

Fall 1991

Dear Tim and Mindy,
      I'm still in Davao for a little bit of recuperation. Riding in any
vehicle is still too much of an adventure for me—even running
over ants hurts—so Art has gone back to the mountains and I will
stay here and soak up the peace and tranquility. Unfortunately
for that plan, the cockfights are in full swing down the hill, and
all the screaming is making my nap impossible. But what a
golden opportunity to write you a letter.
      Excitement—Doug is back from furlough. Jan is still in
the States, having a knee operation, and has the two youngest

Terror Triplets with her. But Doug brought Kerry back to start school, and then I think Jan will home school all of them when she finally gets back. Anyway, Kerry and I are having a good time eating junk food, renting pirated Disney videos (she really liked "Hook," the Peter Pan story, which I think we saw before it was even released in the States), and reading stories.

Doug is slowly adjusting to being back here in Never Never Land himself. He headed back to San Roque first thing to check on his house and see if any of it was still standing. He told us that when he arrived, all the villagers came with their machetes and home-made guns, and warned him not to go into the house—a huge snake was in there, and some of the cult people said it was a roaming evil spirit, just waiting to attack. Despite knowing the number one lesson of all Hollywood horror movies (*never* go into the haunted house alone, especially after being warned), he barged right in there and . . . found nothing. But then he heard the dreaded noise they were all afraid of. It turned out that the battery in his smoke alarm was going bad and it was programmed to make a special beep at certain times every day. So he had them all come in and demonstrated it to them, but most of them still insist there's a supernatural snake in there.

He and Art had an equally interesting time here in Davao when they came back a couple days ago. They'd gone downtown for the mail and usual errands but an hour trip turned into almost a full-day saga. When they finally battled their way back to the house, they said they'd been stuck in the biggest jam-up traffic snarl they'd ever seen. Cars were abandoned, outsiders were pouring in, and crowds had crammed into one of the busiest downtown areas, with everybody trying to get a look at one tree. Doug guessed that maybe there was an actual bird in it (no chance—they've all been shot for food long ago) but it turned out that someone reported seeing a dwende. That's a one-foot-tall enchanted dwarf, usually invisible, that, depending on its color, will either be your friend and bring you presents, or steal and eat your children. Apparently the crowds had been coming to gawk for two days. Hopefully without bringing their children. Just in case.

Art reports that my garden is looking great, and I can't wait to see it. The beans are huge, and the upo squash plant is threatening to attack the neighbor's house. Oh, and all our papaya trees are *finally* getting big. When we first put them in, the neighbors' horses would eat them down to stumps, until Art got to casually mentioning how he was going to make tasty horse barbeque out of the first one he caught eating the trees. That seemed to do the trick, and now we have nice fresh papaya. Although I was kind of looking forward to horse barbeque.

All this food talk is making me hungry so maybe I'll go downstairs and whip us up a batch of that good ol' Southern favorite: camotes n' gravy. Bye for now, Love, Debb and Art

❧ Journal Entry

I was finally able to hike back into Lumabat with Art. Actually, I'm in better shape than I thought, and made the hike in the usual 2 1/2 hrs. Everyone came out to greet us and say how they missed me. The porch was crammed all afternoon. All the regulars came by to say hi, drink coffee, watch their kids pee on the porch, ask for medicines and catch me up on all the latest tismis (gossip). It felt like I had been gone forever—and it's great to get back!

❧ Journal Entry

The sky was cloudless so Art sprayed all our veg with the recommended stuff from the ag center, then went around to do the other gardens too. In the early afternoon it started pouring rain, to wash off all the stuff he'd just sprayed. How do real farmers stand it? Had noodles for supper. Using the solar light has been causing millions of tiny black bugs to rain down on our heads, and into our food every night, so we're back to using the kerosene lanterns instead. So much for that stab at the modern world.

❧ Journal Entry

There was a big batch of kids on the porch today, so I gave them some Cebuano Bible comics. Although most of them are enrolled in 3rd and

4th grades in the village school, none of them can read yet, so they love the comics. They colored pictures for me which I pinned up to the pantry curtain. Folks came by with bananas all day—they must be in season. Not sure where to put them all.

🦋 Journal Entry

Ester stopped by yesterday to get pills for Viktor's grandchild—two are already in the hospital, and this one has a high fever. She herself told them to take the piles of blankets off, keep the child cool, give water just like I told her about two years ago. I am so proud of her! People are starting to remember and do the right thing. I heard later the boy is improving.

🦋 Journal Entry

Ned and Paul, the big mission bosses from the States, arrived to tour our area and see the progress of the mission. We picked them up in Dadiangas, went on to Doug and Jan's in San Roque, and will all hike into Lumabat tomorrow.

🦋 Journal Entry

Dragged everyone out of bed at 4:30 a.m., loaded the cargo horses, and got on the trail by 6. The trail was pretty muddy due to rain but not the ankle-deep soup we've come to love so well. We took it slow and easy for the desk-bound gringos. Had folks cut some green coconut for us in Caputian for the refreshing coconut water. In Kiabol, met some of the literacy class women, and were led onward by a tiny ancient crone in tribal dress who blazed ahead of us, and kept telling us we were so slow because we were wearing shoes. Arrived in a bit under four hours. A flock of people came over to welcome the guests, with programs planned for the next day. Had a good discussion of mission strategies on the porch until late. Before sending them on their way, Art and I wanted to talk about our post-Philippine future too. Doesn't sound encouraging. None of the places we'd like to go are open to us at this time.

❦ Journal Entry

In Manila, we had a farewell meeting with the big bosses, and got ready to head out on our last little vacation trip. On the way to the market this afternoon, I stepped on a dead rat, and coming back, had to choose between the rat again or where someone had thrown up all over the street. I just love Manila.

❦ Journal Entry

Finally made it to the airport. We battled through a massive crush of people on their way to the provinces, complete with kids, dogs, sleeping mats, radios, mah jongg sets, rice pots, and the favorite foods of their dead relatives. They're heading out to the big All Souls celebrations in the cemeteries. And we are on our way to India and Nepal!

15

Interim III
The Far Reaches: India and Nepal
Fall 1991 (continued)

Dear Tim and Mindy,

So here we are, safely back in Home Sweet Lumabat, ready to give you the whole requested scoop on our latest Adventure. Fasten your seat belts. And by the way, which of you guessed we were going to Antarctica for this vacation? This is *me* we're talking about here. Was it me who used to say every April, "Oh, I'm so *glad* it's snowing again—it's so invigorating being out here with my face freezing off, trying to shovel snow over the top of my head, so I can get my car out (if it starts) and go drive it into a ditch somewhere!" How soon we forget. No, it was going to be India and Nepal since last March when we saw an ad for the trip.

We had a great time—especially Art—he likes bizarre trips. India is only about a six-hour flight from here, with just a 2 1/2-hour time difference, so there's little if any jet lag. I like that extra half hour in the time difference, and then Nepal adds fifteen minutes, so their time is always 45 minutes off Greenwich time. Our group was only 20 people, but we were diverse. They were all long-term expats, like us, who had been living in places like South Africa, Singapore and Bali before even coming to the Philippines. Not many Americans, so at least they weren't whining about the dirt and looking for hamburgers all the time. There were a couple Israelis, a grey-haired granny from Vienna, a rather intense couple from France, a Lebanese guy, a college kid from Argentina, some Swiss folks, some high rankers from

South America including an ambassador and his wife, a few embassy people from the good ol' US of A, and two local yokels from the backwoods sticks of southern Mindanao who couldn't remember how to operate a light switch or run a water faucet (that would be us).

You know how stressful travel can be, especially when you get outside your cultural comfort zone. So at first I thought we were in real trouble when we got on this Air France plane and they kept feeding us. Not real airline food like plastic chicken or unidentified rubbery things. But flaky little quiches, and pâté, and a cheese plate, and some stunning chocolate dessert (I'm getting carried away) and, of course, wine with everything and wine every time you turned around. I swear if you went down the aisle to the bathroom, they'd ask if you wanted a little wine for your journey. We were all exceptionally mellow passengers. But then we landed in Delhi and I was mightily reassured that my comfort zone was safe and India was going to be just like the Philippines after all.

We got on this rattletrap bus that miraculously made it to the hotel, after passing half a dozen assorted broken down things that were jamming the roads. We got to our room and Art almost zapped all his hair off by just trying to turn on the lamp (it must've had a wire loose). At least at that point there was functional electricity, which didn't happen too often during the rest of the stay. I especially liked the elegant morning wake-up call, which was some guy tromping down the corridor pounding on doors and hollering. All was lovely again, though, when I discovered our room had a real and true bathtub, complete with working faucets, out of which came genuine hot water! Who knew that such wonders still existed?

Our trip was going to include sites in Jaipur and Agra, so back on the bus for the long haul. Wait . . . first there was breakfast. Art decided to try some kind of vegetable pancake with curry sauce, which caused his eyes to bulge out and his teeth to start melting. And I learned, by observation only, that real Indian curries are highly flammable, sort of like powdered charcoal lighter. OK, *then* on the bus and out into India. I was ready to be dazzled, but the landscape had all the thrill and natural grandeur of Nebraska, and you could almost think you were coming up on Omaha if you ignored the camels plodding around plowing the fields, and the big circles of cow pies drying in the sun to be used for fuel. Actually, sights like that could improve Nebraska, and somebody ought to drop them a hint.

We finally got to this place called the Amber Fort, which was up quite a hill (what a unique, defensive idea) and we saw that they were going to haul us up there on elephants! Art was thrilled right down to his toenails. I didn't realize that he was the last remaining human on earth who had never gone on the elephant ride at the zoo when he was a kid. This beast, though, was about three times the size of those little zoo babies and looked like it could crush whole trucks with a single step. What we could do with one of these in Manila traffic. Anyway, we sat atop the elephant on a little platform and inched our way up the hill, swaying back and forth like a rowboat in a hurricane, and causing us all to truly regret breakfast. We arrived alive, just in time to join a crush of school kids and tour the Fort. I was finally impressed! The décor was like Disneyland on speed: the rooms were huge with gems and bits of mirror built into the walls and ceilings so when you lit candles at night it would look like a million stars all around. If I'd had the brains to think up something that cool, I would've had it built into our house in Lumabat.

I guess I better tell you about the Taj Mahal too, since that's the number one tourista spot in the whole country. Yes, it looks exactly like that 3-D jigsaw puzzle of it that you built, Mindy, and all the National Geographic pictures. But it was a lot bigger than I thought it would be. And it *felt* good. We had to take our shoes off, since it is a tomb and a Muslim sacred place. So wandering around barefoot on all that white marble on a hot day was delightful. And I've fallen in love with Moghul architecture—it's sort of like very early Victorian, with doodads and thingamajigs everywhere. Never leave a space alone if you can slap curlicues and embellishments all over it. And have slaves to dust it.

We saw a bunch of other stuff—I'll send you some pictures— but I think the people and just the scenes of daily life are what

I'll remember most. Even after Hong Kong and Manila, I've never seen so many people crammed together in one place like that before. Every day we had to inch our way through some massive, grid-lock traffic jam that made Manila look deserted. And it's the daily normal—just a huge crush of people, donkeys, ox-carts, bicycle rickshaws, vendor wagons, regular bicycles, scooters, cows, trucks and cars.

We're fairly used to poverty by now so the slums and general wretchedness weren't as appalling as they might've been before we got toughened up, but naturally the beggars are major fierce. Every time our gringo bus stopped, and we were dumb enough to get off to take pictures of camels or water buffalos in a seemingly deserted wasteland, the ground would just open up and hundreds of kids and emaciated small persons would rise up out of nowhere and attach themselves to our arms and legs and clothing. It was an experience. I really liked the snake charmers, though. As soon as they'd see us coming, they'd whip the tops off their baskets and start tootling away on their bulgy flutes. Most of the snakes didn't want to be charmed and would try and make a break for it. One old guy had a snake that I think died about three weeks before. He'd play his music with one hand and wave this limp snake around with the other. Even his mongoose wasn't interested.

So besides stopping at every camel to take a picture, we also had to stop at every tourista shop and knick-knack stand owned by the bus driver's endless relatives. But the group seemed to love it. Speaking of shopping frenzies, do you remember those old pictures of a school of piranha fish attacking a cow that wandered into their river, and stripping its bones in seconds? You get the idea. I swear those folks would buy somebody's stuffed grandmother if given a good enough price.

Well, you've been reading this for days now and need to take a break for some food and sleep. I'll tell you about Nepal in my next letter, if I can afford all the stamps. Bye for now, Love, Debb and Art

Dear Tim and Mindy,

I figure that by now you are both up from the nap induced by my last massive volume, so I'll press on with all the details of Nepal before I forget them. And I guess one of these days I ought to get back to real life and do some financial reports or administer some literacy or something, but as we say here in our most famous and well-used phrase: "unya na lang" (just later).

To get to Nepal we had to take another flight, although just a short one—only 45 minutes. But they fed us dinner anyway, probably so the flight staff could all huddle in the back galley having their silently screaming, knee-slapping laugh of the day. Dinner was a piece of chicken, a pile of veg., and some kind of fritter. I thought, "this is Nepal, not India, and it's just airline food, so how hot can this stuff be, and besides, what can they do to vegetables?" On that moronic misunderstanding, I took a bite, whereupon my hair caught on fire, and as my dying senses failed, one by one, I could hear the coughing and choking all around me.

We recovered enough to make it to our hotel. It had the wonderfully improbable name of "Yak and Yeti" (neither of which I saw on the grounds), and was built onto an old palace, with lovely gardens in the back. Kathmandu is quite a place, and I learned it's a hot-spot haven for aging hippies. Groovy and far out! I would've worn my beaded headband and fringed jacket, except I don't own any kind of jacket anymore, and all my hair fell out due to the curry on the plane. They say that Cat Stevens lives here, and other icons of our flower-child days. I'll have to flash the peace sign a lot and look laid back.

Our first visit was to a microscopic little village with a major Hindu temple. Folks were already lining up with a goat or chicken stuffed under one arm, waiting a turn to have their animal sacrificed. Sure enough, a festival was going on, and this day was the one to honor and worship all the dogs. So each Fido had a garland of flowers and a special red bindi (head-dot). I got to thinking how my old collie Megs (you remember her— a.k.a. Banana Nose) would've loved all the attention. Although I'm positive she would've demanded a garland of bacon treats instead of useless flowers.

You know we live in the mountains on Mindanao and are pro hikers now, but had heard the mountains in Nepal were even taller, so that's where we went next. Yup, they are taller. Our new thrill was to make our way up to the Annapurna region of the Himalayas and . . . hike. Well, we weren't anywhere near as high as the first base camps but it was still no stroll in the park. We edged ourselves up the torturous path inch by inch, hauling ourselves over the stone slabs, trying to breathe—while little kids from the villages jumped all around us chattering a mile a minute and begging for candy and coins. We finally achieved the remote lookout post, with its every square inch covered with vendor stalls and snack booths, and while we were checking to see if we were still alive, the Sherpas came buzzing through. They are squatty little people, men and women both, loaded with at least three tons of junk apiece, in head-strap baskets the size of large refrigerators. They came trotting up the mountain, passed us like we were standing still, and headed up into the clouds. OK, so we're not mountain climbers, but we have other good qualities (maybe).

Besides large mountains, Nepal also has jungles and wild animals (also large). So to say we'd covered every square inch of the place, we had to go to a safari camp next. Getting there was fun. They piled us onto an elderly (I'm putting it kindly) aircraft that looked like it was once a crop duster before it crashed into something. They finally managed to clear all the cows off the grass runway and we took off. Art and I were crammed into the front seats and there was no door between the cockpit and the cabin. The pilot, who looked like he was about twelve years old (maybe he was) had a cocktail napkin with Nepalese writing and a hand-drawn map pinned to the steering wheel. At first we figured it was instructions on how to fly the plane, but then we saw he was watching the map and then checking the ground below for all the little villages, to see where he was going. Good thing it wasn't raining or we might've ended up in Bangladesh.

The jungle camp was large tents (filled with spiders, of course) around a central hut made of bamboo grasses with a cooking fire outside. I was wondering why we came if it was going to be just like home, when they brought the elephants out so we could ride around and look for tigers. OK, that was good. Our elephant was pretty smart. While we were out in the tall grasses, the granny from Vienna dropped her camera off the back and was quite distressed until the mahout (driver) gave a few commands and Beautiful Girl, our elephant, reached down with her trunk, picked up the camera, and handed it back.

Naturally we didn't see any tigers—they're nocturnal and besides, they eat gringos for breakfast. But we did come up on a giant old rhino. The elephant driver figured we'd want a good look (and give him good tips) so kept edging the elephant closer and closer while the rhino, who was trapped by the river behind him, kept getting madder and madder at having his personal quiet time invaded. So the rhino put his head down to charge, which upset the elephant, who raised her trunk and started trumpeting, and it looked like innocent (but stupid) tourists were going to die in the upcoming wild animal free for all. Fortunately, the rhino figured it was too much effort, and ambled off, and the rest of us could quit mentally making our wills and funeral arrangements.

Back to Kathmandu for one more adventure. We were given (and grabbed) the chance to take a flight along the very edge of the Himalayas to see each mighty peak up close, from the air. It was sunny and miraculously clear—the pilot said we even saw peaks which are almost always hidden in clouds. And could we marvel over them with the fellow travelers in our group? No. All the rest of them elected to bypass the flight and *go shopping!* Well, I guess the mistake was mine. Now they all have carpets and brass pots to show for it, and what do I have? Just a picture stuck forever in my head of this most massive mountain blazing in the light, with the sun gleaming off its snow fields, outlining its jagged edges, and a little banner of cloud like a proud pennant floating off its top. In Nepal, it has the grand name of Sagarmatha—Mother of the Universe. The rest of the unimaginative world calls it Mount Everest.

So that's about it from the Far Reaches for the globe-trotting duo. Travel is fun but it's always great to get back again, settle in, and do those comfy and familiar things we all cherish, that make us love home sweet home. You know how it is: pump up the water tank and restock the sardine shelf, patch up the sickies on the porch, haul some nails out to the schools and bring back some chickens, thin out the papayas and put a little bat guano on the garden, wash the horse, fill the lamps, and catch up on all the gossip. And we'll be back to sending you all the boring, home-front news in our next letter. Bye for now, Love, Debb and Art

16

Bye!
Reaching the End: Lumabat, and Out
Winter 1991-1992

🦋 Journal Entry

Back from vacation and over-nighted in Manila. Went to bed early but the neighbors below our window had a huge screaming match, miraculously without gunfire. Got up at 3:20 a.m. to go to the airport, and the plane was even on time! Jan had kindly said she'd pick us up in Dadiangas but wasn't there when we arrived– must've had one of the usual mountain disasters. Luckily, one lone tricycle was left to take us to the highway, where we picked up a Yellow-Bus right away. The driver was your standard devil-possessed maniac, tearing around corners and crashing through pot holes, flinging people and animals around with abandon. Reminds me of what clothes must feel like in a tumble dryer. Art only managed to stay in his seat by holding onto what he thought was a bus pole but was actually the barrel of his seat-mate's ancient rifle.

🦋 Journal Entry

Awakened by a rat chewing through the wall in the kitchen. He ran through the kitchen rafters again in the afternoon so I whacked at him with a broomstick, for all the good that did. I didn't know rats could laugh. It started pouring rain about midnight, so we sprang out of bed and rushed to the downspout behind the kitchen to collect the rainwater in buckets by flashlight. Poor Art's undershorts are now so worn from hand washing with rough soaps that they kept falling down, so he had to hold them up with paperclips while getting water. The neighbors are sure going to miss us.

Dear Tim and Mindy,

We're in Davao for a couple days and there seems to be electricity for awhile, but this letter is still going to be choppy. Every ten minutes another batch of ragamuffins starts bashing on the gate, bleating out tunes that might once have been Christmas carols—even though Christmas is well over. So I go hurtling down the stairs, leap over the coin box while grabbing a handful of cash, rush the gate and try to get all the coins handed out before they can start another verse. This makes all of us happy as they can scurry to the next house (more intake) and I can have a few more precious moments of quiet. Although I have a feeling that broken legs (mine) may be a later feature of this letter.

Our Christmas back in the hills was great—big gatherings at the Sunday Schools and Bible classes, lots of songs and happiness, and gifts all around. Folks kept coming with bananas, eggplants, munggo beans, cashews, coconuts, papayas and veg (mostly from my own garden) and a few stopped by with chickens that got tied under the house for later. So finally Art, Leks and I organized ourselves to do rounds of the village and hand out our presents. Art dragged the sacks to every house, while Leks and I handed out the health kits (bags of combs, soaps, real towels, toothbrushes, etc.), caps and kiddie clothes, and special goodies for the teachers. I can't think of a Christmas that has ever topped it . . . or ever will.

Thank heavens for the people that donated all that stuff and had it shipped over—including yourselves. The teachers almost had the heart attack of joy when I handed over more books and the microscopes at the high school. Consider yourselves arm-hugged and cried on again. Then the teachers told me the kids had won the last regional science meet, due to their new books, where before, they weren't even remote contenders. That was good. Reeeeeally good. We also noticed the terrific 'for us' items you sent, which we latched onto right away. We've been out of reading material for a long time now, and have been reduced to this boxful of clutch-books (semi-clothed individuals clutching each other in various contorted poses on the covers) donated to the office by the military bases, with titles like "Tender Savage," "Passion's Prisoner," "Sweet Savage Heavy Groping," etc. The remnants of my brain were starting to fall out. We're saving the ones you sent us as treats, and will probably parcel them out to ourselves as rewards for driving through town without purposely killing anyone.

Back again. I think that's my fourth trip on the stairs since I started. Thanks for all the news and we were thrilled to hear that Barb is expecting. But if she's truly going to name him Fievel, in honor of the mouse in her favorite "American Tail" movie, she better wait until she's had four more. There is really a family out in San Roque that has seven kids (so far) and their names are One, Two, Three, etc. Actually, they're all boys except for the last one, so they've taken to calling her Seven-Girl. Makes for interesting overheard conversations: "Where's Two?" "Down at the river with Four, but he's supposed to be watching Six." For my money, it makes more sense than Chelsea or Lyndsey.

OK, I'm old, and I know I'm not going to survive one more trip up and down the stairs. So I better end and just go sit out there by the gate for awhile. Hope your own Christmas was extremely fine! Bye for now, Love, Debb and Art

🦋 Journal Entry

We heard that the Dadiangas post office had a fire and saw the damage— the entire interior of the parcel room out back was all blackened and charred. I wonder how many of our packages went up in flames. On to Kimball's and found a great birthday gift for Doug, a nicely hand-painted Bible verse plaque to hang on his wall. Usually the verse reads, "Come unto Me, all you who labor and are heavy laden, and I will give you rest." The copyist was a tad off, and this one just said, "Come unto Me, all you who labor and are heavy, and I will give you rest." Since everyone has been kidding Doug about the weight he packed on over furlough, this should be perfect.

❧ Journal Entry

Malungon. The latest drought is really gaining steam. I couldn't sleep about 3 a.m. so got the water bucket and went out to the yard tap to fill it. The whole town water system is now turned on only from midnight to 4 a.m. every day, but at a real slow trickle. My legs were getting tired and dogs were barking at me. At least there's always somebody else out there in the dark waiting for water too.

❧ Journal Entry

Art heard that the electrical power supply is critically low on Mindanao due to the drought and no planning, and it's been announced that 12-hour power outages will officially be starting now. So what's different about that? I hauled the last batch of books out of the storeroom and started getting them ready for distribution, along with all the other stuff: preschool items, toothbrushes, Sunday School materials, Kaulo primers, literacy supplies, etc. One last big push, if we can survive it. I made supper in the dark, but knocked my candle over and then doused the couch with water when I dropped my glass. Not the calmest of days: saw two giant spiders (one on the water jug the whole time Art was pouring from it), and one giant toad in the bathroom.

❧ Journal Entry

Coming back from Dadiangas, we passed a wreck on the killer curve—a truck had overturned and cartons of Tanduay rum were spread all over the highway. Sure am glad we got by before the expected riot started.

Spring 1992

Dear Tim and Mindy,

You may not remember us, but we're still here. Yes, I know it's been forever since we last wrote. We have been running around like chickens without heads because . . . (drum roll) the countdown has begun, and the end is in sight! It's months off yet, but at least plans are in place to leave, transitions are being started, and massive reports are being crafted—you can't beat a bunch of preachers for hot air.

Unfortunately, part of this paperwork binge had to take place up in Manila, and you know how I love that dear city. My sinuses are backed up just thinking about it. We were going to stay a couple days with Roy and Sandy, so when the cab dumped us out at their house and they weren't there, we were a tad surprised. Not to worry—Vilma and Rosalia, their helpers, made us comfy and plied us with grilled cheese sandwiches while we waited. And waited. Finally in early evening they returned with their own adventure story. Roy was leading a church service in a town up north and was doing the children's message while standing on a box—for some unexplained reason. Anyway, he fell off the box and broke his arm. There was no medical facility available so they drove back to Manila, broken arm and all, and on the way, of course, had a flat tire. Fortunately, someone stopped to help them and they made it to the hospital to get Roy a temporary cast. Some days are just like that.

In the office, we got to ask some initial questions about shipping our stuff (the pitiful remnants thereof) back to the States. I wonder if I can have one of those sidewalk stands rewire all my appliances back to 110 electrical current. Over the years we had them all converted to 220 when we'd forget the difference, plug them straight into the wall and blow them out, usually accompanied by a spectacular shower of sparks and the eye-watering smell of scorched wiring. Then we learned that any shipment we sent would have to go surface and take two and a half months to get there. Hopefully, wherever we end up, I will not immediately need baggy skirts, a manual typewriter with bent keys, a machete, a shortwave radio, or my best rice pot.

The good news is that Steve and Cathy, the translator couple we told you about, are going to move to our area. While the mission office back in the States continues the futile task of finding someone crazy enough to take our place, they'll live in our house and keep a lot of the projects going without a break. Cathy is particularly interested in literacy and they both need to learn the Kaulo language fast, so . . . what better way to get acquainted with the area than to pay it a visit? And see all the nice normal events of daily life. And Lumabat Fiesta Day was coming up. That would be fun.

We hiked out to get them and met up at Doug and Jan's place in San Roque to spend the night and go in all fresh and rested up the next morning. Sometime in the middle of the night, my bed collapsed and I ended up on the floor, probably crushing dozens of poor cockroaches in the process. Didn't sleep much after that. Had to get up at 4:30 anyway to eat, dress, jam everything we owned into rice bags (a record 6 cargo horses), and get on the trail before the sun fried us to a crisp. Everyone and his dog was going in for the fiesta, and Jan and the midwives arrived to do a medical clinic. I started by going out to pump up the water tank, but something seemed clogged, so we had to haul all the water (slowly trickling) in in buckets. The town folks were trying to get a horsefight going for entertainment but the negotiations with the horse owners were taking forever. We finally figured they got it started, judging by all the screaming, and then afterwards they brought over the deaf guy who had gotten trampled by one of the horses—broken ribs and cut face. Good thing the midwives were still there to patch him up.

Then the pump broke completely. We figured it was only a gasket, and Art and Steve could fix it in the morning. So after participating in the evening fiesta festivities and coronation, the car-battery disco cranked up out in the field until about 3 a.m. Would that lead us to sleep in the next morning? Of course not. Someone had tied a baby water buffalo up to a post in the next yard and then taken Mama Buffalo out to do some work, with the resulting bawling and moaning being a real racket. But it gave Art and Steve a nice early start to fix the pump. After tossing down some yummy sardines for breakfast, they went out and pried and pulled to get it all apart, replaced the gasket, tried to find all the pieces and wedge it back together again. Steve learned many new Kaulo words. None of them useable. They got one slow bucket of water and then the real problem surfaced: the well just flat went dry. Nothing down there to pump. So we hired a bunch of kids, with big smiles all around, to bring us water from Reginia's well across the village, for drinking and dishes, and just used the river water for everything else. We'll see what interesting digestive mutations we get from that trick.

After several more fun events, such as wading with Steve and Cathy down the middle of the Tarzan river for an hour to get to the literacy class in Balobo, it was time for them to leave and we waved a fond farewell. As I said to Art, "Such nice folks. Too bad we will never see them again in our entire lives. If they have a single brain cell between them, they will be on a plane by this afternoon."

Still no news on any prospects for our future, but what's a little detail like that to us? Art can always go back to delivering groceries or sign on for the pea harvest up in northern Illinois, like he used to do in the olden days. I have also learned a lot of fool-proof techniques which could turn me into a formidable beggar. We'll keep you posted. Bye for now,   Love,   Debb and Art

❧ Journal Entry

I told Midwife Maribel she could have Hope the Horse when I leave, causing great squealings of joy—from Maribel; I don't know how Hope feels about it. Now we're in the middle of another hassle as the neighbors bought a pig from Leks's brother and never paid for it, but have already butchered and eaten it.

❦ Journal Entry

Reginia came over from the school to check out the stuff for the kids—she will take over and lead the Sunday School. We had coffee and one of our usual good chats. She told me about being a poll caretaker at the last election in some small village further back in the mountains (all the teachers have to do it), and how she had to make a run for it with the ballot boxes at the end of the day, with gunfire coming closer. She also told me of the almost-war at another polling place where a woman teacher had to fingerprint all the voters, and her jealous husband stormed in and threw a fit over her holding hands with all the guys.

❦ Journal Entry

I still have a fever. Got up at 4:30 a.m., and put Leks in charge of hanging the chickens off the horse. It was a slow trek out, and I had a tough time getting over the hills. I've been tending Jun's wife for the last several weeks. She's in a rough pregnancy that ought to be her last, but won't be. We almost lost her the last time, too. After she started the vomiting and diarrhea, I sent her out to the Dadiangas hospital. Better check up on her. Our headlight fell out again.

❦ Journal Entry

I got all cleaned up and even washed my hair so that barely half an hour later I could crawl under the truck and stick my head in the wheel well to copy the chassis number. We're still trying to get our truck papers duplicated. While Art went to struggle with that, I did a bunch of wrap-up computer work and added up my book totals. We've given away more than 3,400 so far!!

❦ Journal Entry

Heard news reports that the American who was kidnapped several days ago was finally freed, but now an Australian missionary and his family down on Jolo have been kidnapped, and two visiting teachers were kidnapped also. Must be fund-raising season again.

Hi Mindy and Tim,

As usual, things are churning away in their own science-fiction sort of way. Steve and Cathy, the translator couple, are still (amazingly) around. Nice folks, full of enthusiasm. And I hope they're not too mad that a lot of the village kids now say OK, and bye! and other Americanisms that they picked up from us. But Steve and Cathy are also given to asking questions every other minute. Not easy ones like where do you buy rice or how do you work the solar panels, but stuff like: what are you supposed to do when you see the neighbor's giant carabao in your yard eating the leaves off all your banana trees; where do the giant fruit bats go; is the Datu's third wife more important than the head teacher; and how do you make pig blood stew? How do I know? We always kind of punted everything anyway. So we do Art's specialty: make up answers.

Then we went out to pick up the mail and got this nice note from my Dad, mailed three weeks earlier, saying he had been diagnosed with a tumor in his brain and would be operated on the next day, but not to worry because he made sure that his will and all his legal papers were up to date. Great. We rushed over to Dadiangas to the phone company to call my brother Peter, waited in the usual endless line for over an hour, and when we finally got a call through, could only get their answering machine (yes, true, it was in the middle of the night for them). Nothing else we could do but go on and run a few errands, but after those we went back to the phone company and finally got through to Peter. Found out that Dad came through surgery fine, was at home recovering, and our dear friend Ruth was helping him with the radiation and therapy. So much for that crisis of the day.

For the rest of the time, I bet you're thinking that, as these last months go by, things are winding down and all is finally getting quiet and peaceful. Well . . . no. Not by a long shot. A few weeks ago, Art was chatting on the front porch with some folks in Malungon, when he said his heart felt funny. So we trotted over to the Malungon 'hospital' where they put on the blood pressure cuff, which is the full extent of their cardiology equipment, and told him he better head down to Dadiangas for an EKG. So off we went, with me driving—and by that I knew something was really wrong. We saw the one and only cardiologist in the whole city of Dadiangas, which has several hundred thousand people. But she actually had a baby EKG machine, and slapped Art right into the hospital 'for observation.' His heart was beating   irregularly, each minute missing several beats, during which his chest would tighten and he'd have trouble breathing.

So there we were in the hospital, and I was Art's 'watcher.' I probably mentioned that every hospital patient in the Philippines has to have a watcher to go out and get the medicines—the doctor only prescribes them, but you have to run around to five or six pharmacies to actually get them. And the watcher also provides the towels, silverware, pajamas, and in some cases the linens and food, and boots the dogs out into the hall. Art's heartbeat got worse and they decided they didn't have enough equipment for testing either, so Art had to go up to Manila. Then the fun started.

The mission office had just bought this evacuation insurance policy and wanted to test it out. And besides, the commercial airlines were refusing to take Art unless he was carried up the plane stairs and had an attending doctor. So we were going to go with this high-tech American outfit. First they thoroughly enraged everyone by calling in the middle of the night (can't Americans figure a time difference?) to make arrangements, and the operator in Washington was practically crying because it took her four hours of constant dialing to get through. I could've told her that. Welcome to the real world.

They hired this little charter plane and I only warned them 500 times: come before dark, Dadiangas has *no* runway lights, and there's a sunset curfew. We loaded Art into the ambulance, which was a battered 1960 VW van on its last legs, went to the airport, where it proceeded to get darker, and then pitch black. I guess they thought my warning was Filipino humor. Everybody in the baby airport went home except one guy on the radio. The pilot insisted he was still coming in. Pretty soon we heard the engine in the blackness. The guy on the radio went out and got in his truck, drove to the end of the runway and switched on his headlights so the plane could get an idea of where the runway was, and the pilot, through no fault of his own, lived to tell about it. They loaded Art in on the floor, there was a doctor from Hong Kong—doubtless cousin to Fu Man Frankenstein who did my operation last year—to accompany him, and we took off. The pilot figured where the runway was by his little headlights, and we lifted off just as we were about to dump it in the ocean. Then we bounced all over the sky while I proceeded to be about as airsick as a person can be. We landed. I staggered out saying, "Thank God, Manila at last!" And the pilot said, "Sorry, this is only Cebu, but we're almost halfway there." Well, to mercifully cut this short, we finally made it, and got Art to the hospital (a big city hospital—no dogs in the halls, only cats).

So Art had his million and one tests including a stress test and a fun video sonogram of his heart. Turns out he has an abnormal heart valve which he's had since birth, which just picked now to act up. He's on medication three times a day and the doctors say he can just go back to doing whatever he did before *except* smoke, drink coffee, have more than two beers a day, or get stressed. Fortunately he doesn't have razor blades, since he doesn't shave, and I was able to hide his belt and shoelaces for a few days until he could adjust to that idea.

We headed back down to the mountains and Mr. Stubborn decided he was going to hike back in anyway, like he's always done. The folks all along the trail said they were ready to carry him out real fast in the mat slung on a bamboo pole (mountain ambulance) but fortunately that last thrill was unnecessary. Take care of your own health and we will all sit around and swap ailment stories one of these days. Bye for now, Love, Debb and Art

Summer 1992

❦ Journal Entry

Malungon. I went with Art to get water at the tap, and don't like it that he's doing all that heavy hauling. Then we took all our old files out back of the house and burned them, getting way overheated. I cut Art's hair, taking time out occasionally to rush upstairs and pound on the wall to scare off the rats, which always works for about 15 seconds. Food supplies are low in the drought, and the walls are full of them now.

❦ Journal Entry

Davao. The moving company came by to estimate our shipment and build a crate. It's a good thing I kept a lot of our old cardboard boxes and packing paper, as the company said they didn't have any. Interesting. Were they just going to heave everything loose into the crate? Don't ask. We're leaving most of it behind for Leks and Marisol anyway.

❦ Journal Entry

Leks came to Davao and stayed with us a few days. We've got the paperwork, finances, and everything in place now for her to go to college. Made sure she had her uniforms and enough to get a really nice bedspacer (shared apartment). She's going to take the business curriculum and is smart enough that she'll probably own half of Davao someday. God speed, Leks.

❦ Journal Entry

Manila. Wayne called to talk to Art—there's a job opening at the Lutheran Hour office in the States that he can apply for. He'd be in charge of planning and training for some of Lutheran Hour's world projects, and helping various international offices get their programs started. Probably based in St. Louis. Sounds perfect for him.

❧ Journal Entry

We couldn't sell our monster truck down in Davao, so brought it up to Manila with us. The Baptist office called and they have bought it! They ended up paying just about the entire amount that we spent on it in the first place. I guess the mechanics must've fixed it up pretty good. At least we hope the battery is done bouncing all over the engine compartment and the headlights don't keep falling out. And it must *still* be the only four-wheel-drive truck in the whole country, for them to want it. Art took it down to their office, signed a couple papers and was handed a check, just like that. Amazing.

❧ Journal Entry

Onward now to reports and reorientation. When we get back to the States, they're sending us to a mandatory re-entry seminar out in Fresno, to learn to be Americans again (although what kind of cultural reality can one expect to find in California?) It ought to be a really fun learning experience: don't shovel in your food with your fingers, don't carry your groceries on your head, don't practice kamikaze driving, learn to stand in line, and learn that those loud noises on the 4th of July are only firecrackers, and not someone trying to assassinate you. I don't know if we can handle it.

❧ Journal Entry

We went out for one last lunch with the mission office staff. A nice lunch, a nice chat. They finally gave us back our passports, and we're cleared to go. Time for one last letter.

Dear Tim and Mindy,

Can it be? Might this be the very last letter from these golden shores of the Philippines? Since we will probably be back in the States before this letter reaches you, that's a good possibility. But I couldn't leave without giving you all the highlights of our last days in Lumabat and our great Farewell Extravaganza.

There we were, peacefully finishing up our last days. Steve and Cathy were already moved into the house, and Leks was helping us sort through our last bits of stuff. Our well had run dry over a month earlier and we'd been getting water from Reginia's well across the village. But then *her* well finally dried out too, so we were all getting water from the river and trying to boil it with a limited fuel supply. Challenging. But there we were on the porch one afternoon, everyone having a nicely boiled cup of coffee and a snack when someone hollers, "Fire! The school is on fire!" Sure enough, that cogon grass roof was burning, and flames were shooting way up into the air. So Art and Steve rushed over, along with all the other guys in the village, and started trying to poke down the burning thatch with long bamboo poles to save the rafters, while others started dragging water from the river. It was only about 5 billion degrees in there, and I worry about Art now, but after an hour they finally managed to smother it out, and at least half the school was saved.

Then it was time to go, and time for the final goodbyes. Excitement was in the air and people were pouring in from everywhere. Our house started bursting at the seams—Doug and Jan were there with the Terror Triplets, of course, and Steve and Cathy. Leks and Riza were bustling around, Rolando and Asterio and all the literacy teachers came, all the midwives rode in, and then everyone else from every village for miles around along with their kids, relatives, friends, dogs, and horses arrived. Huge rice bags everywhere, a ton of chickens (all squawking from under the house), and of course a pig or two. It was lively.

Then our old neighbor, Juaning, died. He had gone buang (crazy) some time ago and taken to hollering and leaping naked around his garden in the full moon. Neither the midwives nor I could diagnose him and he refused to go out to the hospital.

Finally he refused to eat, even my energy and rehydration drinks, and died. So as night fell, the women started keening—this kind of high-pitched wail that cuts right through your brain, the guys droned dirge Kaulo songs all night, and that got everyone nicely in the mood for . . .

Our own farewell event! Everyone who had poured in the day before, and the last stragglers from every other village in the hills, packed themselves into the big, open-sided shed across the field behind our house that is our gathering place. Doug started out with prayers, and then came the usual endless boring speeches, giving everyone a chance to say how we were the greatest thing since sliced bread, interspersed with everyone else getting a chance at the microphone to render their favorite endless song. All went well until about halfway through, when Reginia, the head teacher and my personal friend, got up to speak. She broke down in the middle of her talk and from then on everyone was awash. Since the teachers were crying, all the kids started crying too, and could hardly make it through their little songs. All the mothers carrying babies were wiping their eyes on their kids, and the barrio captain was over by the railing sobbing into his handkerchief. The literacy teachers all had their heads down on their desks, wailing away, and then Art had to get up and give our farewell message. He told them his heart was sick—not like before, when he needed a doctor, but because we were leaving, and they would always be in our memories and prayers. More general bawling. Finally Leks led the Sunday School kids up to do my favorite action songs, and then I was a goner too. Somehow, we all managed to recover just fine to pack away the special yummy rice n stuff laid on for the day. Everyone agreed it was a wonderful occasion.

Then the next day, we had to hike out, and that was even (if possible) worse. We got up at 4:30 in the morning and soon the porch was jammed with folks wishing us well. We had to cut across the whole village to get to the trail and people were standing out in every yard, waving goodbye. Every few feet, as we passed through town, we were stopped and hugged by someone, especially the old ladies of the literacy class. We finally made it to the trail, and halfway up the mountain we could still hear the kids hollering BYE! at the top of their lungs. I turned for a last look down at the village, but I couldn't see it. I think maybe it was raining. Which is odd, since we're having a drought.

And, just like that, we are gone. Time for me to quit and get this letter in the mail to you. Soon it will be at your door—and so will we.

Listen! Can you hear them? .... BYE!

Love, Debb and Art

🦋 🦋 🦋

S S D

Salamat sa Dios

(Thanks be to God)

Newsletters

Following are the official newsletters we sent to churches, friends, and supporters, highlighting our mission's progress and requesting project helps.

The first page of each newsletter is on the right, to simulate turning the page over.

Your Mission to the Tagakaulo Tribe in the Philippines
Rev. Art & Deb Simmons, PO Box 56, Davao City 9501, Philippines
Winter 1987-88

"JOY TO THE WORLD!" On Christmas Eve we gathered at Our Redeemer Lutheran Church here in Davao City to sing our praises to our Christmas Lord. We began with that most wonderful of stories, the Christmas Gospel from St. Luke. We were overjoyed that we could understand God's beautiful message, even though it was read in Cebuano, the local dialect. Then each family of the congregation was invited to share a song, drama, dance, some special offering to the celebration. We even had a puppet show! Deb and I sang a Cebuano Christmas carol that Deb wrote, using a tune that we learned at our language school. Nobody laughed or walked out, or threw any sort of vegetables, so we must have done alright! It was a joyful time!

IT'S TRUE! We even have pictures to prove it! We are now proud graduates of the Maryknoll Institute of Language and Culture here in Davao. That means we can speak just enough Cebuano to get into real trouble. We ask our very slow and careful questions— and people answer with fast and furious paragraphs of big, long words. We still need a lot of practice, but are grateful for what we were able to learn. Now we need to broaden our knowledge of Cebuano so that we can use it to learn the Tagakaulo dialect of the people we'll be working with.

SPEAKING OF WORK . . . Now that we have our diplomas in hand, we'll be starting our real mission. The Tagakaulos are making slow but sure progress on getting our house built in the mountains. The lumber was all cut and finished by hand, and all other materials will be hauled in on horseback. I'll  be going there quite often now to encourage a speedy finish to the project. Then we'll move to the village of Lumabat and begin learning all about the Tagakaulo tribe. I'm sure that for a long time we'll learn more about them than they learn from us. It's a different and fascinating culture, and the more we learn, the more successful our mission will be.

BUT WE WON'T BE ALONE! We're confident that God will go with us as we begin our work among the Tagakaulos . . . And He's also sent another missionary family to help! Doug and Jan have arrived in Davao and have just started language school. By the time they're finished at Maryknoll, they will have picked out a place to live and gotten started building their house. They and their two children, Kerry and Danny, seem to be enjoying their first few months here.

. . . AND A FEW WORDS FROM DEB:

The Christmas decorations are back in their boxes, the plastic Christmas tree is folded up and put away (there are no real pine trees here on the island of Mindanao), the carolers have stopped coming by (I love it when they sing "dashing through the snow" with the sun beating down a strong 90 degrees), and it's about time to get busy about the new year.

We had hoped to be able to move to our village as soon as language school was finished, but construction on our house is slow. As usual, though, the Lord makes it work for the best. Local elections are coming up throughout the country soon, and it would be wiser to stay where we are until they're over. Politics is almost more popular than eating here, and their democracy works a little differently from ours. Vote-buying is taken for granted, and so far there have been 58 election-related deaths and 18 kidnappings (the newspaper runs a little scorebox every day.) You might want to keep this country and its people in your prayers for the next few weeks.

The days of waiting will give us a good opportunity to continue preparing our outreach to the Tagakaulos: gathering materials—pictures and flannelgraph are important to people who are largely illiterate; working with music—their instruments are brass gongs and a 4-string guitar; making contacts; exploring literacy and health programs—their closest health care is a three-hour hike out of the hills, then a two-hour bus ride to Dadiangas; and other concerns. And for myself, I ought to start learning something about raising chickens and goats. For a city kid like me, that'll be interesting.

*****BUT MOST IMPORTANT OF ALL, WE BOTH THANK YOU***** for all your delightful holiday greetings and for your warm and friendly letters. They meant so much to us, especially at Christmas, as we missed you all so badly. God blesses us richly by giving us friends like you! Please keep on keeping in touch—and keep us in your prayers!

THAT'S ALL FOR NOW . . . May God keep you under His remarkable care, safeguarding you until we meet again!

PEACE!

Art & Deb

REQUEST CORNER: If you still have any leftover Christmas seals lying around, please send them over to us—they're especially popular with the kids and a great reminder of the Good News!

MINDANAO MEMO

Your Mission to the Tagakaulo Tribe in the Philippines
Rev. Art & Deb Simmons, PO Box 56, 8000 Davao City, Philippines
Spring 1988

Greetings from tropical, sunny Mindanao! We thought we'd send along a few notes to keep you up on the progress of your mission here and to thank you for your continued and invaluable support of our work on your behalf. As you will see, the Lord is indeed blessing our work and leading us into new and very challenging kinds of service in His name.

Construction continues on our home in the remote mountain village of Lumabat. The foundation is laid but actual building has been delayed by rainy season and trouble sharing our needs over long distances. We'll be able to spend more time in the area soon and hope the building process moves along much more quickly!

The good news is that there are now <u>two</u> roads into our village, eliminating the 3 1/2 hour hike we used to have. There are a few problems—one road is very steep and narrow, hard to travel even in a 4-wheel-drive truck, and the other crosses the river no less than 7 times, with water up to the doors! Still, we're grateful we can haul in materials and help ease some of the problems faced by the Tagakaulos. We hope the government will make provision for maintaining these new roads (dirt and gravel).

We enjoyed a real cultural experience with the Tagakaulo tribe recently. One of the main tribal leaders of our village hosted the wedding of his eldest daughter, child of his first wife. I was asked to officiate the ceremony, along with Pastor Tinong of the Lutheran Church in Davao, who is our constant help and traveling companion in the area. The wedding was done in Cebuano, the main dialect of Mindanao, following the traditional format of Christian weddings. We consider it an excellent witness to the tribe of our beliefs as God's people.

We're now putting together the initial strategies for our mission. At our core will be Bible Study programs, geared to introducing the Tagakaulos to the Christian faith. We'll begin a literacy program, using simple Bible stories and life-based situations (signs, transport, the market, health) so that the older people will finally be able to read in their own dialect. Later we'll begin a regular program of worship services, start a Sunday school program, and train lay leaders for the congregations we'll start in different areas of the tribe's land. We'll need your prayers, your continued mission support, and all your encouragement as we begin to get things rolling!

 We just finished an important language survey of the Tagakaulo area with a team from the Summer Institute of Linguistics (SIL), a Bible translating group which closely cooperates with Lutheran Bible Translators. They wanted to determine which language is favored in the tribal area—Tagakaulo (the tribe's own dialect), Cebuano, Ilongo, or a mix of those three. I sure learned a lot working with them. They get tape recorded stories from a number of different villages, which they then play to people in other villages, to see if the language on the tape is fully understood.

In the process, we discovered many things about the Tagakaulo tribe. They live over a much broader area than we'd been led to believe—a territory about 20 miles wide and 125 miles long. There seem to be about 65,000 people in this group, although it's hard to know. Accurate census statistics don't exist in tribal areas because it's too difficult, costly and dangerous for the government to send in official census workers.

As soon as our survey results are tabulated, we'll have an excellent resource to determine which language is favored in the area. We can then use that to plan our literacy, Christian education and worship programs, and how best to reach the most people with the Good News of Jesus Christ.

. . . AND A FEW WORDS FROM DEB:

As Art mentioned, the wedding of the tribal leader's daughter was a big event for us. So many people came up to us to ask what this "religion" was all about that we would be teaching—lots of interest and eagerness to begin. His middle wife, who will be my next-door neighbor and who is quite a powerful person in the community, also chatted with us for quite a while and offered the use of her carabao (water buffalo) so I could clear garden space.

* * * * * We think of you all often, and can't begin to tell you how much we * * * * * appreciate your prayers and your letters.

In the love of our Easter Lord,

REQUEST CORNER:

First, <u>many</u> thanks to all who sent over leftover Christmas seals– they're a great teaching tool, Christian reminder, and fun for the kids!

Now we'd like to start building a collection of posters and large Sunday School pamphlets showing Bible story scenes. Any materials with simple plays, activities, puppet shows, etc. would be a terrific help in spreading the Gospel to those who can't read.

Sending things surface mail is fine—takes a few months, but it gets here. Thanks for the help!

Art & Deb

MINDANAO MEMO

Your Mission to the Tagakaulo Tribe in the Philippines
Rev. Art & Deb Simmons, PO Box 56, 8000 Davao City, Philippines
Summer 1988

LIFE IN THE SPIRIT! With the celebration of Pentecost, the birthday of the Christian Church, we are reminded once again of the beautiful and priceless Life we are given by God's Spirit! It is by the Spirit's power that we are able to live as God's people in the world that is often troubled and torn. It is by the Spirit's power that we are given the gift of being able to share our faith with others, no matter where we are or what we're doing. We pray that you, too, feel the Spirit's power as you carry on your mission as a forgiven and redeemed Christian!

CAMP MIZPAH '88 — The youth camp of our Mindanao District was held recently in Davao. It was really inspiring to see 150 young people talk about witnessing to their Christian faith. They all came out to our mission house for an evening campfire and naturally it poured down rain. It was quite a trick to jam them all into the house, but they sang Praise songs, enjoyed themselves and then went out to have their campfire when the rain ended. I gave one of the presentations, about witnessing to friends at school or at work, using some of my experience in campus ministry. The kids, loaded in the back of our truck, also took field trips to the beach, the Coca-Cola plant, and a farming resort in the area. A really memorable experience for all concerned.

ANOTHER STEP CLOSER! We are now renting a house in Malungon, the nearest town to the village of Lumabat, where our mission is located. Here we can keep a closer eye on the building of our house, make even more contacts with the people, and get intensive practice with our Cebuano language. We sometimes head back to Davao for supplies but we feel our progress toward finally moving into Lumabat has really moved forward.

WHEN IT RAINS . . . It's rainy season right now and have we been catching it! We get a heavy tropical downpour almost every night that lasts from half an hour up to two or three hours. The ground is saturated and there is some flooding in the lower areas of Davao. It's amazing to drive down the road and watch people pulling fish a foot long out of the flooded places in the street! It has really hampered our ability to get into the mountains to visit our mission site.

A REAL TREAT! We were recently able to travel to the Baptist Rural Life Center, an agricultural training center out in the province. We learned many things that will help the Tagakaulo people. There were examples of SALT: Sloping Agricultural Land Technology, a method of farming steep slopes that holds the soil with terraces made out of densely planted trees. We saw dairy goat projects, important for nutrition and health, and were even able to buy some fresh goat's milk! Most vital were the faith gardens: Food Always In The Home, a way for rural mountain people to have a constant supply of fresh veggies for their families. Now we have to go to work to use and teach all that we learned.

. . . AND A FEW WORDS FROM DEB

SCHOOL DAYS are just about to start up again; hot season and summer vacation are just about over. Since I used to work in a school, I've been fascinated by some of the things I've learned from the local teachers: Malungon High School last year had 372 students in six classrooms (with bamboo walls and dirt floors), and just seven teachers. President Aquino just announced this year that high school is now going to be free, as opposed to the very limiting fee system currently in place. That's expected to *double* enrollment. But there's been no time or money to build new classrooms or hire new teachers.

If any of the kids want to go on to college or trade school, they have to know English (college texts and classes are in English) and pass the National Exam. Only eleven kids passed this test in Malungon, where their English is at about our 3rd or 4th grade level, and in some barrios, nobody did. One reason is the lack of materials: there are only 12 textbooks for all the seniors (no, not 12 for each child; I mean 12 total), no magazines, library books, reference books, or anything at all in English. The school kids are hard workers and want to learn, so I've been thinking of ways to get them some books and magazines. I'll let you know the plan in our next newsletter, and if you have any ideas on this, please share them with me!

Your prayers, support and letters are still the things that keep us going— it's hard to explain how very much they mean to us. We thank God for your encouragement, and ask Him to constantly watch over your own lives and service in His mission there at home.

    In Christ,

    Art, Deb

MINDANAO MEMO

Your Mission to the Tagakaulo Tribe in the Philippines
Rev. Art & Deb Simmons, PO Box 56, 8000 Davao City
Fall 1988

LET YOUR LITTLE LIGHT SHINE! Wow! Is it dark out there! Inky, thick darkness. Not a light anywhere—no electricity, kerosene is very expensive, candles too short-lived. That's what it's like on a cloudy night in Lumabat, our village. It gets you thinking about all those images in the Bible about light and darkness.

There's plenty of darkness in our world. But Jesus was thinking of each of us when He said, "You are the light of the world." He's given all of us the task of venturing out into that darkness, speaking of God's grace and mercy, living lives of hope and encouragement. Don't forget to let your little light shine—make God's mission a part of everything you say or do!

HERE'S WHAT'S IN THE WORKS . . . We've been making all sorts of plans with our mission team, and we'd like to share these plans with you, our partners.

SURVEYING: Doug and I are all set to do some hard hiking into them thar hills. As we survey the whole Tagakaulo area, we'll locate all villages not accessible from the road, see if the people can read and write, learn what they know of the Gospel, see if churches have ever been established there, check on existence of schools, health care facilities, marketplaces, etc. We'll then know our mission target well, and they'll have a chance to meet those strange foreigners they've been hearing about.

LITERACY WORK: Deb has been busy as our contact person on the literacy program. She's been investigating production and cost of primers and other materials to teach adult Tagakaulos to read their own language. In this, she's been working with Asterio, a Tagakaulo school teacher, in redesigning some of the materials, and getting ready to select and train the literacy teachers.

MEDICAL MISSION: Jan has been our primary contact person in the area of health care. She's been contacting doctors, hospitals, nurses and midwives to decide the best strategy for our medical work. She's now collecting materials like books, pamphlets, pictures and posters that will be helpful as we begin health education. She'll also concentrate on nutrition and sanitation—the causes of most health problems in the poorer areas of the mountains.

BUTIKI
(HOUSE LIZARDS)

ON THE ROAD AGAIN! As we travel through the mountains for contacts and plans, much of our time is also spent hauling things. We'll load up with cement blocks, sand, tin roofing, school desks, whatever's needed, and set off. We can only go when it's dry, as the road is very steep and made of clay, which is treacherously slippery when wet! On arrival in the village, people are already waiting for a ride back out—with all their corn, rice, firewood, chickens, bananas, and bat guano. Bat guano? That's bat dung, a rich, potent fertilizer harvested from the large fruit-bat caves further up in the hills. We're trying it on our garden.

AND IT'S FUN ALONG THE WAY . . . with all the interesting things to see. People scurry to move the corn, coffee or cacao they have drying on the path, water buffalo plow the fields, fires roar up the hills from below as farmers burn off their fields. Many of the packhorses have never seen a vehicle before, and have to be passed gently, at a crawl. Laundry is done in the rivers, and people carry huge bags of corn on their heads, on the way to market. We even saw a real live Bayanihan, the way to move your house from one area to another. The bamboo hut is slung onto poles, picked up by twenty or so men, and slowly carried to its next place.

TAKING SHAPE! One of the features of our Lumabat home will one day be a solar energy system, generous gift of the Lutheran Women's Missionary League (LWML). It will power a few lights and whatever small machinery we need to use, such as typewriters or radios. We'll still haul in cooking gas for our hotplate, and may soon have a kerosene refrigerator! Yes, they still make them, as an electric one would be too big a drain on the solar panels. Refrigeration will allow us to store vaccines and various medications, and finally allow the nurses and traveling vet clinics to come through.

And finally, SPECIAL THANKS to all of you who have so generously sent Sunday School materials, money for projects, books of all kinds, and other useful items for our mission! You can't imagine how happy the people are to have these things! We could still use more books—easiest primers to about grade 7 reading level, with most emphasis on the easier books— any kind of story books, Bible stories, school books, kids' magazines, etc. Ask your post office about M-Bag mailing, which is by the pound. Things get here slowly, but they *do* get here—and are received with much joy and thanksgiving!

We think of you all often. Don't forget to keep us in your prayers, in your thoughts, and on your letter-writing list!

Peace in Christ,

Art & Deb

Rev. Art & Deb Simmons
P.O. Box 56
8000 Davao City, PHILIPPINES

Winter 1988-89

Natawo ang inyong Manluluwas

GRASSROOTS EVANGELISM! One of the finest projects we've carried out so far was our Christmas evangelism effort. We printed a small pamphlet with the Christmas Gospel story in both Cebuano and Tagakaulo (the tribal dialect), also featuring a picture of the manger scene. The young people from the Davao City church went with us, sang many Christmas carols, and helped to give out the pamphlets in the hill villages. Tinong gave a short talk about Christmas, and Doug and I talked with many of the village leaders. A lot of interest was shown among the people who heard the message, along with some curiosity and many really good questions. What a joy that so many of them could hear the real Christmas story for the very first time!

A <u>REALLY</u> NEW YEAR! Because the Tagakaulo tribe lives in the mountains, very far from government offices and hospitals, it's common for members of the tribe to have no birth certificate. If you ask them how old they are, they say they were born in the year of a certain war, or the year their village was struck with disease, or the year that the house of a family member burned. They seem to mark the years of their lives by catastrophes. Thank God for our mission here and for your prayers and support! Now there are some who will say they were born in the year their village learned about Jesus, in the year they came to know that God was living among them!

And for our mission, the new year brings lots of exciting plans, as we are in our third year here! The groundwork is all laid, and contacts made, so we're starting new Bible study programs in several villages. Two literacy programs are beginning, to open the world of reading and writing to many. Life-giving health care and health education is ready to go. And we'll continue to say, in small ways and large, in whispers and shouts, in music and prayer . . . Jesus loves you!

AND THE RAINS <u>KEEP</u> COMING! Sounds like a broken record! Right now, carabao (water buffalo) are hauling all materials and supplies into the hills, as the road is washed out and covered with landslides– on our last trip our truck slid into a gully and almost tipped over. Carabao seem to make more sense for hauling, and hiking those miles will keep us fit!

A LITTLE LEARNING GOES A LONG WAY! Another dimension of our mission will be agricultural education. The Tagakaulos still live by "slash and burn" farming, which means using one piece of land until it's eroded or leached out, then moving to the next plot, slashing and burning all the trees and plants, and starting a new field. In result, the land is barren and unfertile. They used to get by with "slash and burn," but now they're out of new land. They must begin the hard work of learning new methods of growing their food. As Christians concerned with the welfare of the whole person, one of our jobs will be to help that process. We're partnering with the Baptist Rural Life Center to present workshops to the Tagakaulos on good farming methods for mountainous land. They can also learn more productive methods of raising goats, chickens, ducks, fish and snails.

AND WE LEARN, TOO! In our yard, we've planted our first little garden. We have a few onions, tomatoes, camote (the edible leaves are like spinach), green peppers, and alugbati (again for the leaves.) And every-thing came up! Not bad for a couple of city kids! We're constantly amazed at how fast things grow here. The tribal people get three harvests of corn a year. Also in our yard, three of our five pots of orchids, which are very common here and need no special care, are in bloom again too.

. . . AND A FEW WORDS FROM DEB . . .

You know that right after Christmas it's time to sit down and write the thank-you's. So we'd like to tell you how richly the Lord has blessed us this past year—through your help—with these gifts:

- Sunday School materials collected to teach Bible stories
- Christmas and Bible stickers to witness to God's love
- books, to start the very first library at the Malungon High School
- pamphlets in Cebuano and Tagakaulo, to share the Good News of Jesus Christ
- teaching trips to the Agriculture Research Station
- hymnals to replace worn, torn copies in many Mindanao churches
- a sewing machine, for use by the High School and livelihood groups

May God bless you all—we miss you and think of you a lot!

In Christ,

Art & Deb

Your Mission to the Tagakaulo Tribe in the Philippines
Rev. Art & Deb Simmons, PO Box 56, 8000 Davao City, Philippines
Spring 1989

JUST FOR THE JOY OF IT! What an event we have to celebrate! God's only Son, through the miracle of God's endless love, left His sad and lonely tomb to rise to life again! And because He lives, we shall also live forever with our God. That's the JOY of Easter, and we're able to share it with one another because God, when He created us, made it possible for us to have and share feelings. We can experience so much more of life because of our feelings—all the joys and sorrows. We invite you now to share some of our feelings about your mission here in the Philippines, the highs and lows that make the spreading of the Good News such an adventure.

CELEBRATIONS OF GLADNESS! It's fiesta season now in the Tagakaulo area, with each village celebrating a two- or three-day extravaganza. In Lumabat, they all got together to remember Datu Manambay, their first tribal leader, who lost his life by drowning many years ago. Hundreds of people, including many tribal leaders related to the old Datu, poured into town for the carnival, the games and dancing, the cockfights and horse fights, and all the feasting.

And missionaries Art and Doug were by no means idle! Gathering so many people together presented an excellent opportunity for us to do evangelism work. We prepared a beautiful brochure, printed in both Cebuano and Tagakaulo languages, featuring Bible passages about Jesus' resurrection and our own eternal life promised to us at Easter. As we hiked in the mountains, stood in the local plazas, visited the many small villages along the trails, we presented those brochures to all who were able to read them.

✚ · · · ✚ · · ✚ · · WHAT A RESPONSE!

Many of the people immediately started reading the brochure aloud so that those who couldn't read could also share in its message. People would gather around, discuss the meaning of the passages, ask about our mission and its plans, and praise the Lord for the goodness talked about in the Bible passages. What a way to celebrate Easter and share it with others!

BUT CELEBRATIONS OF SADNESS TOO. Filipinos are proud to be very emotional and caring people. Is it any wonder that one of their favorite days is Good Friday, with its deep sorrow? As you drive through the provinces on Good Friday, you'll see many processions, headed by a man carrying a cross, sometimes wearing a batik robe or crown of thorns, imitating our Lord on His way to the cross.

 OR GLADNESS AND SADNESS ALL JUMBLED TOGETHER! Doug has now baptized his first infant Christian, the first member of the Tagakaulo tribe to be baptized by our new Lutheran mission. But let's not have them all be so exciting! Doug's neighbor Ernesto rushed into their house, announced that his infant daughter was dying, and asked that she be baptized. Doug hastened to comply. Then baby and family were thrust into Doug's truck, rushed down to Dadiangas, many miles away. The tiny baby stopped breathing several times on the way and gave all the adults heart attacks while she fought for her life . . . but she survived, has recovered, and has gone down in the history of the Tagakaulo Lutheran Mission . . . Praise be to God!

PURE PRIDE! Picture yourself at the elementary school graduation ceremonies in Lumabat. One young gentleman, bursting with fear and pride, is valedictorian of the class, wins several other awards . . . for sure he's the star of the day. But his pride is nothing compared to that of his Tagakaulo father, with no schooling of his own, called forward to place the medal of honor around his son's neck. Conquering warriors, triumphant athletes, great heroes—none of them could strut like that father did.

. . . AND A FEW WORDS FROM DEB

How do you like our new computer? It's smarter than I am, that's for sure. After two years of saving your generous donations we finally bought one, and already it has been a tremendous help with all our programs—especially the literacy project. Asterio and I are now working hard on the primers, tabulating surveys of the villages that want literacy classes (so many!), evaluating teachers, finalizing training seminars, and so much more. It's exciting to see such progress.

SCHOOL'S OUT! Hot season (March to June) is here, and the kids have vacation but our planning goes on. The response to the books you sent has been overwhelming—great gratitude mixed with joy and a little unbelief (that it's really true). I've talked to the teachers about a few other needs, so here comes the . . .

 REQUEST CORNER: The kids know the world is round but can't picture it. We could use some large plastic blow-up globes, which I've seen in novelty stores, as well as wall maps or educational posters. And *Kansas City* friends: do any of you have a simple small microscope, as in a kid's science set, with specimen and blank slides? If you have one to donate, I'll make arrangements with you to get it to my dad and we can bring it back personally. Yes, we'll be visiting family for an all-too-brief couple of weeks soon—our first trip back in 2 1/2 years! Please keep us in your prayers!

Joyful Easter blessings to you all!

Art & Deb

MINDANAO MEMO

Your Mission to the Tagakaulo Tribe in the Philippines
Rev. Art & Deb Simmons, PO Box 56, 8000 Davao City, Philippines
Summer 1989

YOU THINK SOLOMON HAD IT TOUGH?   Our friend Asterio, in his job as tribal consultant to the government, has some days that would try the patience of a saint! Instead of taking their disputes and crimes to court, the Tagakaulos gather in Asterio's office to settle the cases within the tribe. Imagine hearing a divorce case with all the relatives (three or more generations!) getting into the act and each one having their extended say. Or how about determining the compensation  paid, in number of horses or water buffalo, when one tribal member kills another? Asterio, who became a Christian years ago when the first Bible translators came, says the most important lesson he's learned from the Bible is the prayer of King Solomon for wisdom— wisdom to hate the sin but love the sinner, to patiently listen to days-long arguments, to trust the Lord to give His help and guidance. Read 1 Kings 3:5-12!

EVANGELISM NOTES:
The Executive Director of Lutheran Bible Translators was just here in our area for a short visit. He agreed we should have a translator working in the Tagakaulo area, finishing the work begun years ago. The new worker should be here by January!

We're continuing to produce fine brochures, which are very popular, to explain the basic teachings of the church, the various celebrations through-out the year—showing the love and care of our Lord in so many ways. These are read and always discussed with interest whenever we hand them out. It's a real blessing that the Tagakaulo people love a good, deep discussion and will gather for one at the drop of a hat!

Thanks to the Philippine Lutheran Hour, we now have some great Bible study materials in Cebuano, soon to be translated to Tagakaulo. The people in our village are anxious to begin using them. We'll have two types of classes: one for those who can read, and another, using pictures and story-telling, for those who can't yet read or write. Be sure to say a prayer of thanks that so much progress has been made in our outreach efforts.

LITERACY NOTES: Deb and Asterio are continuing to work on the literacy primers and have plans for training more class leaders. Requests have been steadily pouring in from many areas to include them in our literacy outreach. And exciting news! Thanks to your prayers and generosity, we finally have full funding for the program!

Walking through our village the other day, I was stopped by a woman who was very troubled and shaken. "Come, Pastor, and help," she said, "my children are very sick." In her small bamboo hut I saw four children lying in bed—two were breathing very fast, fighting to stay alive. They had had measles, then pneumonia, and were too weak to fight anymore. We tried to hurry them to the hospital, which is two hours by horse, then an hour by truck, but the youngest, the only son, died on the way. His sister was able to recover. So many times the people are just too poor and far away from help, so their children die. I often thank God He loves us so much, through the death of His only Son, that He is waiting to welcome them into His home with open arms, and give them rest from their struggle. I also thank Him that with your help we're here to give them the encouraging hope of life . . . everlasting!

MEDICAL NOTES: As you can see, we're having a difficult time in this area! Last year we had a doctora, but she dropped out to return to Manila. Now it's almost impossible to find a doctor willing to live way back up in the hills. We're still looking. Keep us in prayer!

One of our biggest health problems comes from contaminated water. Diarrhea and amoebic dysentery are severe illnesses for all the villagers, especially the children. We're working hard now on a water project to drill new wells and help provide safe water for all.

AND A FEW WORDS FROM DEB . . .

BOOKS: We've been thrilled with your generous response in sending us used storybooks and textbooks for the village schools. Some of the kids are getting to take home a book for the first time in their lives— they're so proud and excited. And the teachers are grateful for this tremendous help to their teaching in all areas. So many schools have asked us about getting books (more schools than we knew existed) and are building cabinets to keep the books safe.

WHAT A VACATION! Our big "foreign" trip to the States was wonderful! We ate too much, laughed too hard, stayed up too late to catch up on your news, visited, played, relaxed and grew strong again, worshiped and rejoiced at all the remarkable gifts God gave us when He gave us you. Thanks for the memories. It was a very special trip home.

REQUEST CORNER: We haven't been able to stump you with a request yet, and are always overwhelmed by your generosity and willingness to help. Here's a new one for you: can you check those old closets in the church basement and find us some Bible story film-strips? Through your generous donations we have a battery-powered filmstrip projector coming, and filmstrips will be a big draw and teaching tool for both adults and kids.

We ask God to constantly watch over you, keeping you in His perfect peace!

Art & Deb

THE MINDANAO MEMO

Your Mission to the Tagakaulo Tribe in the Philippines
Rev. Art & Deb Simmons, PO Box 56, 8000 Davao City, Philippines
Fall 1989

O GIVE THANKS UNTO THE LORD
FOR HE IS GOOD, AND HIS MERCY ENDURES FOREVER!

What a priceless treasure it is to live in the love of a merciful God. For the Tagakaulos, life is full of fears and taboos. You can't leave your house if a certain bird sings, or the spirits will bring disaster. You can't give your dog a name, or talk to your horse or carabao, as you'll upset the spirits by treating animals like people. How marvelous that we have a God who loves, forgives and cares for us! We no longer have to live in fear. He welcomes us, cleanses us from our sins and treats us as His own dear children. That's the message you're sharing here through your partnership in our mission. *Give thanks!*

WOULD YOU BELIEVE IT?
Our humble home in the hills is finally done—we have a roof, walls, floors, doors, all the comforts of home, including indoor plumbing (well, sort of). We still have to boil the water from our well, patch a few cracks so the big bugs don't get in, and plant the yard, BUT right now we're too busy giving thanks to the Lord to let any of that bother us. Here's what it looks like, as well as we can draw it:

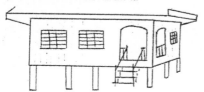

AND WHAT A PARTY!!

Yes, we had a house-blessing party and the whole Tagakaulo tribe was invited! Some of the sights and sounds:

—We rigged up a temporary "cook shack" in the front yard and got ready to prepare dinner for several hundred folks. Like all work here, it turned out to be a community effort ... everyone had to comment on the skills of the cooks and grab a taste of this or that to check the quality.

—We owned, for only 5 short days, our very first pig! Alas, when the party came, the pig departed, to be the main meal course.

—The tribal leaders also donated a lechon, a roasted pig served whole and cut into chunks for eating. The crisp golden skin is the favorite of Filipinos—what a taste treat!

—Many of the older tribal leaders came in their beautiful native dress. The hand-embroidered, beaded blouses of the women would be the envy of even the most skilled needle worker. They also wear strings of small bells that make such a pleasant tinkling sound when they walk or dance . . . as they certainly did at our house-blessing program.

CAUSE FOR REJOICING!

As you read recently in "The Lutheran Witness", we've received funding from the Board for Social Ministry Services for our literacy and medical programs. Officials from the BFSMS and from Lutheran World Relief came to our mission site to meet the people involved in the programs and to wish us God's blessings. We thank them for their interest and for your continued support of Synod's outreach programs in social ministry.

BACK TO SCHOOL TIME

Deb, Asterio and Rolando earlier opened the first literacy class of our mission, starting with 20 students. They're already prepared with four more teachers to begin requested classes in other villages. The Tagakaulos will soon be able to read the Bible for themselves, and all their evil spirits will be on the run because of God's Truth.

AND SOON IT'S GRADUATION TIME

Our first three rural health workers will complete their training and officially graduate from their schooling. What a blessing they will be to the people of the villages. Through your generosity we were able to help fund their studies and provide them with all their equipment. Many thanks for your concern!

THEY SHALL KNOW THE TRUTH

Our evangelism outreach efforts continue as we have begun formal Bible studies in our own and surrounding villages. We're excited about being able to share the Gospel, to grow with God's people in their search for the truth, and to touch people's lives with God's love.

TRIBAL CHURCH PLANTERS' CONFERENCE:

We had a chance to share successes and failures, learn from the experience of others, and enjoy fellowship with other missionaries at work with tribal Filipinos. Deb met with literacy people, Jan got to talk with health care personnel, and Doug and I learned much about tribal cultures and how to reach into them with the Good News. Now we're better prepared to plant (and nurture and care for) Christ's church in the homeland of the Tagakaulos.

PRAY FOR US!

The rain is still turning the trails to soup and making hiking difficult—it seems we've got permanent mud under our toenails. One of the Tagakaulos told me, "Your white hair and skin are pure American, but those muddy feet of yours are pure Tagakaulo. Welcome to our tribe!"

So please pray for open hearts and dry roads as we go from village to village with our Bible study and Sunday School programs.

REQUEST CORNER: We've got a new one for you: *Toothbrushes*—lots of simple new toothbrushes. Dentists never go back into the hills and the people don't know anything about dental care, so rotten teeth are a common and painful problem. We're looking forward to starting some dental hygiene sessions—so thanks for your help!

God's richest blessings to you all,

Art & Deb

THE MINDANAO MEMO

Your Mission to the Tagakaulo Tribe in the Philippines
Rev. Art & Deb Simmons, PO Box 56, 8000 Davao City, Philippines
Winter/Spring 1990

THE JOY OF SHARING!

Never is a person's faith richer, clearer, more exciting than at those times when faith is shared with someone else. That's why the Church Year opens so many doors for us...Advent, Christmas, Lent, Easter, Pentecost...so many joyous opportunities to share the gift of everlasting Life to those we love and serve. It's our prayer that you find many chances to share your own faith, now and throughout the year: "For God so loved the world that He gave His only begotten Son, that whoever believes in Him should not perish, but have everlasting life."

YOUR GIFTS ARE WORKING WONDERS!

Nita and Fe, our mission's two new midwives, just gave the children a complete instruction course:

"This is how you hold your new toothbrush, and this is how you move it, and this is what you DON'T do with your toothbrush, etc." And now all the kids in Lumabat, and later in other villages in our area, will have happy, healthy smiles. Thank you for sending all the toothbrushes we've received so far...and for those you might be sending in the future (yes, we still need a lot more to cover all the villages!) It makes a big difference in the lives of these kids!

WHAT A WAY TO DO SUNDAY SCHOOL!

It all starts when Deb and her fellow teachers head off through the village for Sunday School  class. Soon all the kids are tagging along like they're following the Pied Piper! They start by raising the roof with their joyful (and LOUD) singing. Then things quiet down a bit for the Bible story for the day, using the pictures and flannelgraphs you've sent us.

Now for the hard work...if you memorize your Bible verse for the day, you get a sticker [thanks for all those Christmas and Easter seals!] that you can take home with you...or stick on your forehead or cheek or school books, or ??? One thing you DON'T do: when you go out to play the games you don't put down your lesson, or your sticker, or the picture you colored...who knows who could get their hands on this valuable stuff!

But the funniest part of all happens when Mum Deb turns into the WakWak (legendary old witch) who chases the squealing kids all over the schoolyard in a rousing game of tag (and they won't let her quit!) Of course they don't see she needs a backrub, a long nap, and several hours with her feet up to recover from all that exercise. Sure wish Art and his adult Bible study group could have that much fun...but you know how it is with grownups.

BID A GRAND WELCOME TO . . .

Jemma, Orlando, and Angel, three brand new members of God's family! They were baptized in our home in Lumabat after their parents and godparents were taught the meaning and the joy of Holy Baptism. We rejoice with them and their families at the wondrous grace and mercy of our God.

OUR VILLAGE just celebrated "Day of Lumabat", our Founder's Day festival—with noise and fun being the main ingredients! It began with a grand parade of schoolkids, followed by a ribbon-cutting at the new school classroom. Our midwives and new village health care worker offered a free clinic; there were games, horsefights (the most popular event at any fiesta), a car-battery-operated loudspeaker for the "disco," all topped off by the crowning of the young village queen and her attendants.

It was a great time, with our mission called on to take part in everything—from leading the invocations and prayers, to marching in the parade, to cutting the school ribbon, to pinning the sashes on the winning 'princesses'! What a day!

WHAT'S THAT HORRIBLE NOISE?

That's what happens when the Ag. Dept. Animal Officer comes to vaccinate the pigs against cholera. Each one squeals his little heart out when the mean man grabs its ear and jabs the needle in. We helped arrange the visit and provided the vaccine and transport, but did NOT grab any pig ears!

THE JOY OF LEARNING!

Literacy classes are now ongoing in seven different villages, for about 200 adult students with many other villages on a waiting list. Deb is really pleased, but wasn't ready for such an over-whelming response. Now we'll prepare additional materials, arrange the training of more teachers, find room for more classes. What a great problem to have!

PRAY FOR RAIN??

After months of rain and mud, we're now in a severe drought. Locally, all the farmers are in serious trouble. They have large debts for seed, fertilizer, etc., coupled with large families of 6-8 children, and will have great difficulty weathering the drought if it should last much longer. Most of them can't even afford to buy rice anymore. They're eating corn gruel—what we'd call field corn—as their main (and only) food. Please pray for them and their families in this crisis.

LOOK OUT, HERE WE COME!

The Lord is making possible a very special chance for us to share our mission with many of you who have so long and faithfully supported our work. In a few months, we'll be leaving for a furlough to the States, and our time will be spent traveling around to express our thanks for the support that has made this work possible.

JOY AND PEACE IN OUR RISEN LORD!

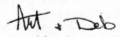

The Lord has done great things for us!

Summer/Fall 1990

Rev. Art & Deb Simmons
P.O. Box 56
8000 Davao City, PHILIPPINES

How long is forever? It's flying from Kansas City to Detroit to Tokyo to Manila all in one day. It's spending over 24 hours huddled in a tiny airplane seat wishing your feet were on the ground. It's crossing the Dateline, losing a day, losing all track of time and place. But God is great and His mercy went with us the whole way. Now we're back to work at our mission and thankful to the Lord for His help in getting us here!

SALAMAT, SALAMAT, SALAMAT SA INYONG TANAN! That's how our Tagakaulo friends would say . . . "we don't know how to thank you enough for all you've done for us!" Your warmth and hospitality as we visited made us feel good about the work we do. Your many gifts to support the mission encouraged us to work that much harder. All the help you extended to our mission programs — evangelism, literacy, medical, well-drilling, etc. — filled our hearts with hope that we can really share God's love with the Tagakaulo people. So as we thank each of you, we also give thanks to God for giving us such beautiful mission partners.

THE SIMMONS BOOK OF WORLD RECORDS or WHAT WE DID WITH OUR SUMMER VACATION: Call us the Overland Park Globetrotters. In a small Mercury Lynx, hijacked from a kind-hearted niece, we visited eight different States, spoke to 16 congregations, ate at least 7,000 pot-lucks, gained back all the weight we lost (Deb: 15 lbs., Art: 22 lbs!), visited with family and friends until the wee hours each day, and learned (we think) what a Teenage Mutant Ninja Turtle is.

Not until we got home to the States did they tell us that we needed boosters for all those horrible shots we got when we started this job. Add trips to the dentist, the eye doctor, the dermatologist, several physicians, and we certainly got our fill of the medical professions.

Highlight of the trip for Deb was buying out every rummage sale in sight (for wonderful things to send back to the Philippines) and stuffing herself with chocolate. For Art, it was shouting, screaming and crying as the Kansas City Royals made fools of themselves. All wonderful times that we'll never forget!

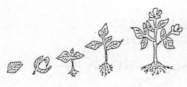

THERE IS GREAT JOY IN MUDVILLE . . . for the rains have come again! When we left Mindanao, we were suffering a severe drought. Now things are sloppy and slidey and covered with mud, but the people here will have food again. Small price to pay for wading in mud wherever you go.

IT MAKES A BEEHIVE SEEM LAZY!

Our loving sisters and brothers came with warm hearts, big smiles and open hands to welcome us back to our village. Some brought flowers to brighten our empty house. We all shared a basket of luscious tropical fruit for an afternoon snack. A freshly roasted chicken popped up just in time for  our supper. In all these ways, our neighbors demonstrated to us the love of our God. Believe us, it makes a person feel great to have such a warm and busy welcome!

HIGH HOPES AND DREAMS!

Now that we're at work again, we hope to keep moving forward in many areas. Your prayers are desperately needed if we hope to succeed. Please pray that:

PLANT LOVE.
HARVEST FOREVER.

- we can begin Bible studies in 3 new villages by the beginning of next year
- we can train teachers and open 6 new literacy classes
- our plan to expand the medical mission to 4 midwives goes smoothly
- we're able to purchase and begin using well-drilling equipment so that the people will have safe drinking water
- we can identify and train Tagakaulo evangelists so that God's Word might spread far and wide
- the agriculture education classes sponsored by our mission can make a real difference in people's lives
- over 500 children (+ more all the time) will keep brushing and smiling brightly because of the toothbrushes you offered

That's a lot of praying, but we hope you'll continue so that our mission might prosper!

WHOA . . . WHO'S THIS? It's our new horse, a sturdy white mountain pony with a lot of energy for getting up and down steep hills. Her name is Hope, because she'll be bringing a lot of love and hope to the village kids when our Sunday School assistants ride out to lead classes in many different villages. (And we city kids also HOPE that we won't fall off very often when we ride!) Many thanks to all the Sunday School and VBS groups who gave us donations—we used your generous gifts to buy Hope.

YOU ARE ALWAYS in our thoughts and prayers . . . Please keep in touch!

Art & Deb

MINDANAO MEMO

Your Mission to the Tagakaulo Tribe in the Philippines
Rev. Art & Deb Simmons, PO Box 56, 8000 Davao City, Philippines
Winter 1990-1991

O ME OF LITTLE FAITH!

Ever bite off more than you could chew? That was sure the case for me when we decided to hike across the mountain to visit a village called Pantang. First we climbed a very steep mountain. Then we scrambled down the other side, slipping and sliding on the *really* steep trail. We spent time talking with the village leaders, then turned around to head home. First we waded in the river, then we climbed up several small waterfalls, then crawled—yes, literally crawled—up some of the toughest trail I've seen yet. Hot and tired, I grumbled to Banoy, one of my companions, that I didn't think I could make it to the top. What a refreshing answer he gave me: "If the hill is big, Reverend, your faith and trust in God must be a little bit bigger!" Those words, coming from a new Christian, gave me all the energy I'd need for the rest of the trip...and how well they apply to all the problems we face in our lives.

ART'S ANTICS—OR, THREE MONTHS IN THE LIFE OF A MISSIONARY
It's hard to imagine what a varied and exciting three months it's been since we last wrote to you! Let me share some of the great new directions in our ministry here:

• Doug and I have put together a seminar program for training the Tagakaulo church leaders. That way they'll learn to provide leadership for their own church and not have to rely on missionaries. Looks like we've got a good start. We're inviting village leaders, local pastors and new Christians to grow in their faith.

• I've been invited to work as a consultant to the staff of the Philippine Lutheran Hour program. Their previous director has been promoted, so now I'll be trying to help out. They've got a great ministry, including plans for a new radio program in our own tribal dialect!

• Part of the work with the Lutheran Hour is to write a Bible correspondence course on Christian ethics. It's helped me do a lot of thinking about our lives as God's people. And at the same time I've been studying new materials for the Bible study courses in our villages, planting our roots firmly in God's Word.

THE BIG PICTURE
We're working hard on a Five-Year Plan for our mission, plotting which directions to take, how to get there, and what resources we must have. Pray for God to give us the mission vision we'll need, and the courage to take giant steps forward in His Name!

DEB'S DOINGS—OR WHAT ELSE IS GOING ON AROUND HERE?

It doesn't seem possible that three months could fly by that fast! Must be the result of all the different directions our lives have taken:

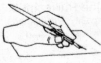 ** Our literacy classes are still going strong. At Art's last baptism, many of the sponsors, who before could only make an X on the certificate, were able to sign their names! They were so proud! We're now adding math and 'life skills' words, as well as doing the groundwork for next year's expansion—seven new classes!

** Thanks to your generosity, we were able to get out several new batches of books to the schools. In one village, the kids were so excited by the books, they wouldn't go home for lunch—they wanted to stay and read!

 ** Sunday School is back in action, and the kids are happily belting out their songs and coloring their pictures. School is out in March, so we have plans to present Vacation Bible School classes in several villages. This should be a great outreach tool, and we hope many of the parents will get interested via the stories and pictures the kids bring home.

** "Nurse Norma" . . . that's what Art calls me when I'm out on the front porch giving medicines and consulting with the sick and injured. We've had a big wave of flu and bronchitis lately along with cuts, burns, skin infections, and several cases beyond my poor knowledge, which I send out to our clinic. The medicines  and bandages you send are a HUGE help! Art says he feels like his father, a rural Texas pastor in the late 1930's, when we discover vegetables and fruit on our porch in 'payment.'

 ** Our own garden is bursting out of the ground (no snow here!) and we get squash, eggplant, munggo beans and bitter cucumber to share with the community. We're urging the villagers to begin planting gardens, too, and are helping out with seeds and know-how.

REQUEST CORNER
You've given so much but the need seems endless. We could sure use:

antibiotic cream, tolnaftate (anti-fungal) cream, and hydrocortisone cream (available here but *so* expensive—maybe your Kmart will have a sale); Telfa bandages with adhesive sides; crayons; stickers; flannel-graph stuff; Bible pictures to color; old reading glasses; etc.

WANTED!

St Paul expresses our **Thanks** so much better than we can. Take a quick look at 2 Corinthians 9:11-15 to see the results of all your mission involvement. God's richest blessings to you all!

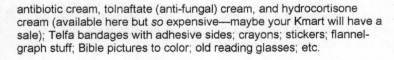

Art & Deb

Your Mission to the Tagakaulo Tribe in the Philippines
Rev. Art & Deb Simmons, PO Box 56, 8000 Davao City, Philippines
Spring 1991

"Buhi, buhi, buhi sa kanunay!" The kids sing it out at the top of their voices and you can hear it all over the village. In fact, you can hear it all over the world because it means, "Alive, alive, alive forevermore!" Easter morning again brings the good news that our Jesus is alive! What a joy it is to hear new Christians shout out that message to each other—and to us!

IT'S TAKING SHAPE!
As we've mentioned before, we want the Tagakaulos to be leaders of their own church, and to do that, we'll have to provide training for them. The process continues!

Working with our Missionary Counselor in Manila, members of the seminary faculty from Baguio City, and pastors from here on Mindanao, we're designing just how that training will take place. What kind of workers will we train? Who will teach the courses? What courses will we need, to equip the Tagakaulos for ministry? Will we have full-time school, or periodic seminars, or—? What kind of training center will we want to build so that all this can happen?

As you can see, a lot of important questions stand between us and our goal. But we're finding answers to them, and with God's help will be able to provide a secure foundation for the vibrant and growing Tagakaulo church.

WE WISH YOU COULD'VE BEEN HERE!
What great joy as the adult literacy classes ended for the year! The closing ceremonies had something for everybody...so everybody came! There were native songs on the 3-string guitar; dances around the big wooden drum; dramas written by the students on how literacy helps you read signs, not get cheated, and sign your name; there was even roast chicken, lunch for all, and a special basketball matchup!

There were so many heartwarming scenes: Adela proudly wrote her name up on the blackboard for all the world to see—the first time in her whole life she could do so—and the whole crowd stood up and cheered. Little grandmother Vida marched proudly to the stage to receive her Certificate of Achievement and then, with her own shy gracefulness, showed it to each and every member of her family. A father stood in embarrassed pride as his son pinned on his ribbon for being the "Most Industrious" student in his class.

Over 130 students completed this year of hard work, and our hats are off to each and every one of them. And to you, too, for making the classes possible in your support of this project through Lutheran World Relief.

BEEN PRACTICIN'

I'm a city kid—always have been. But last week I went to an agriculture seminar with 25 Tagakaulo farmers. We learned how to get top production out of steep hillside farms—which are the only kind found in our area. The seminar was a huge success and very popular with the farmers. All received certificates, including me! So now I've been trying to get the look of a farmer down pat—chewing on a blade of grass, squinting off into the distance when asked a question, checking to see what's on my shoes before entering the house. You better add me to your prayer list, too—I've got a long way to go!

GUAVA LEAVES?

Next week our current mothers' classes end in four mountain villages. Our mid-wives have spent three months teaching nutrition, sanitation, basic health care and herbal medicine. As you can see from the above illustration from one of their booklets, the leaves of the guava tree can treat anything from coughs to cuts! Now mothers know how to treat fever and diarrhea, how to plant and cook vegetables, and how to provide a healthier life for their families. Thanks to our healing Lord for the ability to spread this knowledge!

THE HEAT IS ON!

HOT hot season has arrived at last, so it's only fitting that we send our WARMEST thanks to all of you who have so lovingly sent personal letters and cards, supplies, and helpful items of all sorts to us and our mission here. Everything is very gratefully received, enthusiastically used, and does more good in a million ways than you'll ever imagine. Daghan salamat (many thanks)!

IN THE HEART OF THE WHIRLWIND

Sunday School classes continue, and keep growing and growing! The Bible classes provoke thought and discussion. The Lutheran Hour radio program is taking shape. The Bible Correspondence Course on Christian ethics is nearing completion. Books are received, processed, and presented to area schools. Our eagerly awaited Vacation Bible School begins this month in many of the surrounding villages.

Sometimes it feels like being in a whirl-wind—what a beautiful place to be! Join us in thanking God for the opportunities to touch the lives of others in so many ways.

JOY AND PEACE IN OUR RISEN LORD!

𝔐𝔦𝔫𝔡𝔞𝔫𝔞𝔬 𝔐𝔢𝔪𝔬

Your Mission to the Tagakaulo Tribe in the Philippines
Rev. Art & Deb Simmons, PO Box 56, 8000 Davao City, Philippines
Summer / Fall 1991

WATCH OUT!!

It's contagious! One child catches mumps and soon it's all over the neighborhood. And we all know how fast bad news can spread. BUT...the same is true of good news, as we know here. One day you teach a new song in Sunday School and the next day you hear kids singing it all over the village. Our midwives share God's love through their Mothers' Classes and soon other mothers are learning how to care for their children. Walking around the village, you can hear people discussing last Sunday's Bible Study lesson. Jesus tells you that YOU are the light of the world. If you share His Good News, soon it will spread everywhere. Try it in your own life!

 ...

SHOW AND TELL TIME!

Simple, clear communication—the only way to reach people who can't read or write. Show a picture, tell a Bible Story, teach a song, and people will get the message. That's the basis of our leadership training program. We design pictures, teach people to use them in sharing God's plan of salvation, and send them to their own villages to become worship leaders and Bible Study teachers. In that way, many churches are planted, the mission expands into unreached areas, and God's Word goes forth!

OVER THE RIVER AND THROUGH THE WOODS . . .

to VBS we go! Every morning Deb and her helpers Leksa and Riza would gather their crayons, guitar, juice mix, stickers, pictures, etc. and load it all on poor Hope the Horse. Then off they'd go across mountains or rivers until they reached the little hut where they'd hold VBS that day, and all the kids would be waiting! They sang songs, played games, colored pictures and told the story of Jesus' love to over 250 kids—and many parents too, who came to 'watch' but ended up singing and coloring along! Classes were held in 4 different villages, everyone had a great time and are asking that we come back again next year!

STRANGERS IN A STRANGE LAND

Is it possible to be a stranger in your own country? It is if you come from the city, have a lot of education but no experience working with people in the mountains. Six seminary students just visited our mission to get some cross-cultural ministry training right here in their own country. They hiked the hills, learned about Tagakaulo culture and shared their Christian faith with people in many villages. Now they've met those 'hidden' people who live in the mountains—people with an aching need to hear the Good News—and how will they hear if no one will preach to them?

ALL SYSTEMS ARE GO!

...for another great year of adult literacy classes. Our seven original classes have doubled now to 14! We recently held a training seminar for the 14 enthusiastic teachers so they could learn how to motivate their students, conduct their sessions, and keep all running smoothly. When classes started in mid-June, over 300 students were enrolled, with more expected to attend after the harvest. Young mothers with toddlers tugging at their skirts write their first letters on the board, and old folks peer proudly through their new reading glasses (thanks, donors!) to decipher this strange stuff we call words. We'll keep you posted on their progress.

LET THERE BE LIGHT!

Evening comes. Every child in the village, plus every bug within miles, gathers at our house to peer in the doors and windows. What is this strange light that draws them? It's electric light! - the first ever seen in these mountains since God created the sun. Our solar equipment, donated by the LWML, has finally been installed. Now we can teach classes in the evening, get our paperwork done, hear the kids gather to sing on the porch, even lounge in the sweet breeze of a ceiling fan. What a miracle! It's tough trying to explain solar energy to the tribal folks—especially since we don't have any idea how it works ourselves! We just thank God (and the LWML) that it does!

THE TIME OF THE BANANA

When times are good in the mountains, it's the time of rice. When things get a little tough, it's the time of corn. And when times are really hard, it's the time of the banana—because that's all the people have left to eat (raw, hard, cooking bananas). Due to a severe drought from January to May, the farmers missed a harvest and a lot of belts got tightened. With help from our mission partners like you, we were able to get out at least some rice to several villages in the middle of the crisis. Now the corn is tall and hopes are high for harvest. The time of the banana is almost over. Thanks for helping to make it a little easier for the Tagakaulos.

NEWS 'N' NOTES

MOTHERS' CLASSES have begun again in four new villages and are going strong. They're learning child care, herbal medicine, sanitation and nutrition. Next week the mid-wives are teaching them to make soap.

VOLCANO UPDATE: No, we're not buried under ash and mud, but thanks for your prayers and concern. The volcano is 600 miles to the north of us, and our only inconvenience was missing our mail and papers for weeks when the planes couldn't fly. But damage is heavy up north—please contact your church for relief effort news.

PEACE IN CHRIST!

Art & Deb

MINDANAO MEMO

Your Mission to the Tagakaulo Tribe in the Philippines
Rev. Art & Deb Simmons, PO Box 56, 8000 Davao City
Winter 1991-1992

a time for joy

Colorful paper Christmas lanterns decorate the front of many homes. Every day, carolers sing out from house to house. Midnight services are held each night in churches. The joy of Christmas is in the air! As we celebrate this joy of Jesus' birth, we take time also to celebrate all the other joys that God has placed into our lives . . .

The rains finally came, and the corn grew tall and prospered, and the farmers had a harvest to remember—and to celebrate! And celebrate they did, as they sang and danced at village fiestas throughout the hills. Joy like that just had to break out in noise, and fun, and good times.

The smiles of happy children filled the village of Angos, as our brand new Christian Preschool got off to a great start. They, too, made noise, singing songs of Jesus, their new-found Savior. This pre-school is such a big success we'll be starting another one next month in Balobo, just down the river. If you listen carefully, you can almost hear them singing, "Ang Kalipay Sa Dios!" (The Joy of the Lord!)

Ever experience joy so intense you hesitated to believe it? That's what has happened to us as we await the decision of translators Steve and Cathy, who *might* come to finish the Tagakaulo version of God's Word. Besides their translation skills, Steve has an interest in radio ministry, and Cathy would like to be involved in literacy. We've waited five years, and now—we pray and hope and trust in God's guiding hand.

So we've known and celebrated many joys, not only this year, but throughout our time in the Philippines. Soon it will be time for us to bid a fond but tearful farewell to our ministry here. When our term of service ends in the summer of next year, we will be leaving. We finally decided that the physical and emotional demands of life in a remote rural area call for younger, stronger folks. Our replacement is on top priority, and the mission will

certainly continue, grow strong and prosper in God's grace. We planted; now someone else will water, and God will cause the whole plant to grow (see 1 Corinthians 3:6,7).

TESTING . . . TESTING

We're still hard at work on the program for training the new Tagakaulo church leaders. Right now materials are being field tested, making sure that the Gospel message comes through loud and clear. It has been a long, slow process, but in this way, we're making sure that the new Tagakaulo churches continue—long after all missionaries are gone and forgotten. God will indeed cause these new plants to grow and flourish.

CELEBRATE!

Listen to the prophet Isaiah: "The people who walked in darkness have seen a great light. They lived in a land of shadows, but now light is shining on them. You have given them great joy, Lord!"

Our darkness has many names—despair, suffering, pain—to say nothing of Luther's infamous threesome: sin, death and the power of the devil. Our lives were without hope, we lived in fear of the eternal darkness to come.

But hear Isaiah again: "Unto us a child is born! Unto us a Son is given! And the government shall be upon His shoulders, and He shall be called Wonderful Counselor, Almighty God, the Everlasting Father, the Prince of Peace!" Our Light, too, has many Names. Our lives are full of hope and promise, and we live in the eternal light of our Father's love. Unto us a child is born!

HALLELUJAH!

Rejoice ... your Light has come !

Peace in Christ,

Art & Deb

THE MINDANAO MEMO

Your Mission to the Tagakaulo Tribe in the Philippines
Rev. Art & Deb Simmons, PO Box 56, 8000 Davao City, Philippines

SUCH SWEET SORROW . . .

When we close one chapter in our lives and move to the next, there is a bittersweet feeling. We'll miss so many of the things here, but will celebrate many of the things we've been able to accomplish. We're sorry to part with our Tagakaulo friends, who have so lovingly accepted us and helped in our mission. But as we get ready to return to the States, we also know the work here will continue, many more of the Tagakaulo people will come to know the love and mercy of God, and your commitment to missions will remain strong and vibrant.

UPDATE!!

The translator couple, Steve and Cathy, *have* accepted the task of finishing the translation of God's Word into the Tagakaulo dialect, and will soon be moving into our house in Lumabat until they can get their own place built. We'll spend time in the hills with them, introducing them to the area, the people, and the tribal leaders. We're excited, as they join the mission!

WATER, WATER EVERYWHERE . . .

The water projects to provide safe drinking water for the mountain villages are really moving along! Lots of study has been going into spring development, types of wells, and other systems. Our coworkers will continue to work hard to get pure, healthy water to the Tagakaulo people.

CONGRATULATIONS

. . are in order for over 300 students of our adult literacy program! They had a truly wonderful time at their closing ceremonies—they wrote short dramas about the joys of being able to read, put together some new songs about their classes, and showed their skill in many of the traditional dances. Some of them finished the two-year course, while others finished their first year, but they were all beaming with pride at their new skills. The program will continue next school year—beginning soon this summer—under Cathy's guidance, ably assisted by Rolando, our literacy supervisor. Please keep them all in your prayers.

POOR TREES!

We sure feel guilty about what we're doing to the remaining forests in the Philippines. We're cranking out so many reports, evaluations, guidelines and summaries that we must be killing a lot of trees to provide all that paper! But we're also quite committed to providing this information to others. It's an important step toward assuring that the work we've helped begin here will continue, prosper, and grow! Still . . . those poor trees!

DON'T FORGET THE LITTLE ONES!

Our friend Reginia, the head teacher of our local school, has volunteered to keep the Sunday School program going in Lumabat, and Mariolito will keep the children in his village of Manipis busy learning all about Jesus. Thanks to the materials you've provided, they will be able to share God's love clearly, with confidence and joy.

... OR THE VERY LITTLE ONES!

Our dream of having Christian preschools in the mountain villages has become a reality in two places—Balobo and Angos. We've trained teachers, provided materials, and the classes are going *very* well. Requests are coming in from many other places to expand the program. Again, Cathy and Rolando will be overseeing the growth of this beautiful outreach.

MAYBE IT MULTIPLIES IN THE DARK!

That's the only way we can figure out where we got all the junk we're now busy packing for the trip home. Deb gathers, sorts, and puts in boxes. Art lifts and hefts and hauls, and we seem to make a little progress now and then. It's especially hard, as all our belongings are scattered in three different cities or villages. We don't even want to ask how much of it we really need. And also, come to think of it, there can't be too many people that move who start out loading horses instead of a moving van!

AND SPEAKING OF THE DARK . . .

we seem to have plenty of that! The island of Mindanao has now returned to still another drought, and that means daily power outages—16 hours every day! The only place we have dependable electricity is in our mountain village, where we make our own power with the solar equipment supplied by the LWML. That'll show all those city folks!

 WE CAN'T LEAVE without one more heartfelt word of * * THANKS * * to all of you who have helped so much over the years. You've sent books, clothes, medicines, health supplies, Sunday School and preschool materials, globes, stickers, toothbrushes, microscopes, a sewing machine, letters, donations, prayers . . . the list is endless! YOU have truly been God's blessing to us!

THAT'S ALL! We will thank God for you always, and pray that He keeps you under His loving care until we meet again!

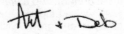

Gallery

Words can't always fully capture the reality. The following pictures give you a few glimpses of your own into what our work and surroundings looked like.

The author

Art makes a standard river crossing

To Vacation Bible School on Hope the Horse

Porch medicine

Singing at Vacation Bible School

Jeepney – country style

Art with Dopey, Dumbo, and Bob

Art picks mangoes while Bantay the
Brainless hunts chickens

Jeepney – city style

Edel, the traditional drum for dancing

Plowing our yard for corn

Horse fight

Bayanihan – house moving

The tough-stuff truck, filled with
Davao church kids

Daily market

Lumabat house construction

Lumabat house finally finished

Malungon house kitchen

Malungon house bathroom

Weeding our back yard corn

Acknowledgments

After our return from the Philippines, many suggested I write a book about our experiences. Such a book, I was told, would not only be cathartic, but would also help others to share in a time and place they'd otherwise never know. And so it came to be. But this volume would not exist without the generous help and encouragement of so many people.

My most grateful thanks: to Tim and Mindy Borchardt, for generously listening, and for the simple act of stuffing all my letters into a shoebox and presenting them to me on my return; to Susan Goldammer, for reading the original letters and ceaselessly badgering me to turn them into a book; to Bennie Ruth Gilbert and Kathy Turner, for critical reading and invaluable help as I waffled over many a decision; and to all the other readers, including Elinor Knodel and Judy Alexander, who encouraged, suggested and guided. I am also indebted to Yolanda Ciolli at Compass Flower Press/AKA Publishing for skillfully navigating me through the maze of the publishing process.

And finally, thanks, love and ice cream to my husband, Art Simmons, for remembering details, proofreading, correcting, encouraging, general longsuffering—and for companionship on the journey. We walked the edge together.

About the Author

Deborah Simmons prepped for cross-cultural mission work by coming from a family steeped in pastors, and growing up in New Jersey, Ireland, and Norway. She and her husband later traveled extensively, with only a tent, a duffel bag, and a willingness to eat anything.

Her training was in church parish work and administration, but her jobs have also included library clerk, secretary, Special Education instructional aide, literacy administrator, and a sprinkling of others lost to memory.

She lives with Art Simmons, a retired campus ministry pastor, and her husband of almost 50 years. Together, they are authors of *Create in Me: Growing in Faith Through Young Adult Bible Study.*

After years of jumping at loud noises, checking her shoes for scorpions, and scanning dim corners for giant spiders, she now lives in the relatively undisturbed peace of Columbia, Missouri.

CPSIA information can be obtained
at www.ICGtesting.com
Printed in the USA
BVOW09s0846290418
514723BV00002B/193/P